MEMOIRS OF A MURDER MAN

Inspector Byrnes (left) looks on while a rogue is "mugged" for the Rogues Gallery in the good old days of "The Forty Immortals."

MEMOIRS OF A MURDER MAN

BY ARTHUR A. CAREY

LATE DEPUTY INSPECTOR IN CHARGE OF THE HOMICIDE BUREAU, NEW YORK CITY POLICE DEPARTMENT

IN COLLABORATION WITH HOWARD McLELLAN

DOUBLEDAY, DORAN AND COMPANY, INC.

GARDEN CITY NEW YORK 1930

PRINTED IN THE UNITED STATES AT
THE COUNTRY LIFE PRESS
GARDEN CITY, N. Y.

FIRST EDITION

TO MY FEARLESS, LOYAL ASSOCIATES

AND OTHER GOOD POLICEMEN,

EVERYWHERE

CONTENTS

LIST OF ILLUSTRATIONS

INTRODUCTION

Deputy Inspector Arthur A. Carey was retired from the New York Police Department on December 21, 1928, ending on this day a police career of thirty-nine years and nine months.

Thirty-three years of this career were spent, almost exclusively, upon the investigation of suspicious deaths in the country's largest and richest city, whose police department numbers nearly eighteen thousand men and is maintained at an annual cost of more than forty-five million dollars.

For almost a quarter of a century he was chief of the Homicide Bureau, an innovation in murder inquiry of which he was the author. This bureau has been referred to in more recent years as a Murder Clinic. Its object is not only to detect murder and apprehend the slayer but to control murder through a clinical study of homicide.

Probably no man living has had more to do with murder and its authors than Inspector Carey. The number of homicides which engaged his attention may be measured in a general way by the expression of his colleagues at headquarters that "Carey's murder cases are somewhere in the thousands." Definite figures are not available, for in the course of thirty-three years every death in the city to which suspicion might attach, and very often prove unfounded, was passed on to him as a matter of official routine. If the truth were ascertainable it probably would reveal that the total number of homicides which had his personal attention, either as an investigator or a director of operations, is in excess of ten thousand. As a record for murder inquiry by one man this figure probably stands alone.

From this fact the inference has been drawn by observers of the inspector's work and his career, that he is the world's foremost police expert on murder. This statement need not rest upon the premise that the great number of cases he handled entitles him to special distinction. One may examine into the effectiveness of his work as chief of the bureau and determine the bearing it has upon control of murder.

In this connection the facts are these: with the exception of Los Angeles, New York City has the lowest homicide rate of any large city in the United States, in spite of its wealth, population, and the cosmopolitan texture of its masses. It offers to the criminally minded of all types abundant temptation to kill and steal, while its geographical situation and facility of travel, and its congested masses, provide the opportunity and means of escape which the criminal always seeks. The lowering of the city's homicide rate began to make itself apparent with the establishment of the inspector's Homicide Bureau.

It is interesting to note by way of a commentary on murder control that Inspector Carey and his staff had not been out of office two months when the chief prosecuting officer of New York County announced with some alarm that there had been more homicide cases in those two months than during any two months in the history of the prosecutor's bureau, whose duty it is to present to courts and juries homicide evidence gathered by the police.

Of the inspector's personality, which seems vital in a narrative having to do with detectives, a thumbnail sketch, being brief as well as modest, like the man, appears best to suit the occasion.

Though sixty-three, he is easily taken for a man on the tender side of fifty. He is of average height and build, quick in movement and restless. He might be taken for a man in any walk of life, and this, of course, is the unfailing requisite of the successful man of his calling who must be all things to all men, and at the same time remain inconspicuous. His hair, while thin, has not grayed, which disposes of the presumption that a man long engaged in unraveling the tangled skeins of the phenomenon known as murder has an inordinately worrisome job. His face too is boyishly plump and almost unlined. His hands are thin and soft, his fingers taper, which invites the surmise that he has artistic ability. Which he has, as one perceives in his memoirs that his job has been painting one picture after another—murder pictures.

His eyes are blue and constantly in motion. They seldom betray eager interest, but, then again, this is the mark of the long-trained detective, never to appear too anxious for information—an emotion which if expressed by a crime ferret is likely to inspire fear, surprise, or reticence in the person from whom the investigator seeks hidden and often damaging information. A most noticeable quirk in his deportment is that he never turns his back in the presence of someone about whom he knows little. This may be charged to caution.

And he bears the inevitable "tag," that mannerism with which the inventors of the fictional sleuths invest their manhunters. Inspector Carey is possessed of two voices. Now his speech is soft and sympathetic, almost soothing, but in the twinkling of an eye it shifts, becomes shrill and demanding, penetrating. He is hardly aware of the change. It is not a trick but habit, a part of a technique, acquired instinctively through the countless hours of verbal combat with murderers with whom it has been his practice to sit and talk things over.

This duality of voice is paralleled by another uncanny "tag." When his voice is soft and soothing his face is alight with a pleasant smile. Suddenly a hand moves quickly to his forehead, covers it, then comes slowly down across his face. With this movement the smile vanishes. His features become stern and unyieldingly serious. And when he sits his audience is aware that he does so solidly and intends to remain sitting until the business in hand is finished to his satisfaction. These mannerisms, of which he is quite unconscious, have been acquired in the process of searching the consciences of his suspect subjects.

Outside, on the man hunt in the field, he betrays another characteristic mark. He comes, for the first time, upon the scene where murder has been done. He looks about with an all-inclusive glance at the body of the victim, the setting, and invariably in a quiet voice remarks: "Well, this is the picture I get."

Whereupon his deductive faculties, working upon patterns which years with murder have planted in his memory, build up the picture of what probably happened. With uncommon, uncanny precision he almost always gets the right picture the first time, and with quite reasonable frequency gets his man.

At home he has his family, his dog, and his pipe and books on poisons, weapons, and wounds. But he is most at ease on the murder hunt, and when they ceased officially for him he began to live his cases over again.

Hence this book.

HOWARD MCLELLAN.

New York City,
January 1, 1930.

MEMOIRS OF A MURDER MAN

CHAPTER I

SMALL BOY AT THE MAN HUNT

ALTHOUGH present at the most transcending event in my life, my testimony about it is based wholly upon information, belief, and hearsay. It took place in July, 1865.

It was a warm day, although, I am informed, cool ocean breezes swept in through the open windows of a summer cottage where Mr. and Mrs. Henry C. Carey, along with other New York City folks, were sojourning temporarily to escape the sweltering heat of the big city. In the front room of this cottage, not far from the ocean beach on Staten Island, was a cradle. In this had just been placed an infant whose face, I am told, was round as the moon's.

A tall, well-set man came into the room, looked into the cradle, and, according to those who stood by eagerly watching him, said:

"He's a strapping youngster. Set up like a policeman. I think he'll make one."

The prophet was my father, Henry Carey, and the moon-faced infant he was looking at for the first time, and whose destiny he was mapping, was his son, author of these memoirs. Family tradition always has insisted that I was born a policeman. To prove this the record of my father was cited to me. He had been a policeman on the New York force and left it to go into business. He did well in business, but never could get away from the call of the police. He quit business and rejoined the force a short time after I was born. He never left the force after that.

My older sister seems to have watched the instinct to be a policeman grow within me. She has told me that almost as soon as I had on my first short pants, made of navy blue cloth like my father's uniform, I used to stand in front of our home in lower Manhattan swinging a policeman's club, reduced size. I have, of course, no recollection of this.

Eventually my father became a sergeant on the force and he passed on long before I was being referred to in the public prints as a murder man. My mother was an Acker descended from early Dutch settlers who came to Manhattan in the Seventeenth Century.

There are several possible deductions as to why my father picked me out to be a policeman. He was born in Ireland and came to the land of promise while he was a small boy. At that time nearly all Irish fathers wanted their boys to be policemen, firemen, or politicians. None of my father's ancestors had been policemen. But his male descendants of the second and third generations have been policemen, and two are now. I joined the force in 1889 and left it on December 21, 1928. Two of my sons are now members of the same force. One is a detective. Certainly the New York Police Department did well by father Carey and his chickens. For that matter, there are many men now on the force who can trace back to grandfathers and fathers who preceded them in the same line of service.

My own preferred deduction is that the Irishmen who arrived in America in earlier days knew where and how to butter their bread and wanted a chance to try their hand at governing, having had at that time little opportunity in the old country to test their talents in that direction. They were the governed rather than governors.

Here in America the opportunity opened up to them, starting with police duty. They were equipped by nature, too, for the job. The Irish are not great worriers and they were possessed of that smile which often takes the sting out of tight, temper-trying situations.

And the American police in those early days played a much more important part in governing than they do now. They ran the street-cleaning operation, fed and lodged the poor, kept down criminals, and conducted the elections. And they wore beards like Lincoln's, which seemed then to be the proper insignia of the governing class.

Police pay wasn't high but it was certain to be forthcoming, and a man's job, if he kept away from snags, was good for a lifetime. So all round it looked good to the Irish. Nearly half of the police captains on duty in my father's time were born in Ireland. The rank and file were Irish, too. You couldn't walk two city blocks without running into a bluecoat named O'Brien, Sullivan, Byrnes, O'Reilly, Murphy, or McDermott.

Gaelic influence ran strong in police affairs. I recall hearing a tale about this when I was a boy. In 1844 Mayor Harper of New York City went to England. He was much impressed by what he saw of the London police. He brought back a star-shaped copper badge such as the English bobbies wore and installed it as the official insignia of the New York force. A handful of Irish patrolmen, sporting the new badges, walked proudly into the Old Bowery Theatre. A tough spotted the new badges and yelled, "Take a look at the liveried English lackeys, the coppers." A riot ensued. It was not fomented by the slang term "copper," which came into use in this country for the first time at this riot (and which no policeman cares to hear himself called), but rather because they had been dubbed English lackeys.

So I say that deep down my father's desire to make me a policeman was ruled by the Irish blood in his veins, even when I lay in my cradle. I have never regretted the choice he made for me and have been glad more than once that he didn't choose to make me a politician.

I went along policeward without knowing as a boy, or caring to know, why. Just what influences worked upon me as I grew I can't now recall. The days of my early youth are obscured by the ramifications of some uncounted thousands of homicide cases which occupied my mind during the span of nearly forty years I was on the force. It's not an easy matter now to look into life's mirror and recall what kind of a boy I was when the glass is alive with the faces of men and women upon whom it was my duty to fasten murders, and the grinning faces of others, some still alive, who I am positive were murderers but who beat the law. It's an uncanny pattern to look upon at the age of sixty-three.

Boyhood seems to have flown past me like a phantom. At seven there was no doubt that I was on my way. At about that age my father toted me with him to the Chambers Street station house where he was on duty. It stood in the Third Precinct, an old red brick building. It was in the center of what was then one of the busiest sections of Manhattan Island. New York City's business and residential district had not reached Forty-second Street on the north. In the Third were many hotels and retail shops and docks along the Hudson River where wharf rats and pirates had their playground. To the east several blocks was the squat, gray courthouse that Boss Bill Tweed built and went to jail for building.

My father's custom was to let me have the run of the station house while he was on duty at the desk. One of the first impressions which I remember was the assort-

Drilling a Squad of Policemen.

The bearded policemen of Carey's boyhood.

ment of beards I saw in the station house. Nearly every policeman wore one, and crooks that were brought in were adorned likewise. Lincoln undoubtedly set the style. Beards lasted with policemen until Grant's time, and when the John L. Sullivan type of walrus mustache came along police beards came off, but mustaches remained and flourished. It was possible for even a small boy to judge the status of a policeman by the beard he wore. The rank and file wore long chin whiskers while the higher-ups sported side-whiskers, or Lord Dundrearies as they were called.

Among the eighteen thousand men on the New York force to-day not a beard will be found and scarcely a mustache. When they disappeared quite a few years back nimble-witted bunco men turned many a trick selling to gullible but ambitious barbers the exclusive franchise to shave the members of the force. Police beards are mentioned not alone because they were a first impression with me but also to show that the policeman is quite a stylist. I don't doubt that if President Hoover were to appear with a Van Dyck police beards too would reappear. Or if professional crooks began again to conceal cunning grins under beards, the police, at least detectives, probably would follow suit upon the theory that a hunter in the woods should not dress like a volunteer fireman on summer parade.

If there was ferocity hidden under the beards of the Chambers Street men it never fell to my lot to see it. They liked children. It was part of their duty to care for a share of the seven-thousand-odd youngsters who were lost each year in the city and also to look after the precinct's quota of some one hundred thousand homeless and penniless persons who were quartered during each year in the city's station houses. The old-time policemen got a closer view of life's seamy side than do their modern successors. Or perhaps in this prosperous day there isn't such a seamy side to American life.

Sometimes I mingled with the lost children, but most often the basement in the old brick house held my attention. There was a sitting room in this basement, in the center of which was a long, low oak table. Around this sat tall, square-shouldered men in civilian clothes. These were the precinct detectives and patrolmen assigned to plain-clothes duty. They stood aloof and apart from uniformed men. They were very mysterious to me at first. But after a while I was sitting on their knees, and from this point of vantage I heard and saw something of the man hunt.

I got to comprehend more of what these men did by what I saw upstairs at the sergeant's desk. I can't recall all that went on here, but I have a recollection of having seen my fill of action. To this desk the men in plain clothes brought their prisoners. While the captives stood at the desk the detectives ran their hands through the pockets and clothing of their prisoners and out upon the high desk tumbled rings and watches, money, nippers, keys, billies, jimmies, gold bricks, and the other paraphernalia of the thief. There were seldom any guns taken, and when there was the face of the sergeant came alive. A man with a gun was a good capture. Thieves of the old days were not gun carriers. I suppose I remember the tools and occasional guns because of a boy's instinctive interest in them.

Prisoners were taken from the desk to a corner. I have quite a vivid recollection of gruff police voices hurling questions at the thieves. Sometimes the captives lunged at the detectives or struggled to get away. Guns flashed, clubs whacked, and men fell. Action and conflict, and I saw most of it as a fascinated onlooker.

It was a world which was closed to other boys. No matter where he is put a boy will find his heroes. I was now about nine or ten. I am quite sure that by this time I had given up carrying the miniature policeman's club, for there was nothing fascinating in that after I had watched these plain-clothes men. There was the strangest fascination in watching them search their prisoners; in the way they seemed to know just where to put their hands to find the thieves' gear and of flashing things at them that fairly took the prisoners off their feet. They seemed to be privileged above all men; to be permitted to wander about in ordinary clothes with the magic power to haul men in.

Being accorded the privileges of a mascot, I listened to their tales, which they told with many gestures and in excited voices. They used a language all their own. Honest men were "citizens" in their vocabulary. Every wrongdoer was a thief. An arrest was a "collar"; a pickpocket a "dip"; a stolen purse a "leather." A watch was a "round piece of white or yellow metal." This made the world they moved in all the more mysterious, fascinating, to me.

They talked glibly of professional thieves, calling them by their pet names. They were picturesque names such as would stick to a boy's tongue. There were Tim Oats; Marm Mandelbaum, notorious woman fence; Shang Draper, gambler and thief; Sheenie Mike Kurtz; the Hopes, father and sons who never have been equaled as bank robbers; Funeral Wells, who stole purses while posing as a mourner; Deafy Hunt, expert burglar though deaf; Grand Central Pete, who sold gold bricks to farmers arriving at railroad depots; Hungry Joe, Pretty Jimmie, and Jersey Jimmie, the butcher cart thieves; Banjo Pete Emerson; Paper Collar Joe; Eleck the Milkman, and scores of others. Many of them lived on to meet me face to face in a professional capacity years later.

And these detectives were forever going to or coming from the Burnt Rag, Satan's Circus, Hell's Kitchen, Cockran's Roost, McGuirk's Suicide Hall, the Bucket of Blood, Billy McGlory's Place, the Slide, and other notorious rendezvous where a man was supposed to take his life in his hands when he entered. It gave these men a glamor which uniformed men never had.

Of murder cases I saw little but heard a lot. Precinct detectives spoke of their cases, and occasionally a veteran dropped in to tell of murders in his time which always eclipsed those of a later day. Now and then a still more glamorous figure stepped in to the station house, a Central Office man, one of twenty great men stationed at headquarters in an old gray building at No. 300 Mulberry Street, a spot often woven into stage melodramas and mystery novels.

Central Office and its men were so widely exploited on the stage that for years audiences merely had to hear Spring 3100 mentioned and without another clue recognized it as the telephone number of Central Office.

New York City was reputed in my boyhood to be rashly wicked and untamable. Yet the homicide record then was about sixty a year, and few of them were like the mysteries of later years. There was no such person as a murder expert in the Central Office and hardly need for one. Central Office men handled anything their chief sent them out on and they were paid a patrolman's wage. Glory made up the difference. Their merit was determined in an odd way. When a detective was spoken of as having "375 years" it meant that he had put away criminals for sentences totaling that amount of time and he was considered pretty good.

When a man solved a murder or caught a slayer there was talk, talk not only about his exploit but about all the big murders and detectives of bygone days. Some of the older murders had been woven into elaborate legends, a rich dish to set before a youth who was quite sure that destiny was cutting him out for a police career. I listened eagerly when after school I hurried down to Chambers Street to look and listen.

Boys will be born by the sea and go down in ships.

Other boys will see the first light of day in the home of a policeman and go the way of his father without knowing the whys and wherefores, lured on in his youth by the romance spun on the tongues of his heroes. There was certainly a lure for me in the tales the veterans told about High Constable Jacob Hays. Hays had been dead many years when I was a boy, but in his time he was the one-man wonder in the police world.

High Constable Hays was the first to install a detective system in the New York Police Department. In 1836 he had a law passed creating the post of roundsman, and 192 men were appointed to the Watch Department—the forerunner of the New York force. He assigned twelve to plain-clothes work. They worked in pairs and, besides keeping their eyes peeled for crooks and watching each other, saw to it that uniformed men were not amiss in their duties. Their pay was twelve shillings. The entire Watch cost the city $262,000 a year or about one dollar per citizen. The Watch consisted of 453 men.

At that time I knew nothing about Vidocq, the famous French detective, but he was contemporaneous with Hays. Vidocq organized his Brigade de Sûreté in 1817, but before that Hays was building a reputation in New York City as a single-handed crime ferret. The story-tellers in Chambers Street station house called the high constable a born detective who worked by instinct. He differed from Vidocq in many ways, chief of which was the fact that Vidocq before he became a police agent was a criminal, while Hays, a strict and devout Presbyterian, knew all about crooks but never had been one himself.

His fame reached all parts of the world. Twenty years after his death letters reached New York from abroad addressed to him as the head of the Department and inviting him to visit Europe to work out unsolved crimes. He slept only six hours out of each twenty-four and made his men do likewise. He monopolized the mystery solving and went about unarmed. He carried only a light locust staff with which he knocked off crooks' hats. When they bent to recover them the high constable gave them a push and they fell sprawling upon the sidewalk. There they remained until Hays had given them a brief but edifying lecture on the better life.

The details of one of Hays's great murder exploits, relayed to me by a veteran, were thrilling enough. In 1820 the captain of a sailing vessel was found slain in Coenties Alley on the water front. He had been shot in the temple. Hays arrested one Johnson, keeper of a sailors' hotel, for the murder. The suspect was coming piously out of Trinity Church when Hays seized him.

At that moment the victim's body lay in the rotunda in City Hall Park, a few blocks away. Hays marched his man to the rotunda and stood him in a darkened room beside a table covered with a sheet. Suddenly the window curtains went up and the sheet was pulled from the table, revealing the body of the slain captain.

"Look, my good man," Hays whispered into Johnson's ear. "Look upon the body. Have you ever seen that man before?"

"Yes!" cried Johnson. "I murdered him."

Johnson was convicted, but upon the gallows recanted a confession he had made to Hays. Presently he spotted the high constable moving in the crowd. As the hangman coiled his noose about the murderer's neck Johnson shouted, "I can't lie while that man Hays's eyes are on me."

This was the first actual instance I had heard about of a detective using this method to bring about a confession of guilt. Years later I was to try it myself when our Murder Clinic was established. It met with varying degrees of success. Murderers since Hays's time had hardened. The ghastliness once associated with violent death by murder seems to have been greatly minimized. Slayers nowadays seldom shudder and confess at sight of their victims' bodies. Perhaps the great war cheapened human life, or the advent of the motor car, with increasing fatalities on public streets, has made death a much too common sight to be shuddered at. Then too in High Constable Hays's time the gibbet stood but a block from the common jail, and only a few weeks instead of years stood between murderer and his penalty. Murderers could be made to quail at sight of their victims' bodies when out the window they could also see a gallows.

Death, though I have seen it too many times to count, though I have sent a good many murderers to their doom, remains to me a horrible sight. I have never seen a murderer executed and never shall. Such experience in a murder man's career is unnecessary. I don't know what my reaction would be if I were to witness an execution. I don't care to know. One thing I am certain of—capital punishment is the only effective deterrent yet devised by society. If we have more murders to-day it is because an abnormally large number of criminals who deserve it don't get the extreme penalty. This makes punishment not a certainty but a gamble, and the greatest gamblers in the world are murderers. I don't believe I'm calloused or hard hearted. It is merely because I have seen so much of what is so easily forgotten, the victims of murderers, not only those slain and their families, but those other victims, the murderer's families.

The most impressive murder scene I ever looked upon was not an actuality but a picture. I don't recall how old I was, but I was old enough to be impressed. It was the first I had ever seen. It was a wash drawing from the brush of a newspaper artist. It was labeled "The Unsolved Murder." It depicted in graphic detail a bedchamber in a pretentious home and upon the floor in night attire was the body of a man. The room was in disorder. I was looking at it when a veteran precinct detective saw me.

"Was this a real murder?" I asked.

"Don't you know, my lad, what that is?" he said in surprise. "That was the biggest murder case this town ever had. The Nathan case. I worked on it."

I had heard about the Nathan case, but I was to hear more from one who had been there.

"That's a perfect picture of the scene," the detective went on. "Only one thing wrong about it. You see the uniformed patrolman standing at the bedroom door with his nightstick?"

I studied the picture.

"Well it wasn't a patrolman's job," he said quite pompously. "Murder is a detective's job."

He told me the story of the Nathan case. Benjamin Nathan, a rich merchant, had been beaten to death and killed in his bedroom. His valuables were missing. Chief of Detectives James J. Kelso arrived upon the scene with his assistants. He saw the bloody imprint of a man's hand upon the casing of the door in the room.

"This," said Kelso, according to the legend, "is the crime of a gentleman," and he pointed to the imprint. "Long, thin, ladylike fingers. A dude killer."

The hand imprint showed plainly in the picture.

That, however, was as near as they ever got to the murderer. A reward of forty-seven thousand dollars was offered for his capture. The detective bureau split into factions, each having its pet theory. Superintendent of Police John Jourdan is reputed to have died of broken heart mourning his inability to solve the crime.

It was the sensation of the age. Years later, when I was captain of the Homicide Squad, a letter reached me purporting to solve the old crime. It developed that the writer, who had lived during the Nathan case, had become demented trying to unravel the puzzle.

Suspicions rested upon the dissolute son of the dead merchant. A noted physician of the day offered to put the son under an anæsthetic and in this way unconsciously

High Constable Jacob Hays, the first famous American detective.

draw from him a confession. Public opinion was against this proposal. It was never tried. To-day the modern fingerprinting expert would have determined one thing at least: whether the bloody imprint was that of the hand of the son who died without having the suspicion against him lifted or whether it was the hand of someone else.

The detective held me enthralled. There was a pause as he finished his story. Then he went on:

"Now, if you've got the detective bee in your bonnet take a good long look at that picture. In this game everything is pictures, pictures, pictures."

Long after he left me I was still looking at the picture unaware that destiny was cutting me out then to spend the rest of my life looking at pictures, real pictures of murder and its authors, and, from these pictures, develop whatever special talent I may have in the art, or trade, or profession, of murder inquiry.

Another famous murder case was just petering out when I was about ready to leave school and seek employment. I had first-hand accounts of it from day to day. One Charles Goodrich was found slain in his Brooklyn home, beaten to death. From the precise manner in which two damp towels had been hung on a line in the cellar of the dead man's home, Superintendent of Police Frank Campbell, of Brooklyn, reasoned that the slayer was a woman.

Campbell accosted Kate Stoddard, a public character more or less, on the street after the murder. As he approached her she tore a gold locket from her throat, and as it dropped to the sidewalk two dark red particles fell out. Kate reached eagerly for them and started to put them in her mouth.

"Don't," cried Campbell. "They might be poison."

"Oh, no," said Kate. "They're just dried blood."

He made her yield up the particles.

And that was as far as he got on the Goodrich murder.

He had the particles of blood; suspicion ran against the woman, but no one could determine to the satisfaction of a court and jury whether they were human blood. The chemist of to-day, right bower of the murder man, quickly determines whether particles of blood are human or not. Science was a little backward in those days. But as to Kate Stoddard and the Goodrich crime it hardly mattered. She came to an unhappy end in a madhouse brooding over the crime.

About this time my unofficial study of murder pictures ended. I secured employment in the Western Union Telegraph Company's offices where my brother worked and still works. For me it was just a makeshift; for him a lifetime career. As soon as I had reached the legal age I took the civil-service examination for patrolmen and passed. This meant that I would be in a uniform pretty soon, and while a uniform wasn't the habit of a detective it was one of the things a man had to wear until someone in authority thought he had the makings of a detective.

I waited for the call to join the force. Waiting, I got a shock.

Although George Washington Walling had retired from the superintendency of the New York Police Department in 1885 he still had ideas about improving the force, and plenty of them. His big idea was this, in his own words:

"I have sometimes fancied that it might be wholly possible to endow policemen with those elegancies and courtesies of life which make refined social intercourse so pleasant and improving. Imagine an institution in which the guardians of the peace can learn to make a pleasant bow, to walk with grace, to shake hands with dignity, to lift their hats in a courtly way, or extend their protecting arms to a lady with Chesterfieldian decorum. Such ideas are teachable."

Dude policemen! That was the reaction that met Walling's suggestion. And it almost lost New York City a murder man. It was then and still is my idea that detectives should dress quietly and be unassuming, for the less notice they attract the easier their task. I debated whether to be or not to be a member of a Wallingfied police force.

Walling countered with more details. He would teach all the graces to policemen. He picked Frank Mayo, then a reigning Broadway comedian, as his expert to teach grace of manners; Chauncey M. Depew would have the chair of deportment; William M. Evarts, noted lawyer and after-dinner speaker, would instruct policemen how to "crack a pleasant joke," and in the matter of dress and social usage their teacher would be none other than E. Berry Wall, the town's greatest dandy and social lion.

Former Superintendent Walling was a man who meant well. His grand idea, however, never was put into execution. My shock was over and I was on my way.

On March 1, 1889, I hotfooted it to police headquarters to be sworn in. It was like going after something that by right of inheritance is yours.

CHAPTER II

PICTURE OF A THIEF

AFTER a month of probation duty I was assigned to a regular post on April 3, 1889. It was in the lower section of the city, not far from the old Chambers Street station house, and took in a part of the post my father had walked. I took care of the multiplicity of duties that befall a uniformed policeman in a big city. There were, in addition to the watch kept for crimes and their perpetrators, the duties of guardianship. Women and children had to be helped across streets, guided to their destinations; lost youngsters to be found and returned to their parents. Watch had to be kept for fires, cracked water mains, street lamps that were out; for suspicious characters and unseemly happenings. Traffic had not yet become a problem.

My physical senses were devoted to their task. In a day I walked many miles and sometimes imagined that in time my regulation shoes would wear grooves in the pavement. The uniform was not irksome, yet it was not the raiment to satisfy my ambition. I had set my mind on being a detective, and it seemed that if I remained in uniform any great length of time I would be known to every crook in Christendom, and thus my usefulness as a plain-clothes man would be impaired. But the tradition was, and still exists, that a man is not fitted for detective duty until

On Post.

How the finest looked in Carey's days on Post

he has had at least two years on post. Central Office, which was my objective, seemed a long way off. I figured that if ever the call came to join the hall of fame at headquarters it would be after I had made enough mileage on post to have circled the globe once at least.

Central Office was in command of a man who was being referred to as the greatest detective in the world. Newspapers were calling him "the immortal" and challenging Scotland Yard to produce his equal. He was Thomas Byrnes, chief inspector of the Central Office detectives, and one of the most picturesque thief catchers in the history of the American police.

It was said of Byrnes that if he picked a man to serve under him as a detective and he made good, that man, like Byrnes, would earn immortality. In 1928, nearly forty years later, I read in a newspaper of my retirement. There was a line which said: "Carey, last of Byrnes's forty immortals, leaves the force." Such is immortality. I had never dreamed while walking post that some day my name would be linked with that of the great man at headquarters, or that my retirement would be the means of reviving his immortality.

Probably every young ambitious policeman on post in my time hoped eventually to work for Byrnes. I know I had it, although, while the hope was burning fiercest, Central Office looked as far away as the White House in Washington. There was always this much to keep the fires of ambition burning: Byrnes took on no men for the Central Office who had not walked a post.

During off-duty hours I studied Byrnes's famous book, *Professional Criminals of America,* which he had published in 1886. In this were listed the pedigrees of all professional thieves of the higher rank, together with their photographs and complete descriptions of their methods of operation. It was not only a "Who's Who" of the underworld of that time but a textbook on the technique of the best-known and shrewdest criminals. Byrnes had been gathering the data for years. The book was put into circulation among police departments, banks, hotels, and railroad companies, and became a sort of "blue book" of criminal identification. It was the earliest systematic attempt to establish crime control and crime prevention on a national scale.

There was little in the book about murderers. The reason was obvious. Byrnes did not regard slayers as professionals, and the thieves of that day, unlike the professional criminals of the present era, had not adopted murder as an incidental to robbery. The book was hated by habitual criminals for it advertised them to the world at large. They might not be sentenced to prison as habitual criminals and made to stay there for life, but Byrnes's book sentenced them to lasting notoriety. Then, also, death and life term penalties were more often inflicted than they are now, so there was hardly anything to be gained by picturing and describing criminals who were no longer at large.

Frequently criminals objected to having their pictures taken for the book. There were some mighty struggles to prevent the operation of "mugging," as the rogues' gallery process is termed. Byrnes was very proud of his success in always getting good pictures of professional thieves. If they would not sit peacefully for a photograph they were held down while the camera made a lasting record of their physiognomies. He once pictured the struggles of a crook while being photographed to show the public what the police were up against in working out a system of crime prevention. The picture was known as "The Inspector's Model," and shows a bearded crook being mugged under forced circumstances. The newspapers got hold of it and spoke of the operation as applying the "third degree." But the photograph was only a model.

The crook was a detective wearing a false beard who posed for the picture as Byrnes stood and directed the scene. I believe this was the first use of the term "third degree."

It was generally known among the men on the force that Byrnes would pick out for Central Office duty only those men who had acquired a wide knowledge of professional criminals and their methods. His first requirement was that a man should have "the picture of a thief" well in mind, a sort of mental pattern to fit men and women of the criminal class. The word "thief," I might explain, is a generic term applied to all professional criminals of whatever degree or specialty. Others who have not attained professional status are just "wrong," yet it was Byrnes's belief that, whether professionals or amateurs, men who committed crime displayed the same characteristics. He believed that a patrolman, if he were at all observant and had the knack, with a memory and ordinary deductive faculties to back him up, could get "the picture of a thief" while walking post. He might also, if he were interested in carrying the picture process farther, get "the picture of a crime."

So I proceeded while on patrol duty to acquire this essential, hoping that when I had gotten the knack it would lead me to Central Office. A few months of observation gave me the start on this picture. The mental process which is involved has remained with me through all the years and is the foundation of whatever peculiar skill I may have shown, first as a general investigator of all classes of crime, and later as a specialist in murder inquiry. If there is a science to crime detection it is in the application of this process. The other sciences will help, but, first of all, whatever rules these sciences lay down, or whatever clues they develop, they can bear fruit only when there is a trained mind to put them to practical use.

I'll try to paint the picture of a thief as I built it up in my mind while walking my post looking for the details that composed it.

In his manner of locomotion the criminal betrays instinctive characteristics which set him apart from his honest fellowmen. He will walk along at a jerky pace, although his gait is usually fast. He moves in spurts. At intervals he will pause, or slow up, to look over the scene or passers-by. He will turn his head furtively and make his survey in glances and not by studied, calm observation. In a crowd of normal persons going about their business the crook will hang behind, sidestep, and loiter. When he thinks he has found a vantage ground he will halt in a hallway or on a corner. It is a peculiar twist of fate that he invariably seeks a shadowed spot in which to pause and get his bearings. He avoids looking at anything in a straight, direct way but casts his eyes downward.

On post I followed such movements closely and became able to pick the suspect out in a crowd with ease and certainty. In a crowd the contrast between the criminal and the normal law-abiding person is most noticeable. Almost every move is a betrayal. The criminal stands out like a rank weed flowering above a smooth lawn. If he is a pickpocket his false move is an unnecessary jostle, an unseemly movement of the arms in a crowd otherwise still and preoccupied. If he is a burglar, going to or from a job, he measures his safety by apprehensive glances sidewise or around, and with each movement of the head his gait quickens or slows up.

The reason for this became quite apparent to me. It is the logical working of nature. Crime is an irregular enterprise which reflects itself in irregularities of movement, manner, and speech. A man walking post for days, weeks, and months, with his mind concentrated on catching these peculiarities in men and women, falls as easily into the habit of sensing them as a skilled carpenter instinctively

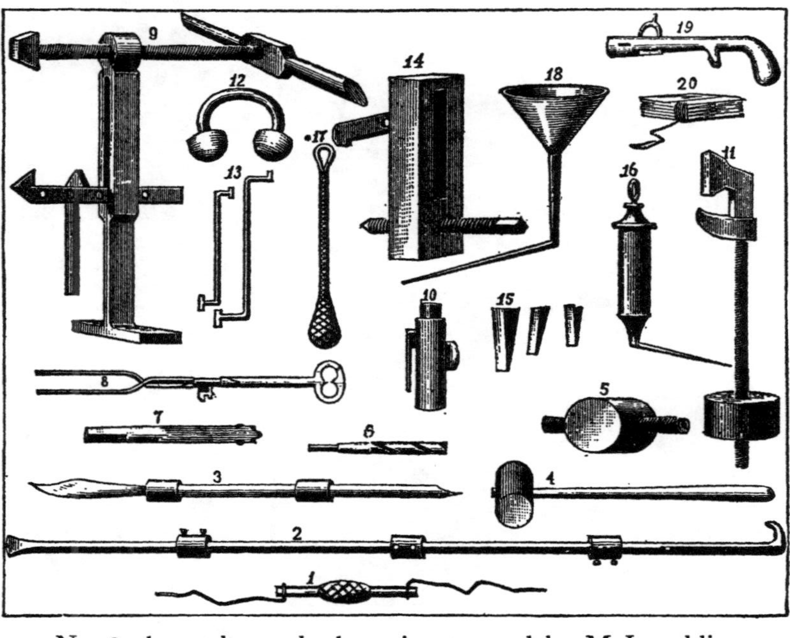

No. 8 above shows the key nippers used by McLaughlin, the hotel burglar

catches the grains in lumber or the tailor, by the feel of fabric, detects its quality.

And the irony of it is that the criminal, self-confident egotist, believes that nature has endowed him with a shrewdness above that of his honest fellows. But nature tricks him. He hangs himself by his own rope, for these shifty, jerky movements, the twisting of the head, the sudden darting off a normal course into a shadow, while supposed to enable him to pick out and thwart his enemy, the police, furnishes that enemy with an unfailing index to his man. Nature seems to refuse to serve as a protector of unlawful enterprise.

I observed early that thieves always gravitated toward certain types of haunts, mingled with one class, and came, as a rule, from one class, the poor and dissolute. If a burglary or robbery occurred on my post it was possible for me, on many occasions, to find the man I wanted by going direct to the places he would likely be, shabby places that would by the same token invite the thief and attract the attention of his pursuer. The finding of loot or thieves' tools in his possession, or the conflicting elements in the thief's story, to me were the daily tests to which this early picture was put to determine its accuracy.

And by the same logical course of studying the illogical, unnatural moments of the criminal I arrived at the picture of a crime. If windows were broken open, doors forced, safes robbed, or sneak jobs perpetrated it was possible to determine their authorship; that is, whether it was the work of a professional or not by the type of tool used, the marks upon the window, door, or safe. From these circumstances a man could map out the course of his investigation and move with very little lost motion.

From what I know of detectives the world over—those in Scotland Yard, Paris, Berlin, Vienna, or Rome—I am quite sure those who have made an outstanding place for themselves possess this basic instinct and operate with it.

It is their science. Froest, one of Scotland Yard's most outstanding detectives, is no great hero to practical police detectives. He was very successful. Since his work was contemporaneous with mine, I watched his career with interest, and from visiting European detectives got more or less first-hand information about his work. The secret of his success, if forty years of police work entitle me to sit in judgment, was this: he had gotten the picture of thieves and crimes and had trained his mental resources to work with it. If he was equally successful in dealing with amateurs at crime as well as professionals, with murderers as well as thieves, it was because of that peculiar faculty which comes to the detective long in service, and who has a never-ending flair for the work—the ability to assimilate two logics, that of the criminal, which is wrong, and that of the law-abiding, honest human being, which is right. The latter is normal, the former unnatural; and by the picture process the detective measures the difference between the two.

How this process works out in murder inquiry is left to subsequent chapters. I did not get the opportunity while on post to apply the process to murder. The first big murder case that attracted my attention during my first years on the force was the poisoning of Helen Nielson Potts, a student at a fashionable New York City boarding school, by her husband Carlyle Harris, a young medical student. I had nothing to do with the case, but read or heard all the details and was absorbed in them. Byrnes at headquarters handled the case. It came to an end in January, 1892, with the conviction of Harris. The trial intrigued me because it penetrated the dark domain of the poisoner, which is the realm of murder most often entered by the educated type of slayer. So to keep abreast of developments at the trial, which were shrouded in the technical testimony of medical experts, I bought a standard textbook on toxicology and at home, after hours, pursued a home-study course in what is perhaps the most fascinating of all phases of murder inquiry.

Captain Edward Slevin was in command of my precinct. He had been one of Byrnes's most trusted lieutenants. He knew from personal contact with the inspector precisely what he required in Central Office men. I had never asked Slevin for plain-clothes work, although itching for an assignment. I had done a little off-duty plain-clothes work just to test unofficially the effectiveness of my picture of a thief. It had worked out quite successfully. The crimes were minor, but they had built up certain suspicions which I wanted to put to the test, and letting the picture guide me I solved them and brought in the offenders to Slevin. He was not a man to say much, one way or the other. If he didn't like a man's work he said little but acted quickly. If he did like it he said less but also moved quickly. I imagine that he thought that by this time, if I had any natural talent for detective work, I should have a fairly workable picture of a thief in mind.

He assigned me to plain-clothes duty, and the opportunity came to put my picture to its first important test. In my rounds I became well acquainted with hotel men in the precinct and made it a point to establish a close contact with them, for hotels in those days were magnets to crooks. The hotel detective had not yet become part of a hotel's complement.

I dropped into the old Hotel Stevens one night and was informed by the clerk that a guest had registered who had been in the hotel on previous occasions. Invariably after he quit the hotel complaints were made by guests that their rooms had been robbed by an unusual thief who, in some unaccountable way, visited the rooms while the occupants were asleep and left the doors locked from the inside. This guest was now occupying a room on the second floor on a hallway leading from the main stairway to a side window. An elevator shaft ran alongside the room he occupied. All rooms on this floor were occupied.

I took it upon myself to solve the mystery. I was anxious to let Slevin know how good a picture of a thief I had. If by chance the crook turned out to be a man with a big reputation among thieves, Byrnes very likely would send for him. The inspector doted on meeting the big fellows face to face; on quizzing them about their methods and their movements. And if, also by chance, the man I was after happened to have his "mug" in Byrnes's book, it would doubtless please "the immortal." He might possibly like to see the man who caught him.

It was impossible to watch the suspect's room from a position in the hallway, for there was no place to stand and observe him come and go without my being seen. So I rigged up what is commonly known in detective circles as a "plant."

I let myself into an elegantly appointed elevator and, pulling down on the steel cable, was hoisted to the second floor. I took off my shoes and fell back into a napping posture on an upholstered settee within the lift. I had to double up my knees to do this. I could see dimly out of a grated opening in the door to the hallway. I left a small light burning in the elevator so that if anyone looked in he would see me and take it for granted that I was asleep. If I left the elevator in darkness a professional thief, not being able to see within, might be frightened off temporarily.

Presently a tall figure in stockings came silently down the hall and halted before the door. He glanced into the elevator and smiled. Then he looked around quickly along the hall in both directions. His shoulders went erect. He started down the hall with a bold step. I caught a glimpse of his face through the grated opening in the door. I was quite certain that he fitted into my picture. I arose and watched him go down the hall. He reached the stairway and looked down quickly to where the night clerk stood at his desk. He straightened up again, looked around, and then stole along the hall: sign number two that he had no business in the hallway, or he wouldn't have gone to the pains of looking down the stairway. He wore heavy underwear, woolen socks, and a blue sweater: indication number three that he was garbed for prowling. A guest would not enter the hall in his under-attire unless it suited a special purpose to do so. A thief might. If anyone encountered him he might easily explain that he was looking for the bathroom.

He disappeared for a moment, then reappeared. He stood still: the little lull of indecision that comes in the preliminary maneuvers of a thief. He walked down another short hall, then started up a flight of stairs. He stepped heavily on the first stair as if testing it for creaks.

I let myself out of the elevator and walked along the hallway in his wake. I turned and went up another stairway and, reaching the top, looked through the banisters and saw him halted at the door of a room. He glanced around. He had a shining instrument in one hand. It looked like a curling iron. Voices sounded on the floor above. He turned quickly, listened, and then started down the stairway. I crept down my stairway to avoid being seen. I wanted to catch him red handed in a room.

He reached the floor below the same time I did. We almost bumped. He smiled. I looked at his hands. The instrument was gone. I seized him.

"Give me that instrument," I demanded.

"I haven't got any instrument," he said, and showed his open hands. He tried to squirm out of my grasp.

"Give me that instrument," I insisted.

"Say, you got me wrong," he said, pulling his shoulders back and eyeing me as one who had outraged his dignity. "You can't do this to me. I'm a guest of this hotel. I'll sue you."

Two men, whose voices had sounded on the floor above,

hove in sight, coming down the stairs in a zigzag course as though tipped off their balance by one too many highballs. They came up to me and insisted, rather volubly, that I had the wrong man.

"Give me that instrument," I demanded once again.

The suspect threatened me. I lifted the sweater up over his head. On the outside of a white woolen undershirt, near the armpit, I observed brown stitches, unevenly sewn, one stitch long, the next short. They were a man's stitches not a woman's. They ran in a sort of egg-shaped design. I felt where the stitches were and my hands closed on a hard object. I felt under the shirt and from a tiny pocket sewed inside the shirt drew out a pair of key nippers made in the shape of a curling iron. These explained how it had happened that the doors of the rooms that had been robbed were always locked with the keys inside. My man merely inserted the nippers in the lock, caught the tip of the key and turned it. He entered and came out by this means, leaving his victims to wonder at the mystery. He was a rare operator who worked as his victims were asleep.

I turned to the two misguided samaritans, then at the man.

"Well," I said to the suspect.

"All right, officer," he said. "You got me."

I looked him over closely. I felt of his underclothing. It was spongy. He had on two heavy suits of woolen undergarments and two pairs of heavy socks. He was dressed for a night of business. He was professional but he wouldn't say who he was. It was the way with old-time thieves. Caught, they admitted their offense, but the one thing they seemed to want to crawl out of was their past record. Perhaps they were afraid of getting into Byrnes's book. At any rate, there was a wholesome fear in them which in later years seemed to have disappeared from succeeding generations of professional crooks.

When I got my man to the station house Captain Slevin

interviewed him. Later I took him to the Central Office. Here Detective John Heard, one of Byrnes's camera-eyed men, recognized him as Charles McLaughlin, alias McClain, one of the best-known hotel thieves of the day. Byrnes came in and had a look at him and grinned. His "mug" was in "the immortal's" book, adorned with a luxuriant growth of beard.

He pleaded guilty to possessing burglar's tools and was sent away.

The picture process had worked. Not only that, but I had enjoyed the rare opportunity of seeing a thief in the act; of watching his moves when the stress of crime was on his mind. It made it possible for me in years to come to put myself in the place of a criminal in the act, a most valuable lesson which I applied with some success when it became necessary for me in more than one murder case to judge between the pictures of faked and real robberies—fakes built up to shield the real murderers.

It was gratifying also to know that Byrnes had seen my first important catch and had expressed, in his blunt way, some delight that McLaughlin's picture was already in his book.

A short time later an order from Byrnes directed me to report to him at headquarters. I was ushered into his presence. He was a man of few words.

"Do you know any thieves?" he put to me.

"Only a few, but I'm willing to learn," I replied.

"That's all," he said with a wave of his hand. "Go back to your precinct."

Whether I had registered favorably with "the immortal" I did not know. My interview was abrupt and indefinite. But that was Byrnes's way. He looked at a man once, sized him up, and expected his men to have the same faculty. He doted on "getting the picture" from his first glimpse of a man, an act, or a scene. He had merely subjected me to this process.

CHAPTER III

IN "THE IMMORTAL'S" PICTURELAND

APPARENTLY I had acquired a workable picture of a thief, for on May 24, 1892, I was transferred to the Central Office, thus coming under the eye of Byrnes, who was now chief of police but still personally supervised the Detective Bureau. There were forty Byrnes-picked detective sergeants and thirty-two detective officers in the bureau.

No man who ever worked under Byrnes could forget him or the picture that surrounded him. He sat at an old-fashioned high-topped desk known in those days as a secretary. It had few papers on it, but this was not strange, for the chief was a man with a long memory who needed few papers to run his job. He had joined the force in 1863; had risen through all the ranks to the highest place.

Byrnes stood five feet eleven inches, a huge man, yet not bulky. His shoulders were broad and erect; his smile was friendly but firm. He had a flowing mustache and was at ease in a low, comfortable Piccadilly collar. He was addicted to the low-crowned derby with wide brim which he wore well down over his large ears. He always appeared in a cutaway coat edged with braid. When he promenaded he went along with military dignity. He was always pointed out by passers-by, but not because of any vanity or self-

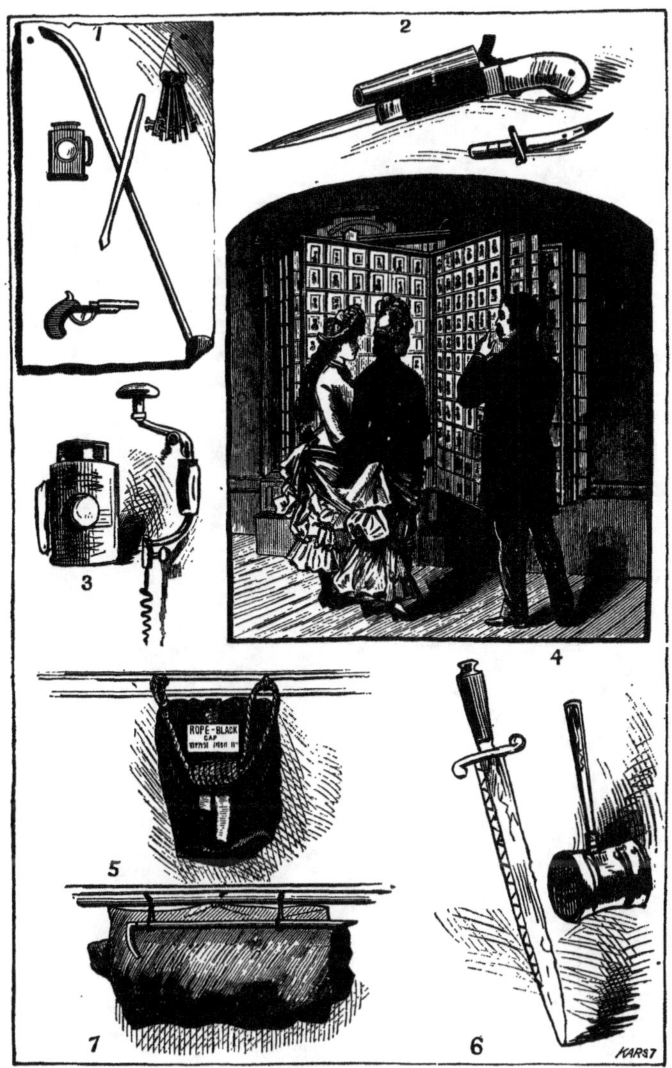

Exhibits in Byrnes's Pictureland

importance on his part. He believed in dignity because it won him respect not only from his men but from the world of professional criminals he was always after. He was one of the pioneers in crime prevention who understood the effectiveness of visual propaganda on active and would-be wrongdoers. He held the underworld of his time in awed subjection.

One look at his offices indicated why he doted on pictures. He himself was not only a picture, but he lived in a world of pictures, the pictureland of rogues.

Opposite his private office was a large room referred to often as a museum and by some newspapers as the "mystery chamber" or "cold room." On its walls were pictures of famous criminals he had caught. In glass-paneled cabinets running the entire width and height of the walls were the tools of thieves and the weapons of murderers, braces and bits, dark lanterns, lock picks, jimmies both one piece and sectional, skeleton keys, spurious gold bricks, and bunco men's lurid circulars for the gullible. There was a weird assortment of weapons—billies, pistols, daggers, slung shots, and vials—that had contained poisons and knockout drops. In the center of these were two black masks and a hangman's noose—both the accouterments of the public executioner which had actually been used.

Also upon the walls facing chairs in which criminals sat while under examination were large pictures of men and women cavorting in low dives. On a large chest which stood in front of the chairs were enlarged drawings, in color, of playing cards, dice, and other implements of the gambler.

"A thief has three weaknesses," was Byrnes's favorite saying. "Wine, women, and gambling."

His museum pictured the story. It was a stirring exhibit in chapters. First the cause of downfall—wine, women, and gambling; the tools which brought about the downfall—thieves' paraphernalia and weapons; and the end—the hangman's noose and the black masks or caps. It was more of his picture propaganda. Amid these graphic mementos Byrnes seldom failed to get a confession from criminals brought before him in this museum. They saw the pictures. He was not a bully. His own idea was to "soften" a criminal, and he expressed it in these words: "Even the greatest ruffians are amenable to the influences of a friendly address. No man is so utterly depraved or lost as not to possess a soft chord in his heart." Byrnes played upon that chord through his assorted pictures.

A thing about him that impressed me most deeply was his expression "Here's the picture I get" when he was discussing a crime, or "Now this is the picture I want you to get" when he was assigning a detective to a case. They are two expressions that cling to my tongue to-day.

Of Byrnes's influence upon the modernization of police departments there is little doubt. When he was appointed chief inspector in 1880 he created the first real detective bureau. At the time twenty-eight plain-clothes men were on detective duty. He sent twenty-one of them back to posts and picked out their successors from men who had done good work on patrol duty. He increased his staff to forty men, made them detective sergeants, and thus built up the first real American police detective bureau. His plan was copied everywhere.

He judged his men by the number of arrests they made and convictions they secured. Explaining his administration to a legislative committee headed by Assemblyman Theodore Roosevelt, then making his début in political life, Byrnes said:

"During the four years before I took charge of detectives 1,943 arrests were made and 505 years of convictions secured. For the four years I have been in charge 3,324 arrests were made and 2,428 years in convictions were secured."

Asked about the murder record he said:

"One man hanged and thirty-five arrested for murder."

He was a great man to hurl facts at people and he expected his men to throw facts back at him. He made a good impression upon the legislators, for they officially voted him a "detective without a peer, comparable to Vidocq, Coco-Lacour, and Mace." His fame spread throughout the world. He sent men to the ends of the earth on man hunts and he boldly asserted that he had a better department than Scotland Yard.

Men working under "the immortal" never became intimate with him. He was a strict disciplinarian. Of all men he required honesty, common sense, and no political pull. He had a pat formula for detectives. They had to be good judges of human nature, or, to put it in his own words, "they had to be able to size up a man for all he was worth and be all things to all men." They also had to have muscular and mental talents for the job. The greatest factors in detective success, he always said, were habitual close observation and great experience, ability to see the most insignificant things, and to fit them together and develop a perfect memory.

They had to be picture builders. He summed this up as follows: "A good detective works like a good physician who sees at a glance the nature of his patient's illness. He gets a picture, compares it with other pictures, and then acts." I don't recall that truer words have ever been uttered about the qualifications of a real police detective. A detective who picks out murder for his specialty is a composite, something of the artist, the scientist, the lawyer, and a little bit of nearly everything that other men are, plus a memory that not only absorbs everything he sees or hears but is facile and unfailing in its accuracy. Otherwise the pictures that he gathers in his daily work are worthless.

In the capture of McLaughlin my picture of a thief was

put to its first real test. Under Byrnes's eye it was put to a severer test. It was the chief's practice to send detectives out in advance of great public gatherings to round up thieves who were attracted by the crowds. My assignment was to mingle with crowds attending an anniversary of Columbus's discovery of America.

I spotted two men weaving in and out of an assemblage. One was about twenty-three, his companion much older. They displayed the usual shifty characteristics which I have described in my picture of a thief. I accosted them.

"What's this?" exclaimed the older man when I caught the arm of the younger one. "I'm not saying anything about myself, but the young feller you got is all right."

"Well, you're not right yourself," I answered, and took them both along. They fitted into my picture, I thought.

At headquarters I searched them. In the younger man's vest pocket I found a registered mail receipt bearing the name Walker and the address 102 MacDougal Street.

"Where did you get this?" I asked.

"Picked it up on the street," said the young man.

I reasoned that men of their type would not stoop to pick up a registered mail receipt. They were held as suspects. At the MacDougall Street address I found a Mrs. Walker who identified the receipt as having been taken from her the night before when an attempt was made to snatch her purse. She identified the young man as the thief. The older thief was a veteran; the young man had made his first excursion into purse snatching with his elder as a mentor. Both were sent away.

I was more than ever certain that I was getting the right picture and using it correctly.

On the same day I made an arrest for murder, a man named August Langner, a farm hand wanted for strangling a woman in Dedham, Massachusetts. But I had not worked up the case. As I have stated, there were not many murders in New York City at this time, but what there

Examining a crook in Byrnes's crime museum

had been were handled by older men in the bureau personally supervised by Byrnes. But such murders as had occurred were built into elaborate legends and were widely discussed by the men. Hearing about them from men who worked them gave me additional pictures for my memory album. One in particular was rated as Byrnes's most notable piece of detective work.

Byrnes had suspected for a long time that the Whyos, a gang of cutthroats and thieves who roamed the Hell's Kitchen district, were hiring out to do murder, and that they had an established price list in which murder appeared as "a big job worth a hundred dollars and up."

The body of Louis Hanier, an inoffensive French saloon keeper, was found at the head of the stairs in his flat above the saloon which was located in Hell's Kitchen. A bullet wound in the head gave Byrnes the picture of how Hanier had been killed.

Byrnes arrived upon the scene with an assistant. On the bar in the basement of the flat he saw three whisky glasses. They were empty but had recently been used. A bit of whisky still remained in them. From this he reasoned that three men had been drinking in the place before or after the murder, probably before, since slayers after killing usually hurry away.

He determined that the gun used was of .38 caliber and he sent men out to find a pawnbroker who might have bought the gun, reasoning again that if the three who had drunk the whisky were Whyos and therefore professionals they would sell the gun and not throw it away. The gun was found in a pawnshop, left there by a man who answered the description of Mike McGloin, notorious leader of the Whyos. This evidence was not sufficient to connect McGloin with the crime. Byrnes assigned a woman to make the gang leader's acquaintance in the hope that he would make incriminating statements to her. He gave the woman some of his own clothing which McGloin wore at times. All the woman brought back to Byrnes was a rather rambling statement that McGloin had made after the murder to several friends, that "a man wasn't tough enough to be a Whyo until he had knocked out his man."

McGloin was picked up and brought to Byrnes. For ten minutes the Whyo chieftain was left alone in Byrnes's museum to inspect the pictures. On a table near him lay the hangman's noose and black cap.

Two of McGloin's companions, suspected by Byrnes of having been his accomplices in the murder, had been smuggled into the prison basement. McGloin did not know of their arrest.

Byrnes taxed McGloin with the crime. He spat back his denial. Byrnes repeated the statement credited by the woman to McCloin, without naming the woman or indicating her part in the inquiry. At this moment the prisoner's two companions were led across the prison yard below. McGloin could see them.

"We know whom you made that statement to, and we've got them," said Byrnes. McGloin's eyes were riveted on his companions in the yard. He sat silent until they disappeared. Finally he cried out: "For God's sake, Inspector. I'll call 'er quits. I'll tell yer. I killed Hanier." Subsequently McGloin made an extended confession. He was hanged in the Tombs. Byrnes had worked this with pictures from start to finish. A good many years later I had a case in which a whisky glass cut the same figure in a murder case.

Byrnes's murder cases were not the factors that built his fame. It was the effectiveness of his crime control system. He established the first police deadline when he sent a squad of picked men into the Wall Street financial section with orders to arrest every crook with a record who stepped across Fulton Street, which was the northern boundary of the financial and jewelry districts. For the first few months the deadline was established he paid the rent for the squad's office out of his own pocket. When he left the Police Department he was able to say that since he had established the deadline "not a ten cent stamp had been stolen in the section." The deadline exists to-day.

He also inaugurated the famous morning line-up at headquarters. Each day at about 9 A. M. all suspects rounded up during the preceding twenty-four hours were paraded before the assembled detectives. By this means the Central Office men got mental pictures of old and new crooks and frequently recognized men they were looking for. The line-up is still in operation at headquarters. It has been improved in only one respect—the detectives wear masks to conceal their faces from the suspects.

Byrnes often talked in epigrams. He once said, "There is no honor among thieves," bursting the old myth that professional criminals live and operate under a mutually protective code of honor. Perhaps it was not original with him. At any rate, Marm Mandelbaum, one of the city's most famous women fences, who disposed of millions of dollars in loot brought to her by thieves, disputed Byrnes on the honor question. He had been after her a long time, but legal evidence was hard to get.

The woman was well protected, relying chiefly upon the so-called code. So, while he could not fasten a crime upon her, he undertook to prove that her ideas of honor among her own class were wrong. One of her most trusted lieutenants was a burglar's banker known as Traveling Mike Grady. Marm had worlds of confidence in him. After many weeks of watching Byrnes caught Traveling Mike taking stolen goods from Marm's best customers and disposing of it on his own account. He was double-crossing the old lady. Byrnes went to special pains to show Marm that she was being cheated by the man she most trusted. It was too much. She packed up, left for Canada, and quit America for good.

One of the last things Byrnes said before retiring was:

"The old thieves are disappearing. Young people of the rising generation are going into crime more and more."

He not only saw pictures close at hand but he could catch their meaning far off. It was not so many years after "the immortal" passed that a rising generation of seventeen-year-old murderers, bobbed-hair girl bandits, and murder mobs chieftained by racketeers came upon the American scene, and are here yet.

Byrnes was a strong influence upon my professional life. He taught me the value of pictures and he gave me my first chance on a real big murder mystery.

CHAPTER IV

MY FIRST MURDER PICTURE

Byrnes gave me my first murder assignment in June, 1892. There were unusual angles to it. First it was approached by me as a shadow job, and few murder suspects are ever shadowed. Usually they are arrested the minute they are suspected. Secondly, it marked the beginning of a strange cycle of poison murders in New York City.

References already has been made to the Carlyle Harris case, and since it has a bearing upon my first murder inquiry I'll give a brief résumé of the facts. Harris was a young medical student. In his classes at the New York College of Physicians and Surgeons he had listened to lectures on morphine by Dr. George L. Peabody. Among other things he learned about the uses of morphine, the symptoms which follow morphine poisoning, and the treatment in such cases. These lectures were delivered in January, 1891. On January 31st Helen Nielson Potts fell violently ill in her room in the Comstock School for Young Ladies and died.

Investigation by Byrnes showed that Harris had given Miss Potts large overdoses of morphine. He was secretly married to her and wanted to avoid a public wedding insisted upon by her parents. He was convicted and electrocuted. A great battle of medical experts took place at the trial. Several lawyers came to fame, including Francis L. Wellman, an assistant prosecutor, who later wrote an admirable book, *The Art of Cross-Examination*. I regretted not having had a try at the Harris case, but I was then on post. However, the shadow job was to give me experience on a still more famous mystery.

My instructions were to follow a short man about thirty-five, white face, close-cropped mustache, and a very red nose. His name was Dr. Robert W. Buchanan. He had lived in a house at No. 267 West Eleventh Street in Greenwich Village, but his whereabouts were not known. He drank a lot, which accounted for his red nose, and after inquiring for him at various saloons I picked him up in a downtown café. He came out of the place with a lawyer named Davison and went to the lawyer's office. The first picture I got of him indicated that he was badly worried. All I knew about him was that he had remarried his first wife after his second wife had died. The district attorney was about to have the body of Number Two exhumed. It was feared that he might flee, and if he attempted to do so my orders were to lock him up. Nothing was said about murder, but I was instructed to observe every movement and keep in close touch with the Central Office.

For days I shadowed him and found he was occupying a furnished room uptown. I "got him up in the morning and put him to bed at night," as the shadower describes an all-day surveillance job.

As the days passed he doubled his visits to saloons and his nose grew redder and his manner more restless. Then he began to buy papers at each newsstand as he passed. He would go into his room with an armful of papers, come out and buy more, and return to the house. Wherever he went he bought papers, visited lawyers' offices, and went into every handy saloon.

He was greatly agitated. The reason I soon learned. The body of his second wife had just been exhumed. The stomach had been sent to Professor Rudolph Witthaus, a noted toxicologist, for analysis. Dr. Buchanan was eager for news of the result of that analysis. My close observation of him gave me something of an insight into the actions of murderers before they are caught. A rare experience, one that comes only a few times in a lifetime. He seemed to have acquired the furtive movement of a thief, yet after each libation, or when he was in the presence of a lawyer, he was as calm as a cucumber. But when the effects of the stimulants wore off or he parted company with the lawyers he became more restless than before.

Finally I was ordered to arrest him. He was in a downtown café with Davison, the lawyer, when I approached him. He had just had a drink.

"Buchanan," I said, "you're under arrest."

"What's the charge?" he asked. His face turned gray as a wet newspaper.

"Murder," I replied.

"Where will you take him?" queried the alert lawyer.

"To headquarters," I said, and started off with my prisoner. He was silent all the way.

Next morning at headquarters, when I brought him out to take him to court for arraignment, the first wife whom he had remarried appeared and walked along with us. We reached a saloon.

"Can't we have a drink?" the wife asked.

"No," I said, "not this time," and went on. If Buchanan had flight in mind I wasn't going to let him go into the saloon and, anyway, I didn't drink and never have.

Next I was assigned to work under the direction of the district attorney, whose assistant, James W. Osborne, was building up the case, strengthening the picture so that it might be laid out on a legalistic canvas before a jury.

The investigation now turned to Dr. Buchanan's history. He had come from Halifax, Nova Scotia, in 1887, bringing his wife and small daughter. He opened an office in the West Eleventh Street house. His practice was small. Suddenly his wife departed, leaving the daughter behind with her father. On November 12, 1890, he was divorced by means of a painless litigation known in New York as an undefended divorce. His wife did not appear in court.

He began to neglect his practice and spent much time in Newark, New Jersey. Just what he was doing here was not known until he asked Robert W. Macomber, a restaurant keeper, to go to Newark with him on an important mission. The two set out for Newark and there Dr. Buchanan introduced his friend to Mrs. Annie B. Sutherland, who, although she was nearly twice the physician's age, beamed fondly on him and he on her.

She produced her will and read it to the two men. It disposed of her property to her husband, but if, upon her death, she were unmarried her "dear friend and physician, Dr. Robert W. Buchanan," was to receive her property.

Macomber was asked to sign the will as a witness, together with another man whom Mrs. Sutherland called in. However, when it was recalled that the day was Thanksgiving, the signing was postponed. Mrs. Sutherland feared that a will executed on a holiday might be questioned. Later Macomber witnessed the signing of the will.

Returning to New York on the ferry, the restaurant man joshed the doctor about the age of his admirer and benefactor, whereupon the physician said it was not a case of love but merely a woman's gratitude for professional services he had rendered. Buchanan had no idea of marrying again. Women were out of his life for good.

A few months later Buchanan told Macomber of great fortune he had fallen into. Mrs. Sutherland had sold her Newark holdings for ninety-five hundred dollars, which she had given him. Adding five hundred dollars of his own money he had purchased the West Eleventh Street house.

Not many days passed before Mrs. Sutherland came to live in this house. Macomber, upon seeing her, winked at Buchanan. He suspected marriage, but Buchanan explained again that he was through with marriage and that Mrs. Sutherland was merely his housekeeper.

Trouble followed in the Buchanan household. The little daughter and the aged and taciturn housekeeper were not mated. The elderly woman, so Buchanan told his friends, used filthy language in the child's presence. Buchanan asked friends to take the girl and they did. This situation forced Macomber to ask Buchanan if there had not been a marriage, and the doctor admitted he had wed the woman. But he hastened to add, if she got worse he "would ditch the old girl." The restaurant owner remarked that if he did that the "old girl would remake her will and ditch him."

It was about this time that the trial of Carlyle Harris opened in New York City and the experts began their testimony as to the effects of morphine poisoning and its symptoms. Wellman, in this trial, had produced evidence to show that Harris had made no attempt to conceal signs of the poison, although there were ways a skilled physician might have concealed them.

Mrs. Sutherland-Buchanan became suddenly ill in the Eleventh Street house on the morning of April 22, 1892. She died April 23rd. Dr. B. C. McIntyre, a physician, called in by Buchanan, signed a death certificate giving cerebral hemorrhage as the cause of death.

The woman lay in her grave for some time. Then one morning a man giving the name Smith called at the morgue to remark casually that he had known Mrs. Sutherland; she had been a healthy and robust person, and he thought it strange that she should die in the home of a physician. Smith also visited the newspapers and made the same casual statement.

Thereupon Byrnes exhumed the body, and Professor Witthaus reported that his analysis showed that she had died from the effects of poisoning. He had found morphine in her viscera; also traces of belladonna or atropine, both derivatives of the lethal nightshade. The admission of this drug, together with morphine, prevented the contraction of the pupils of her eyes, thus counteracting the usual symptoms of morphine poisoning and also confusing for a time the toxicological analysis of the contents of her stomach.

A strong suspicion pointed at Buchanan, yet no evidence had been found to put the deadly dosages in his hands and build the legal case against him. To do this is one of the most difficult tasks besetting the murder specialist, for when poisoners administer the means of death onlookers seldom are around. Circumstances, of course, strengthened the suspicion against Dr. Buchanan. The use of morphine suggested that the influence in that direction had come from the Harris case. And Dr. Buchanan was an experienced physician; Harris was only a medical student.

The process of boring into the mystery by learning what had taken place in the Buchanan household prior to the death of his wife began. Something, the truth of which never developed, suddenly made Macomber talkative about his medical friend. He remarked that about the time Buchanan had sent his daughter to friends he had said "the old lady was getting intolerable." He had taken to eating his meals at a restaurant because, he said, she had threatened to poison his food. Then she threatened to kill herself and Buchanan had told her: "Well, you know where the poisons are kept."

Had the doctor ever mentioned the Harris case? I asked Macomber. Indeed he had, said the restaurant man. While the trial was on and details of the medical testimony were being printed, Buchanan had said that if the medical student had had a real knowledge of morphine he would have administered belladonna with the morphine. This would have confused the symptoms of poisoning both externally and internally, thus baffling the attending physician and the toxicologist.

Precisely this had happened in the Buchanan murder. Yet it was not sufficient to clinch the case against the doctor. It was necessary to find someone who had seen him administering medicine to his wife just before her death. Such evidence would indicate an opportunity to commit the crime alleged. His marriage to the woman and his possession of her property furnished abundant evidence of motive, but not as to the felonious means of death.

At the time of Mrs. Buchanan's death several women lived in the West Eleventh Street house. Ordinary observation and experience teaches that women are quick to minister to the wants of their ailing sisters. So, working along this logical premise, I spent some time rebuilding the picture of Mrs. Buchanan's last days in the house—her final illness.

A Mrs. Brockway was found. She had lived in the house; was there when Mrs. Buchanan was taken ill. She had called in a nurse to attend the doctor's wife and had attended the woman herself. She recalled that Dr. Buchanan had given his wife medicine. She saw him feed it to her with a teaspoon. A bottle of chloral hydrate, which Dr. McIntyre had prescribed, was on the table near the bed. It was the only medicine he had given her. The directions on the bottle called for a dose of one teaspoonful at a time. Mrs. Brockway had given such doses to the ailing woman when Dr. Buchanan was not around.

But when Dr. Buchanan administered the dosage he gave his wife two teaspoonfuls instead of one! Whether from the bottle on the table Mrs. Brockway could not say. In the house Dr. Buchanan kept his drugs. Among them was morphine, belladonna, and atropine. Though the contents of the teaspoons in Dr. Buchanan's hands were not definitely established it added the last touch to the picture. He had the motive for killing his aged wife; also the opportunity and the means.

A jury found him guilty of the murder. He made his fate certain by taking the witness stand in his own behalf. Wellman, a suave but merciless cross-examiner, tangled him in one conflicting statement after another. But, even though he made a poor witness for himself, he smiled through his examination and was cocksure and haughty. He confidently expected an acquittal and said so openly in the courtroom.

He was electrocuted in Sing Sing prison.

Dr. Buchanan was a superegotist, trying to improve upon the poisoning technique of the young medical student. As the reader follows the famous cycle of poison murders in subsequent chapters he will discern that this is characteristic of nearly all poisoners. Each believes himself to be better than the one before.

It was my first experience at building up a picture where the result would be State's demand for the life of a human being. It differed vastly from running down professional thieves with known records and it helped convince me that all criminals act alike; that they belong somewhere in the picture of a thief—seasoned professionals or just amateurs trying their hand at murder for the first time. Crime, an unnatural, illegal enterprise, tars them with the same brush.

CHAPTER V

LITTLE MURDER JOBS IN BETWEEN

THE outcome of the Buchanan trial put a temporary quietus on murder by poison in New York City, although there was an epidemic of such slayings in other parts of the country. Reading about them in newspapers strengthened my opinion that one poisoner always tries to improve upon the technique of some preceding example.

My chief occupation during 1893 and 1894 was running down professional thieves. On the floor, as the Detective Bureau was known, was a detective sergeant of exceedingly gracious manners and dapper dress who bore the name "Chesty." Big Bill Devery, captain in the Tenderloin Precinct, and later chief of police during a violent police upheaval, invented the name. But the possessor of it signed the payroll George W. McClusky.

He had been a detective since 1881 and was one of Byrnes's most trusted men. He had acquired some of Byrnes's technique but ran more to strategy than "the immortal." McClusky looked and acted the part of a prosperous Wall Street broker. He made his unofficial headquarters at Delmonico's famous café. Here he mingled with the moneyed crowd while casting an inquisitive eye at the easy-money men who follow the trail of wealth. In this way Chesty kept in touch with the upper crust of the underworld. He liked to outguess and outwit big, shrewd criminals.

In the bureau at this time also was a modest, hard working detective sergeant, James McCafferty, who had handled most of the murder cases. He too was a Byrnes product. He liked murder cases, and so we just gravitated toward each other, two men with interests in common. We became partners later on. There was hardly enough real hard murder work to employ our joint talents. We worked together on professional thieves. Some laughs came our way and also opportunities to work out strategy as McClusky liked to see it done.

A mob of professional thieves were altogether too busy in uptown hotels. I was assigned to run them down. The methods employed by the gang seemed to indicate that a bellboy thief named Byrnes was the ringleader, and moreover whenever he quit bellhopping in that hotel losses were discovered by guests. I hunted up Byrnes.

He was stepping out nice and high with two companions when I spotted him on Fifth Avenue. I anticipated that he might have loot on his person, so the operation known as "splitting" was performed. I grabbed Byrnes from behind. His two companions fled as I expected they would, hoping they would make for Byrnes's room for refuge. No loot was found in Byrnes's pockets at headquarters when I searched him, but he was booked. He gave me the address of his room and I hurried there.

The savory odor of a cooking steak greeted me in the hallway. I knocked at the door. It was opened by a lanky, hungry-looking man with a large fork in his hand and a pillow case around his front as an apron. The steak was nice and juicy and plenty for at least five persons.

He saw my face at the door. "Wha's all this?" he demanded. "Wha's all about?"

"Never mind whass all about," I replied. "Plant yourself in a chair and don't move." He obeyed. I shut the door.

A huge young Negro was dozing on a bed, stretched out in solid comfort. A row of gold front teeth shone like a sunburst. His eyes opened lazily. He closed them and resumed his beauty nap.

"Up and off that bed," I commanded. He arose and took a chair.

"Mistah, mistah," he blubbered, "wha's all happenin'?" He rubbed his eyes and yawned.

The juicy steak was frying nicely.

There were knocks on the door—three short raps. I opened it.

"Ah," said a young man, looking at the steak, then at me. "What the——" he stammered, and started to turn and run. I yanked him in. Two big Spanish onions, to garnish the feast, bulged in his pockets. I ordered him into a chair.

Another rap upon the door. It opened quickly and the caller, bearing a bag of buns, tumbled into my arms. In a few minutes another visitor came to the door, and I admitted him. He was carrying a bottle of catsup. When he spotted me he started out again, but I hauled him in.

They were all members of the gang Byrnes captained.

A patrolman answered my call for assistance. He was a heavy-weight Irishman. I told him his help was needed to take the gang to headquarters.

"Let me take the black fellow down," he said, moving toward the Negro. There was a roguish glint in his eye. Somewhere, not long before, he had met up with a gang of colored thieves.

"No, I'll take care of him," I said. There was no good putting trouble in an Irishman's way.

I turned off the flame under the steak. It was done to a leathery toughness.

They all went away for long terms, and for quite a while bellhop thieving suffered a slump. This was no outstanding exploit; just another case of getting the picture;

knowing what thieves would do and corralling them in a bunch by the McClusky strategic system.

Then I was on murder again. Just a little case. Two human legs were found in a bundle which had been thrown into a grass plot in front of a Greenwich Village bank. They were identified as the limbs of a dusky matron who had been missing some time from her home in the Harlem black belt. Her gentleman friend was a porter. He too was missing.

The fact that the bundle had been thrown into such a conspicuous place led me to reason that some confusing situation had arisen in the mind of the bundle carrier; that what he probably intended to do was go on farther, which would have brought him to the Hudson River, where bundles of this sort were usually thrown. In the house where the Negress had lived bloodstains were found in a room she had occupied. The slayer had made a great mistake. He had used the wrong fluid in an attempt to wash out the bloodstains. I'll not disclose just wherein he made that mistake, for a little bloodstain often has proved the only handy clue to a murderer.

The porter finally was arrested. He confessed that he had strangled the woman in a fit of jealousy, had cut up her body, and carried it out in bundles. He started for the Hudson with one bundle, found himself on the wrong car, and jumped off. Suddenly confused, he dropped the bundle in the most conspicuous place. His mind wasn't capable of rearranging his plot at a moment's notice. I had grasped the first picture correctly.

He grieved to death, beating the electric chair by one day. His name was Cæsar. His little empire went to pieces, and having killed his dusky queen he was through. This case, quickly disposed of, fell into its appointed place among patterns of murder in my memory. Just an over-dark vignette of murder done and paid for.

Then the cry that all policemen dread. Shake-up! In

Pen and ink sketch made during trial of Martin Thorn for murder of William Guldensuppe. (Thorn is looking over shoulder of his attorney at photographs of the dismembered body of his victim.)

1895 Byrnes retired. His successor completely reorganized the Detective Bureau, and old veterans and young men trying to get a start were shifted. No charges or comments involving my work were made, but forthwith I was walking a post in a sparsely settled section of the upper city where, according to police tradition, a patrolman helped tend the goats.

But murder followed me here. After a time on patrol I was detailed to plain-clothes work in the precinct. On a Sunday afternoon in June, 1897, two small boys with their father were walking through a woods in the precinct. They stumbled upon a bundle containing a section of a human body. The find was reported to Detective Aloncle and myself.

We unwrapped the bundle. When an outer wrapping of brown paper and a secondary wrapping of red oilcloth with bronze figures were thrown back, the lower section of a torso including the diaphragm was revealed. Adhering to the back was a small piece of wet wrapping paper. This paper contained the imprint Kugler & Woolens, Hardware, 277 Bowery, New York City. Both pieces of paper were such as would be used in hardware stores. The thigh bones bore evidence of having been cut with a saw, and from this I reasoned that the saw had been purchased at Kugler & Woolens. At this store I found that sheets of brown paper, the size of that found around the torso, were used to wrap saws. From the agent of the maker of the red oilcloth I learned that quantities of it had been distributed throughout the city. After a canvass of many stores I found that a small shop in Long Island City, along the East River, had sold several yards of the material to a stout woman who apparently lived in the same section. This had been purchased a few days before the torso had been thrown into the woods.

Then word was received that the upper section of a human torso had been found in the East River wrapped in the same red oilcloth. A tattoo mark had been cut from the breast of this. A little later sailors in the Brooklyn Navy Yard, not far from the store where the oilcloth had been purchased, found a man's legs in the East River wrapped in white oilcloth. The soles of the man's feet were rough and thick, indicating that he had gone barefoot a great deal.

The keeper of a duck farm in the vicinity of the store where the stout woman had gotten the oilcloth reported that for some days the water in his duck pond had taken on a peculiar reddish cast and that it made his ducks sick.

The police machine began to grind. The larger picture formed. Tracing the reddish cast in the duck pond, detectives found that it came from a sewer serving a number of new, unoccupied houses in the vicinity of the store. A man and a woman had visited this house about a week before as prospective purchasers.

It was concluded that the calloused condition of the victim's soles was due to his employment in a Turkish bath as a rubber. Detectives were sent out to visit Third Avenue cafés frequented by Turkish bath employees, and here they found that William Guldensuppe, a young rubber, had been missing for more than a week. He could easily be identified. Since he worked in the nude everyone had seen a tattoo mark on his chest. The body was identified as Guldensuppe's. The head was missing.

The woman who had visited the unoccupied house was identified as Mrs. Augusta Nack and her companion as Martin Thorn, her star boarder, while Guldensuppe was also a roomer in her house whom she had jilted in favor of Thorn. She had lured Guldensuppe into the vacant house, where Thorn, hidden in a closet, shot him in the head and killed him, threw the body into the bathtub and cut it up with a saw. The red cast in the duck pond was blood which had run from the bathtub into the sewer.

It was a shrewdly planned murder. The disappearance

of the head showed this. The head was not only the most reliable means of identification but it also contained vital evidence of the felonious cause of death, the pistol wound. The head was incased in a plaster-of-Paris cast and thrown into the river and was never found.

Mrs. Nack turned state's witness and fixed blame for the crime on Thorn. This development threw Thorn's defense attorneys into consternation, and the missing head suddenly became a vital issue. Thorn's lawyer got up one day in court and announced that the body was not that of Guldensuppe! He, the lawyer claimed, was alive in Germany! The reason was apparent why the murderers had gone to such pains to dispose of the head.

Detectives were sent to Germany and reported that Guldensuppe was not there, and ample testimony was produced to prove by the tattoo mark and other peculiarities on the body that it was the corpse of the missing rubber. The fact that he had gone about nude so much made it possible to produce these witnesses.

Thorn was convicted and electrocuted. Mrs. Nack pleaded guilty to manslaughter in the first degree and was sent to prison for fifteen years.

The case attracted wide attention. From a professional standpoint it furnished me with several important fundamentals. First, that in a murder case there is no one obvious clue but that all clues are good if they are direct; secondly, that the police detective machine, though small at this time, functioned with precision and relentlessly, from patrolmen on the beat to executives at headquarters, gathering, piecing together, and analyzing bits of evidence as they came in piecemeal from a hundred different sources. It also convinced me that a woman's refuge in murder, as in other things, is man. Augusta Nack by confessing threw herself into Thorn's arms and at the cost of his life saved her own.

Whether Captain McClusky thought I had a knack for

handling murder cases I do not know. He assumed command of the Detective Bureau in 1897, and from then on I was engaged in murder inquiry most of the time.

He handed me a real tough case shortly after he came in. The details remain clear in my memory because it was one of the few cases in my entire career that offered possibilities of unmasking a mass murderer of the Bluebeard type.

A man giving the name of Braun appeared at the offices of a large life insurance company and presented for collection a five-hundred-dollar life insurance policy on the life of one Zanoli. Braun's name appeared as beneficiary. The man who asked for payment as Braun had a swarthy face and seemed to be an Italian, while Braun obviously was a German name. However, the company paid the policy. Suddenly friends of the dark-skinned man became suspicious when they recalled that whenever death overtook anyone in his employ or in his family he showed signs of suddenly increased prosperity. These friends communicated with the Detective Bureau.

Braun, it appeared, worked in a barber shop at Tenth Avenue and Twenty-fourth Street. I went there. To my great surprise I found that Zanoli was the owner of the shop and still alive! The man Braun had been dead some time, and Zanoli had most solicitiously arranged a quick burial. Zanoli was a queer little man with mixed mannerisms and a strange accent. He had two personalities. He was of German-Italian parentage. In arranging the Braun insurance matter this dual nationality was relied upon to allay suspicion.

I inquired into the little man's history. Some years earlier his first wife had died and he had collected insurance on her life. He married a widow named Werner, who died suddenly, leaving insurance which Zanoli collected. He married a third time, and this wife too passed away suddenly, also leaving insurance which Zanoli also collected. And with each collection Zanoli moved to a better part of the city and opened up a finer barber shop. In the last shop he hired Braun, who did not live long afterward.

I arrested Zanoli for forgery. He was held on this charge while we considered exhuming the bodies of his wives and Braun. However, medical experts decided that owing to the large quantity of poison in embalming fluid it would be useless to exhume the older bodies. The body of the third wife was taken from its grave. The death certificate stated that death was due to typhoid, but no evidence of this disease was found. It could not be ascertained whether poison had caused her death. The same situation was true of Braun's body.

There was not sufficient legal evidence to charge Zanoli with murder, but he was convicted of forgery and sent to prison.

And into the limbo of unsolved crimes passed the mystery of the deaths of the Mesdames Zanoli, second and third, and Barber Braun. My conclusion was that the first wife had died from natural causes, but out of her death, and the ease with which her insurance was collected, had come the idea to murder her successors and Braun. I do not accuse Zanoli of the murders, if they were such. The circumstances are cited merely to support a hypothesis which experience has confirmed that the mass murderer, particularly the Bluebeard type, comes nearest to being the author of the perfect crime, if such a thing there be. With such criminals murder is a career. They live for little else.

And here's a strange thing: If, to-day, a man were to appear and confess to the murders of the two wives and Braun, it is doubtful if he could be convicted. Murder never outlaws, but the evidence of murder in these cases would have to come from the lips of the murderer himself. The law will not accept his plea of guilty to murder in the first degree. He would have to be tried in regular course. And there would be nothing but the remotest circumstances, perhaps none at all, at this late day to establish the case against him.

But at that I don't think many murderers escape. Men and women who I know to a moral certainty have committed murder have beaten the courts, but then as the reader goes along in these memoirs it may strike him that nature invariably overtakes them in the end with tragic circumstances that are even worse than life or death in prison.

During this period in the Detective Bureau I added materially to my store of murder patterns, or pictures, with which I worked on other cases as time went on.

CHAPTER VI

THE MAN IN THE STRAW HAT

CAPTAIN McCLUSKY announced my appointment as a detective sergeant in November, 1897. From this time on, except for a few years of precinct duty occasioned by shake-ups, my days, and many of my nights, for more than thirty years, were to be taken up by homicide cases of all descriptions.

On August 16, 1898, McClusky sent word that he wanted me to meet him in Room 84 of the Grand Hotel, which at that time was one of the most popular hotels in the Broadway bright-light district. It was a gathering place for well-known figures in the sporting and theatrical life of the city. In the room I found McClusky, Dr. O'Hanlon, coroner's physician, and several detectives viewing the body of a young woman lying on the floor.

She was in her early twenties, pretty and stylishly dressed. Beside her lay a piece of lead pipe around the end of which were bound several thicknesses of bicycle tape. It was a homemade bludgeon. From this I caught the first flash of the picture—murder with premeditation. The specially-made bludgeon was sufficient evidence of this.

With Dr. O'Hanlon's assistance—it then being a rule that only the coroner or his representative could first touch a body—we lifted the body to a table and sat it upright, resting the feet upon a chair. The young woman's beauty became more apparent in this lifelike posture, and it was easier to build the picture. Her hat was taken off, and Dr. O'Hanlon removed the outer garments. We found small, superficial cuts about her head, but they were not sufficient to have caused death. There were specks of blood upon the floor where her head had lain. Other than these cuts there were no signs of violence or the cause of death, although, of course, there was the bludgeon. The cuts had not been made by this weapon. Dr. O'Hanlon concluded that death had been instantaneous, and a moment later we found that the young woman's neck had been broken by a bludgeon blow at the base of her skull, dislocating the vertebræ and causing asphyxia. To have effected death in this manner the blow must have been delivered by someone skilled in a knowledge of human anatomy.

As the young woman's white shirtwaist was opened eight dollars and sixty-two cents in currency fell out; also a bank check for twenty-five thousand dollars drawn on the Garfield National Bank, dated August 15, 1898, made payable to Emeline C. Reynolds, signed by Dudley Gideon and indorsed by S. J. Kennedy.

The bank was not far from the hotel. The only name on the check that was familiar to me was Gideon. I knew of a race-track bookmaker by that name, whose headquarters were in the Grand Hotel, but his first name was Dave, not Dudley.

Detective Davis, who was in the room, was sent to the Garfield National Bank to inquire about Gideon, Emmeline Reynolds, and S. J. Kennedy. On the window sill I found a prescription blank such as is furnished in pads to physicians by medicine manufacturers. It was made out to Mr. and Mrs. E. Maxwell, Grand Hotel. These were the names which appeared on the hotel register as the occupants of Room 84. They had registered the day before.

Davis reported that the bank had no depositor named Dudley Gideon or Emeline C. Reynolds but did have a client, Dr. Samuel J. Kennedy, a dentist, with offices at No. 60 West Twenty-second Street, who carried a small account. This office was about nine blocks south of the hotel. Davis was instructed to find Dr. Kennedy and interview him.

Newspapers had been informed of the finding of the body. Scenting a sensational white-light murder mystery, they spread the story on their front pages. They reached the conclusion, which we were not warranted in doing, that the dead woman was Emeline C. Reynolds, whose name appeared upon the check.

Davis returned with the information that he had talked with Dr. Samuel J. Kennedy and that he denied knowing an Emeline Reynolds or any woman of the description which Davis had given him. The dentist was married and lived on Staten Island.

Much may be learned from a minute examination of weapons found at the scene of murder. They have always intrigued me, and this, I suppose, is because they have so often revealed the only clues. I studied the homemade bludgeon. Inside the lead pipe, to stiffen it and make its blow more deadly, was a piece of thin iron rod which had recently been severed from a longer piece. It had been made to kill and not to wound, I reasoned. As I fingered the lead pipe a gray smear came upon my hands, the usual coating that rubs from the surface of lead. This circumstance, of no importance at this moment, tucked itself away in my memory, a matter of habit.

A hotel maid told me of finding the body. It was a busy hotel. Had anyone seen the woman about? Burns, a waiter in the hotel dining room, had attended the young woman at luncheon immediately after she had registered the day before. She had asked that the meal be charged against her room account. Burns went out to inquire at the desk if this could be done and was told that cash would be required, since she had brought no baggage. He went back to advise her of this. She was gone.

That evening the young woman came through the dining room with a man wearing a straw hat. McGregor, the head waiter, called Burns's attention to her, and he then went to Room 84 and knocked at the door. It was opened by the woman. He asked for payment of the check, and she offered him a ten-dollar bill. At that moment a man was seated within the room reading a newspaper. Burns could not see his face. Apparently the woman had not left the hotel after that, for the money which fell from her shirt was the change given for the ten-dollar bill.

Gregory, the hotel night clerk, recalled that at 2:30 A. M. next morning a man wearing a straw hat had come down the stairway. An elevator operator recalled taking a couple up to the room the night before, but he was not certain that the dead woman was the companion of the man he had taken up. Davis, a colored bellboy, told of taking a bottle of wine to the room during the night. He had gone into the room. The man and woman were there. He had asked the man if he should draw the cork and was told not to, but to leave a corkscrew behind. The bellboy giggled to himself over this, for one accustomed to champagne would know that corkscrews were not needed to open bottles of sparkling wine. Thus the incident was firmly imbedded in the colored man's mind.

Yet who was the dead woman and the man who had been with her?

A middle-aged woman from Mount Vernon appeared, who answered this question. She was Mrs. Reynolds, the mother of Emeline C. Reynolds, who had cut loose from her parental home in Mount Vernon and had been living in an apartment in New York City. She identified the body as that of her daughter.

I talked with Mrs. Reynolds late in the afternoon in the station house.

Dolly, as the mother called Emeline, was an unusual type. For a time she had worked in a Mount Vernon candy store, but friends told her that she had too much personality to be behind a counter and that she ought to go into business for herself. She quit the candy store and sold books and, on occasion, did odds and ends for lawyers, serving processes and looking up witnesses. One thing was predominant in her nature. She craved money and thought as much of five cents as ordinary mortals think of five dollars. She made out well with her books. Although she was a book agent, her personality won her audiences. She was vivid and pretty. Men especially welcomed her calls. It was on such a business visit that Dolly met a broker, and thereafter she gave up the family home and went to live in the apartment. This broker had introduced her, the mother said, to a New York City dentist.

This dentist, Dolly told her mother, was treating an ulcerated tooth. His name was Samuel J. Kennedy, and his office, the mother recalled, was on West Twenty-second Street. Dolly also had told her that on one of her visits to the dentist he had told her of a man he knew "who was in with a jockey who rode horses with an electric saddle" and could bring in his mounts ahead of the field.

Mrs. Reynolds spoke to her husband about the jockey and the saddle and wondered if Mr. Reynolds would put money on such a venture.

"It might be a swindle," the father said.

"Oh, no," spoke up Dolly. "The doctor's all right. He couldn't afford to be mixed up in anything that wasn't honest."

Dolly spoke of winnings at odds of fifty to one, which

she had been told might be realized from a small investment in the saddle. Later she drew five hundred dollars from her savings account.

According to my computations, the twenty-five-thousand-dollar check which fell from the young woman's corset might represent five hundred dollars placed on a winning bet at fifty to one odds, an event commonly known at race tracks as a big killing. Whether she actually invested five hundred dollars in such a venture no way existed then, or exists now, to determine. Her withdrawal from the savings account was established, but it was in cash. No check was ever found to trace the course of the money after it left her hands. She did not have it in her possession when her body was found.

My attention quite naturally turned to Dr. Kennedy. I found him in his office, which he shared with his father. He was a slim man, about thirty, with a small black mustache. He greeted me with gentlemanly coolness.

"Doctor, you know Emeline Reynolds," I said to him. "You said you didn't know her. Why, she was a patient of yours."

He hesitated for a moment, then quickly, "Oh, yes, yes. Is that the one you mean? I know her."

I requested him to come to the station house with me. He went to a closet and took out a soft hat. I noticed a derby in the closet and a new bicycle cap. There was no straw hat, although this was New York's hot season.

"Have you got a straw hat?" I asked.

"No," he replied.

"Do you usually wear a soft hat?"

"No. Usually a derby."

"How does it happen that you have both a soft and a derby hat in the closet?" I queried.

"It looked like rain this morning, so I wore the soft hat from my home and carried the derby in a bag in my hand."

It struck me that it was the habit of most New Yorkers to wear hard derby hats in a rain.

I told Dr. Kennedy to get ready to go to the station house. I picked up the cap and found that it bore the label of Smith & Gray, hatters, with a store near by. I took Kennedy to the station house and then hurried to the hat store. Here I found a clerk who knew Dr. Kennedy and who said that he recalled selling a straw hat and a cap to the dentist the day before Dolly Reynolds's body was found. Thus a straw hat was placed in Dr. Kennedy's possession, although he denied owning one.

On my way back to the station house I got thinking about the twenty-five-thousand-dollar check. The name Dudley Gideon had a strange significance. Dave Gideon was, as I have said, a bookmaker. Had this name been signed to the check it would have been forgery. As it was the name on the check was merely fictitious. But I had heard that Dr. Kennedy had a friend whose first name was Dudley.

At the station house McClusky directed me to get hotel employees who might identify Kennedy as the man with the straw hat who had come down the stairs, or the man who had been seen in the dining room with Dolly or in Room 84 with her.

Kennedy was placed in line with a number of other men. The witnesses were brought in. The head waiter picked him out as the man he had seen passing through the dining room with the young woman; Davis, the colored bellboy, who had served the champagne and left the corkscrew behind, picked him out as the man who was in the room with Dolly and who had paid for the wine. And Gregory, the night clerk, identified him as the man who had come down the stairs at 2:30 A. M. wearing a straw hat.

I searched Dr. Kennedy. On the left-hand side of his underpants I found a blue-black smudge like that which had come upon my hands while examining the bludgeon in the hotel room. The night Dolly was murdered had been hot. Lead would soften, and the surface coating would come off easily on any object rubbed against it. Dr. Lederle, a noted chemist, said that the smear upon Dr. Kennedy's underwear was lead.

Kennedy was formally charged with the murder of Emmeline Reynolds.

Whence had come the bludgeon? It was a homemade affair. Its place of manufacture might be found. With the aid of Detective Smith I searched the basement of the Kennedy home. Smith found a piece of lead pipe in a cigar box. On a work bench I found a small section of iron rod from which a piece recently had been cut. A mechanical engineer asserted that the iron rod found in the basement and that inside the bludgeon had been one piece. So much for the history of this homemade weapon.

The motive for this murder was obscure. I sought to establish it more firmly by inquiring into Dolly's past. Here I got a picture quite different from the one first given to us. Dolly, after leaving her Mount Vernon home, had taken up with the broker. Her parents and friends knew nothing of this. He furnished her with money, but she continued to do odds and ends. She had saved every cent she could and had accounts in a number of savings banks. She seldom rode street cars but walked and saved the fare. She was penurious and would quarrel over a penny's change.

The story which has just been related, with many other details too voluminous to be repeated here, was retold in court at Kennedy's trial. He was convicted and sentenced to die. This verdict was reversed by a higher court on the grounds that Kennedy had not been permitted to reply to one of his identifiers in the police station the day he was arrested and also because the trial court had erred prejudicially in permitting a witness to testify to hearsay. Kennedy was tried a second time.

While this trial was under way an incident occurred which shows what a murder man sometimes encounters. A man whom I had never seen claimed that he heard me tell Detective Smith on a ferry boat coming from Kennedy's home that if he, Smith, would make his testimony "good and strong" about the finding of the lead pipe it would be a feather in his cap. No such thing came from my lips. The man did not tell his story on the witness stand, but it reached the newspapers.

The district attorney took hold of the stranger, who denied the story. He proved to be a poor peddler, who, never having seen his name in print, injected himself into the case to get a thrill. In my experience I have met many seeking the same thing. Not all were peddlers. Some came from higher stations in life, but had the same craving for publicity.

The second trial resulted in a disagreement. A third trial ended the same way, and finally the charge against the dentist was dismissed, and he stands cleared of the accusation.

Who did kill Dolly Reynolds? This question has been asked for years.

The reader may ponder the question while I add a sidelight to the picture. Dolly, as has been pointed out, craved money. She had a firm determined chin and a square little jaw. She had brushed against the world quite a bit and had little fear. She went to unusual lengths to earn small fees. An incident in her life shows this. A lawyer had given her a paper to serve upon a clergyman who had avoided service for some months. Finally Dolly arranged to have the minister marry her and thus gained access to him and went through a mock ceremony of marriage, handing the clergyman the process as he was about to bless her. My surmise is that if anyone owed her money and did not pay on demand, or attempted to swindle her, Dolly would have made life pretty miserable for that person.

Dolly died thinking perhaps that a fortune had come into her hands. But the check that fluttered from her corset was worthless. In the room she had a sip of champagne, perhaps to toast her dream of wealth so suddenly come true. A woman scarcely would have put into her bosom a worthless check knowing it to be such. What happened after that no one, I fear, will ever know. It remains one of those unfinished spots that appear in so many murder pictures.

For a time there was such a dark spot in the picture of what had happened to Mrs. Anna Kronman, a woman built in a pattern vastly different from that in which life had cast Dolly Reynolds. A small whisky glass removed the dark spot.

Mrs. Kronman, just past thirty-two, had no great yearning for money. She was prepossessing, always modishly but modestly attired, and took infinite pains to make her little apartment at No. 260 West Thirty-fifth Street attractive and comfortable for herself and husband. He was a wholesale produce dealer. The couple were moderately well off. Mrs. Kronman had jewels and good clothes, but the thing she most desired had come into her life and had gone. She was childless. A child had been born to her but had died.

On August 7, 1899, Mrs. Kronman sat alone in the living room of her apartment. On a table near by was a photograph of her child. Draped over chairs were the clothes the little one had worn. Almost every day Mrs. Kronman locked herself in her apartment and, surrounded by the trinkets and apparel of her dead child, indulged her mother love in reminiscent fancy and tragic contemplation. Occasionally she wept. Relatives and friends remained away from the apartment, knowing that Mrs.

Kronman spent hours in this way. They did not want to disturb her.

Late in the afternoon of the seventh I stepped into the Kronman apartment. The child's photograph, trinkets, and apparel were as she had left them. Some hours before Mrs. Kronman had died in Roosevelt Hospital. She had been beaten to death in her apartment. The murderer had crashed the blunt end of an axe against her skull, causing a number of wounds. Any one of them would have been fatal.

Her jewelry was missing. There were signs about the place of the professional thief's hurried search for valuables.

Other detectives were sent to question the husband. They established what jewelry had been taken from the apartment.

I remained in the apartment to build the picture. If I seem to dote upon building pictures as I approach each murder case it is because of an instinctive mental process. Back in an earlier chapter I told how Byrnes went about getting a picture in the Hanier murder case by looking at three whisky glasses on the bar in Hanier's little grog shop. His exploit had settled into my mind as a pattern.

On the wooden cover of a stationary washtub in the rear hallway of the Kronman apartment I found a small business card containing the name and address of a photographer. Near this card was an empty whisky glass. A sniff of it convinced me that it recently had contained liquor. A look into a pantry above the tub revealed a bottle of whisky partly used.

A detective sent to interview the photographer reported that one of his solicitors had been at the apartment in the morning; had knocked at the door; had canvassed Mrs. Kronman for her patronage and left his card in Mrs. Kronman's hand. He had not entered the apartment. It was obvious that Mrs. Kronman had dropped the card on the tub cover near the whisky glass. Her husband said she was not fond of whisky and that he kept the liquor on hand for visitors.

An ice box stood near the tub close to the dumb-waiter. An axe lay on the floor in the corner, and near its blade was a small pool of blood, where Mrs. Kronman's body had lain. I had seen her body and had concluded after examining the wounds upon her head that the murderer had not hit her to render her insensible but had deliberately attacked her with intent to kill or he would not have struck her repeatedly, inflicting each time a fatal wound.

Now, I reasoned that the murderer was known to Mrs. Kronman and probably well known to her; that he was a man, for the blows were dealt by a strong arm; and that Mrs. Kronman had invited him to a drink. Had it been a woman friend who drank, undoubtedly Mrs. Kronman would have joined her in a libation, and after that the whisky glasses would have been returned to their places in the pantry where Mrs. Kronman had placed the bottle.

This picture came to me: The murderer was so well known to the woman that he had killed her to prevent her from naming him, hence the repeated fatal blows. My idea of murder inquiry, however, is to dwell not too long on the picture process but simultaneously to set the net for the slayer.

The janitor in the apartment house told me of the arrival of ice in the morning. He put the ice in the dumb-waiter, hauled it up, and Mrs. Kronman took it off. The piece of ice was in the ice box. Its edges showed that it had been chipped; that apparently it was too large a piece to fit into the refrigerating chamber and the chipping had been done with an axe, the axe on the floor. Its blunt edge was covered with blood stains.

The picture was unfolding. The murderer standing at the tub near the ice box, drinking his whisky, had witnessed Mrs. Kronman chopping the ice, and that ill-fated act had suggested to him the weapon he would use, the axe in her own hands.

A woman living in the apartment on the floor below Mrs. Kronman's said she had heard no screams or noise of a struggle, but that same morning, while she was leaving the house to get some milk for her husband's oatmeal, a man about twenty-eight years old came up to her and asked her on what floor Mrs. Kronman lived. She directed him to the top floor. He was a stocky man with a black mustache and a large nose. His features were dark.

In a city the size of New York men of that description are as common as lamp-posts and as much alike.

Another witness was found who had seen the same man in the vicinity of the apartment house on the same morning. I was convinced that the man was not a stranger to Mrs. Kronman, so I cut back on the picture and decided to locate friends of Mrs. Kronman.

The woman bore an unblemished reputation. She was above flirtations. She admitted no one except closest friends to her apartment, and none of these had been men. Two of her nieces were found. We questioned them at great length. When we put questions about the possibility of a male visitor with a big nose having been admitted by Mrs. Kronman to her apartment, the two girls were silent, apparently fearful lest whatever they might say would mar the reputation of their aunt.

Later the young women advised us that they had recalled all of their aunt's friends, and that the only person they could think of who resembled the man with the big nose was the son of an elderly woman, Mrs. Neufeld, who lived on the lower East Side. His name was Billy. His mother had brought him to the Kronman apartment on a friendly call during religious holidays, and on this occasion Mrs. Kronman had displayed gifts of jewelry from her husband.

From then on the picture was speedily finished. Mrs. Kronman's jewelry was traced to the possession of Neufeld. He was convicted in twelve minutes by a jury, the speediest result I ever witnessed in a criminal court. He was executed.

The Kronman case became an important pattern which figured vitally in later cases. It had a most uncanny aspect. It was Mrs. Kronman who unwittingly suggested the crime by displaying her jewelry and who also suggested the means by which her end was so horribly encompassed—the axe with which she chopped the ice. This has happened in so many cases that it would seem that pictures often supply the murderer with motive and the means for murder.

CHAPTER VII

THE POISON CYCLE RESUMES

Arm in arm and chatting gayly a young man and woman swept through the lobby of the Waldorf-Astoria hotel shortly after noon on November 29, 1898. They had just been married in a near-by church.

Two weeks later the couple hurried up the brownstone steps of a fashionable boarding house at No. 257 West End Avenue. They were met at the door by Mrs. Bellinger, the proprietoress who effusively welcomed the honeymooners. She knew them both. The bride had lived in the house before her marriage.

The man was Roland Burnham Molineux, a handsome, athletic young clubman and son of a respected former officer in the Civil War. The bride had been Miss Blanche Chesbro, who, sometime before her marriage, had lengthened her name to Chesebrough. She was tall, dark, and in her middle twenties. She dressed stunningly and possessed a voice that won her distinction as a choir singer. She had been taken up by a rather lively gaited social set on Long Island. Young Molineux was credited with having made quite a catch. Miss Chesebrough had been much sought after by men admirers.

Her beauty was remarkable. People spoke of her as the true Gibson girl, a living replica of the Junoesque creation of Charles Dana Gibson's artistic pen. Her beauty was the more striking because, though one of her eyes was glass, nature had made ample compensation for this blemish by accentuating other factors that go to create womanly charm.

Young Molineux and his bride settled down in the West End house to enjoy their honeymoon.

It was soon interrupted by a series of devastating disclosures brought about chiefly by many hours of official toil on the part of Captain McClusky, McCafferty, and myself, and by much newspaper activity.

The cycle of poison murders that had begun in 1891 with the Harris case, followed by the Buchanan case, was again set in motion, this time by a man of scholarly attainments and social standing who knew about all there was to know about the deadliest of poisons and their uses.

On the afternoon of December 28, 1898, Captain McClusky called me into his office and set before me a small, blue bottle, a silver bottle holder, and a piece of crumpled wrapping paper with a name and address sprawled upon it. These articles had been sent to McClusky by the coroner's physician, Dr. Albert Weston, who also had reported that a widow, Mrs. Katherine Adams, had died that morning in her apartment at No. 61 West Eighty-Sixth Street after taking a dose of headache remedy from the bottle. Her body was at the morgue, where an autopsy was being performed.

No Murder Clinic or Homicide Bureau was then in existence in the Detective Bureau, but McCafferty and I had handled most of the homicides. I carried the articles into the general assembly room for detectives and began an examination of them.

The bottle was of dark blue glass, one-ounce size, and bore a printed label, Bromo Seltzer, with the manufacturer's name and directions for using its contents. Apparently it was a genuine bottle of the headache remedy, yet, as I turned it in my fingers, I saw no name blown into the glass as was the manufacturer's well-known practice. The color of the glass was darker blue than the bona fide Bromo Seltzer bottle.

The label seemed to be genuine, but had the appearance of having been soaked in water, removed from another bottle, and pasted on this one. A hurried trip to a near-by drug store placed me in possession of a genuine bottle as an exemplar. This was of two-ounce size and over its cork was a thin, evenly applied coating of paraffin, while over the stopper in the dark blue bottle the paraffin veneer was thick and irregular, as if pressed down hurriedly by human fingers. And the name Bromo Seltzer was blown into the two-ounce bottle!

I dropped the dark blue bottle into the silver holder. It fitted in precisely. The genuine bottle was a trifle too large to go into the holder. An obvious conclusion came to mind. The person who had manipulated the dark blue bottle had discovered that a genuine bottle of Bromo Seltzer would not fit into the holder so had substituted the smaller dark blue bottle, dressing it up to look like the genuine bottle. Why such a person had gone to all this trouble was not apparent. The fact was known that Mrs. Adams, after taking a dose from the dark blue bottle, had died under suspicious circumstances, and this was enough to start the police machine.

The piece of wrapping paper bore the words, "Mr. Harry Cornish, Knickerbocker Athletic Club, Madison Avenue and Fourty-fifth [*sic*] street, New York City." The piece had been torn from a larger sheet and bore postage stamps canceled at the general post office, New York City, and dated December 23rd P. M. But a Mrs. Adams, and not the addressee, Harry Cornish, was dead.

Cornish was found at the Knickerbocker Athletic Club, where he was physical director. He was pale and feeble when I interviewed him. He was in his thirty-fifth year and a man of considerable culture. He had studied medicine at Harvard, but had given this up for a career as physical instructor. He had specialized in the study of human anatomy, hoping, he explained, to become perfect in the cultivation of the human body.

The day before Christmas, he said, he found a package in his mailbox at the club, carried it into his private office upstairs, and opened it, throwing the paper wrapper into a waste basket. Patrick Fineran, his young assistant, came in. Cornish remarked that someone had sent him a Christmas gift. The package contained a bottle of what looked like Bromo Seltzer, a small silver bottle holder, a small envelope, Tiffany embossed, which was empty, and these were packed in a new light blue Tiffany pasteboard box.

Cornish remarked to his assistant that it was odd the sender did not include his card. Fineran laughed and thought it was a joke. He suggested that Cornish keep the wrapper and perhaps by this means discover the joker. Cornish fished the wrapper out of the waste basket and tore off the written address and the canceled stamps.

Later in the day Harry King, a broker, who had been playing handball in the gym, wandered into Cornish's office and complained of a headache. Cornish instantly suggested that he take some Bromo Seltzer. King picked up a water glass and went to the water cooler to fill it. The cooler was empty and he did not get his dose.

That night Cornish went to his rooms in Mrs. Adams's house, where he had been living for several years. In this house was also Mrs. Florence Rogers, a divorcée, the daughter of Mrs. Adams. Cornish also was divorced from his wife. Cornish told Mrs. Rogers of the gift he had received and described the silver bottle holder. The design seemed to match silver toilet articles owned by Mrs. Rogers, and when she mentioned this to Cornish he promised to bring home the holder so she might look at it.

On the evening of December 27th he brought home the silver holder and the bottle of supposed Bromo Seltzer.

The next morning Mrs. Adams complained of a headache. Mrs. Rogers suggested a dose of Bromo Seltzer and asked Cornish for the bottle he had brought home. He gave it to her. She had some difficulty in pulling the cork, owing to the heavy thickness of the paraffin. She called Cornish, and with a fork he pried out the cork and poured some of the powder into a drinking glass held by Mrs. Adams.

Mrs. Adams half filled the glass with water, and as it effervesced she drank quickly. "What a bitterish taste it has!" she said, making a wry face. Cornish picked up the glass and drank the remnant of the dose. He looked up. Mrs. Adams was writhing in pain and ran into the bathroom, where she collapsed. Mrs. Rogers and Cornish went into the bathroom and tried to lift the woman from the floor. Cornish's knees gave. A hall boy was sent for a doctor.

Cornish was in violent pain. He hurried out to a near-by drug store and showed the Bromo Seltzer bottle to the druggist, who said it looked like a genuine bottle of the remedy. He gave Cornish a drink of aromatic spirits of ammonia to relieve him. When he returned to the apartment he found that Dr. E. F. Hitchcock was attending Mrs. Adams, who had fallen into a stupor. Later Dr. E. S. Potter was called. Dr. Hitchcock had tasted of the supposed Bromo Seltzer and was seized with pains in his stomach and a burning sensation in his throat. He took the bottle away with him and later turned it over to the coroner's physician.

In less than an hour Mrs. Adams was dead. Cornish had taken almost as much of a dose as Mrs. Adams. For an hour he lay on his bed retching. His constitution was strong. He had spent years cultivating his body. This strength saved him. He recovered.

Dr. Weston, the coroner's physician, who arrived at the house, detected the odor of bitter almond when he examined the dead woman's mouth. From this odor he suspected that cyanide of potassium had caused her death. That the bottle might have been filled with this poison in the Bromo Seltzer laboratory through error was out of the question. The substitution of the dark blue bottle for the genuine precluded the possibility of error and pointed, in my mind, to a diabolical poisoning plot.

Drs. Hitchcock and Potter reported that they had found traces of "probably cyanide of potassium" in Mrs. Adams's throat and stomach. Her digestive organs were sent to Dr. Rudolph Witthaus, noted toxicologist, for analysis. Cornish hastened to a chemist, who advised him to tell his story to the authorities. He communicated with John H. McIntyre, lawyer for Mrs. Rogers, who also was an assistant district attorney.

Presently Cornish was back at the club, puzzled, and frightened to know who had sent him the deadly Christmas gift and why, if the sending of it was the result of a plot, anyone should have struck at him through Mrs. Adams. He could think of no enemy filled with such hatred for him that he would seek his death. In his contact with club officers and members Cornish had sometimes differed on athletic policies. He rather vaguely recalled that in April, 1897, he clashed with several club members over the conduct of club entertainments, and later a disagreement had arisen over the activities of Bernie Wefers, a noted sprinter, who was a member of the club and one of its star athletes. A member of the club's house committee as a result of this disagreement had demanded Cornish's discharge. This member was Roland B. Molineux. When the club officers refused to discharge the physical director Molineux resigned and transferred his activities to another club. Among members of the Knickerbocker Athletic Club who regretted Molineux's action and sought to have him

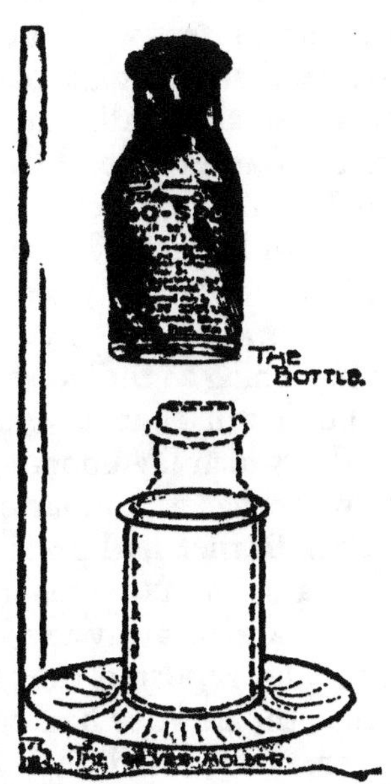

The doctored Bromo Seltzer bottle and the silver holder in the Adams poisoning case.

reconsider it was his close friend, Henry C. Barnet, a broker.

Barnet had died in the meantime. He was taken ill during the preceding October and passed away November 10, 1898. Dr. Wendell Phillips, a member of the club, had attended Barnet and later, when he grew worse, he was attended by Dr. Beaman Douglass, a throat specialist, who diagnosed his illness as diphtheria.

Nineteen days after Barnet's death Molineux married Blanche Chesebrough, who had been seen frequently in the club dining room with Barnet. However, no suspicious circumstances had attended Barnet's death. Dr. Douglass, in the certificate of death, had given cardiac asthenia induced by diphtheric poisoning as the cause of death. Barnet had mentioned to the doctor that he was in receipt of a box of Kutnow powder which lay upon a small table near his bed. Kutnow powder was a popular stomach remedy. The wrapper in which Barnet had received the box was gone, but Dr. Douglass, on November 4th, while his patient was still alive, carried away the box and sent the contents to chemists, who reported that their qualitative analysis indicated that the powder had contained cyanide of mercury. However, Barnet had been given some calomel which contains mercury, and Dr. Douglass concluded that death was due to cardiac asthenia caused by diphtheric poisoning, and moreover he had no knowledge that Barnet had ever tasted of the Kutnow powder. And diphtheric poisoning produces upon the human throat symptoms which are not unlike those which mercury produces.

My immediate concern was not Barnet's death, but to investigate the poisoning of Mrs. Adams. The Barnet matter found a place in my memory and came alive a little later.

On the bottom of the silver holder sent to Cornish I found the letter "L" and a crescent stamped into the silver. With this mark to guide me I found the maker of the silver holder in Newark, New Jersey. Fifteen holders of this size and pattern had been manufactured and scattered among retail jewelers from Waterbury, Connecticut, to San Francisco. But since the Cornish wrapper bore the canceling stamp of the general post office in New York City out-of-town buyers were eliminated. I confined my search to the immediate vicinity of New York City. I found that C. J. Hartdegan, jeweler, Newark, New Jersey, had purchased one silver holder from the manufacturer.

Newark is but a twenty-minute ride from New York City. It is a large manufacturing center, and among its industries was the plant of Morris Herrmann & Company, Nos. 6 and 8 Jersey Street. This firm specialized in the compounding of dry colors in which rare poisons are used. In Herrmann & Company's laboratory Molineux worked as a chemist and color maker.

The date of sale of the holder by the manufacturer to Hartdegan gave me the approximate time at which the latter had placed the article in stock, which was sometime before the Christmas rush. A Hartdegan saleswoman recalled having once polished the holder prior to Christmas. The holder was not now in stock. Sales books were fine-combed to ascertain the date it was sold. Finally a clerk, running through the sales records, came upon an item of five dollars and seventy-five cents, but it represented the sale of a toothpick holder and not a bottle holder. This sales slip was dated December 21st, which was a week before the death of Mrs. Adams and two days before the poison package was mailed at the general post office.

Miss Emma Miller, a Hartdegan employee, had made the sale. I found her at her home. She recalled the sale on December 21st. The young man who had purchased the article had asked for a bottle holder. She knew of no such article in stock. He suggested that the bottle he had in mind using was a Bromo Seltzer bottle. Miss Miller asked the store manager for a bottle holder, whereupon he suggested offering the silver toothpick holder to the young man. It suited him and he purchased it.

"What did the man look like?" I asked Miss Miller.

"I believe he had a beard, a reddish beard," she replied.

Back many years, as I have indicated in previous chapters, I had been given an opportunity to study beards. I reasoned that a red beard probably would be a first growth on a youthful face.

"How old was the man?" I asked.

"In his early thirties," said Miss Miller. "We were frightfully rushed. I didn't see a lot of him."

The discovery of the store where the bottle holder had been purchased was blazed across newspaper front pages, which were filled with sensational accounts of the holiday poisoning mystery. Newspapers were referring inferentially to suspicious circumstances in connection with Barnet's death. Enterprising newspaper artists built up wash drawings of the man with the reddish beard. Along with this were printed facsimiles of the handwriting on the wrapper of Cornish's poison package.

Molineux and his bride, still honeymooning in the West End Avenue house, must have watched these accounts with deepest interest, for Barnet was their mutual friend.

And John Adams, secretary of the Knickerbocker Athletic Club, but not related to Mrs. Adams, also was reading the newspapers. He had studied the handwriting facsimiles most eagerly. His mind ran back to a scene on December 20, 1897, when Roland Molineux, in an impetuous huff, resigned from the club and bombarded Adams with letters protesting against the retention of Cornish.

Adams thought that the handwriting on the Cornish wrapper bore the closest resemblance to the writing in Molineux's letters. Strangely too the word "Forty," which appeared in the address on the wrapper spelled "Fourty," was also misspelled this way in the Molineux letters! But, Molineux had never been seen with a reddish beard! He had worn a mustache, but this had disappeared shortly before Christmas.

On January 5, 1899, Dr. Witthaus reported that Mrs. Adams had died not from the effects of cyanide of potassium but from the effects of a slower but equally deadly, corrosive poison, cyanide of mercury, which is used in the blending of dry colors such as were compounded in the Herrmann color works where Molineux worked.

Now that Molineux's name was openly being mentioned in newspapers he began to appear in the company of an eminent criminal lawyer. This lawyer also was a director in the club to which Molineux had transferred his membership after his tiff with Cornish. It was Cornish's criticism of the lawyer that had caused Molineux to insist upon Cornish's discharge.

The first phase of the poison cycle had brought startling developments. The second phase, even more startling, merits a separate chapter.

CHAPTER VIII

THE POISON CYCLE SPINS GIDDILY

GOING back to Newark to settle the question of the red beard, it occurred to me that if Molineaux were implicated in the poisoning of Mrs. Adams he had made no attempt at flight. Flight is one of the surest signs of guilt, and evidence of it is readily accepted in court of law as a damning circumstance.

Molineux was in possession of newspaper accounts of our work each day. He must have known we were slowly approaching the murderer's door. Yet he appeared much in public, unconcerned and gay, but generally in the company of his lawyer.

Experience will teach a detective that there are substitutes for flight. A murderer may remain close by the scene of his crime, know that he is suspect, but trust himself to the enfolding embrace of his lawyer, whose client's guilt is automatically denied by the mere fact that he has become his defender. The professional criminal appropriately calls his lawyer "my mouthpiece."

Hundreds of times I have had criminals before me who I knew to a moral certainty were guilty. But when I tried to examine them their answer has been, especially in recent years: "Excuse me, mister, but on the advice of counsel I can't say a word."

They become mum as sleeping clams. This, of course, is their legal right, and also it makes flight unnecessary.

At headquarters before leaving for Newark I had heard that Molineux had sent word to McClusky that he would willingly talk to the police at any time, but in the presence of his lawyer. McClusky had smiled at this, assuring Molineux that the police inquiry was being directed at others. McClusky had a strategic motive in doing this. The time he spent at Delmonico's was not wasted.

I interviewed Miss Miller again. Her memory had not greatly improved since our last talk. She was positive that the man who bought the bottle holder had a reddish beard, and that he had come into the store around 5 P. M., for an arc light, she asserted, was burning. She could not have mistaken a mustache for the beard, although it had been my experience that witnesses frequently transpose the two. It was necessary to test the accuracy of her observation and memory. I asked her about other sales she had made on December 21st. She was unable to recall the face of any customer she had waited on and she gave faulty descriptions of persons who had been in the store when I first entered.

Though the beard question was firmly settled in her mind it wasn't in mine. Could anyone else have seen the red-bearded man come out of the store or enter it on December 21st? The Christmas shopping season was at its height on that day. Probably the Newark Police Department had extra men in the shopping section. Talking this over with Detective Farrell in Newark police headquarters I found that he had been near Hartdegan's on December 21st. And Farrell knew Molineux. The detective had been a well-known boxer in his younger days and Molineux had been a prize-fight fan.

"On the twenty-first," Farrell told me, "I saw Molineux walking up from the Hartdegan store. He spoke to me;

said he had just been to dinner with his boss. It was a little after 2 P. M."

"Did he have a beard?" I asked.

"Nothing of the kind," said Farrell.

I step ahead of my story to explain that Farrell testified to these facts and, moreover, the boss, who Molineux had said had been to lunch with him, also testified that no such thing occurred on December 21st. Miss Miller's faulty observation was obvious.

Reading in the newspapers of Newark developments, Molineux hurried with witnesses to Newark and confronted Miss Miller. She declared positively that he was not the purchaser of the bottle holder. She was positive that he could not have worn a false beard. Fresh from this assuring trip, Molineux again presented himself to McClusky—accompanied by his lawyer—and offered to do anything McClusky asked him to do. He wanted to clear himself. McClusky smiled and intimated again that his men were working in another direction.

The fact that Dr. Douglass had sent the Kutnow powder found on Barnet's sickbed table to a chemist kept popping up in my mind. Then from day to day persons I interviewed, who knew both Molineux and the broker, kept referring to the fact that Barnet and Blanche Chesebrough, now Mrs. Molineux, had been on most intimate terms.

Love, jealousy, spite, and one man's desire for one woman above all others furnish the most powerful motives not only for murder but for self-destruction, far more powerful than a squabble two men might have had over the conduct of club affairs. And where the motive is possession of a woman whom another man had won, the murderer, working out his plot under the confusing torments of a frenzied desire, makes glaring slip-ups.

A long way back I had begun a study of poisons. I found the subject most engaging. When the opportunity presented itself I discussed poisons with Dr. Witthaus, who probably knew at that time more about poisons, especially the cyanides, than any other living American toxicologist. Cyanides, I learned, were treacherous poisons; in the hands of a skilled chemist they could be manipulated and mixed with other substances so that death from them might be made to look natural. Their effect upon the human throat might be taken for the symptoms of several fatal diseases.

With McCafferty I called again upon Dr. Douglass, the throat specialist, whose diagnosis of Barnet's death now puzzled me. It was a rather unpleasant interview and a strange one, a police detective taking issue with a skilled medical practitioner on the technical aspects of his profession. Dr. Douglass was quite upset. He demanded to know what Barnet's death had to do with Mrs. Adams's murder, since she had died of poisoning by cyanide of potassium whereas, if poison had been admitted to Barnet's system, it was cyanide of mercury. Just what connection the two deaths had, I advised the doctor, would develop in due course; what McCafferty and I wanted to know was whether the doctor might have been mistaken in ascribing Barnet's death to a natural cause.

Dr. Douglass's face reddened. He admitted that he had taken specimens of the infection in Barnet's throat with a swab and had made a culture but found no evidence of diphtheric poisoning. But, he added, it might have been clinical diphtheria. He was unable to make clear to McCafferty or to me just where the difference lay. Then he admitted that the chemist to whom he had sent the box of Kutnow powder reported that it contained cyanide of mercury. But he was certain that no signs of mercurial poisoning appeared on the swab. Nor could he say whether Barnet had ever tasted of the Kutnow powder in the box or, if he had, that the powder had caused his death. Barnet had received other boxes of the same powder earlier. He might possibly have taken some of this.

I asked Dr. Douglass for the box of powder. It was a small tin box of sample size. The name Kutnow Brothers, No. 13 Astor Place, New York City, was on the box, and across the bottom a small printed label: "This box does not require internal revenue stamps." I took the powder to Dr. Witthaus.

In the meantime an inquest into the death of Mrs. Adams had begun on February 9th. At each session Molineux was present with his lawyer at his side. He appeared also as a witness.

A visit to Kutnow Brothers' office revealed that the tin box was genuine. It was a sample box such as the firm had been giving away on written request, and to passers-by on the Boardwalk at Asbury Park, New Jersey. The label on the bottom indicated an important fact. This particular box had been mailed, or given away, after the federal government had decided that samples of patent medicine need not bear revenue stamps. Reference to the bill submitted by the printer who had made the labels established that they had been printed and delivered to Kutnow Brothers some time before Barnet's death.

For the best part of a week I sat with several assistants at a desk in Kutnow Brothers' office running through thousands of written requests for samples mailed in from all parts of the world. Finally a young woman who was helping me came upon a sheet of robin's egg blue note paper with three interclasped crescents embossed at the top. The handwriting seemed like the penmanship on the Cornish wrapper. I read the letter:

GENTS:

Please send me a sample of salts to 1620 Broadway and oblige

Yours, etc.,

H. CORNISH.

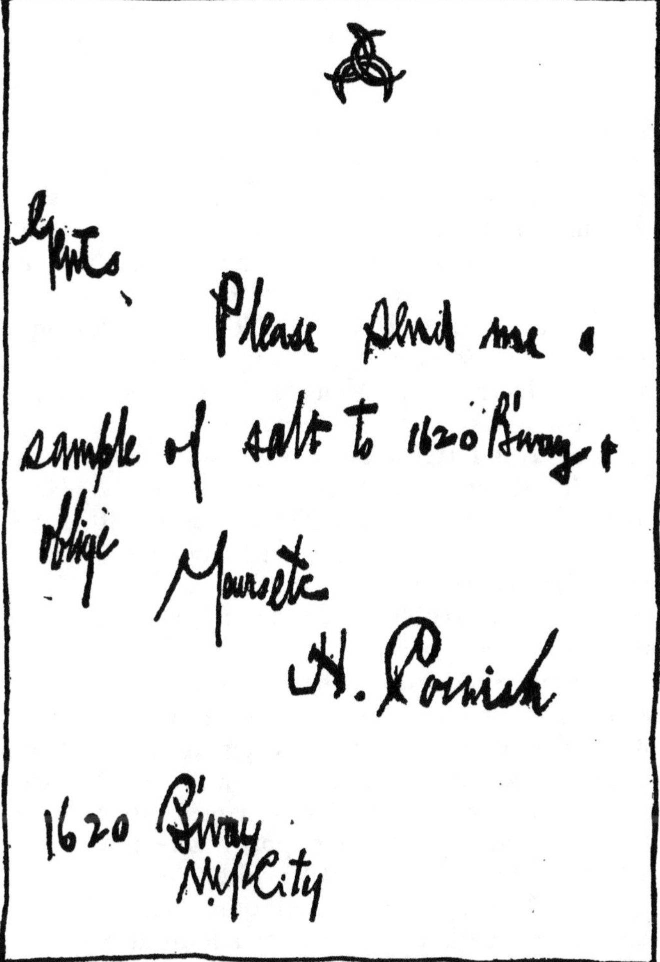

Gents,

Please send me a sample of salt to 1620 B'way & oblige

Yours etc

H. Cornish

1620 B'way
N.Y. City

The fake Cornish letter on robin's-egg-blue note paper with interclasped crescents which Carey found in his long search through patent medicine letter files.

Cornish again! And an address—1620 Broadway. To this address I hastened and found it to be a small store where newspaper want ads were taken in and where private letter boxes were rented to persons who preferred for their own reasons to receive mail here rather than at post offices or their homes. A man named Koch ran the place. He rented boxes to whoever wanted them and asked no questions. On December 21, 1898, he had rented a box to a man who gave the name of Cornish. And in the box at the present moment were two unclaimed letters addressed to Cornish. These I found to be correspondence from Frederick Stearns & Company, manufacturing pharmacists in Detroit and Von Mohl & Company, patent medicine manufacturers in Cincinnati.

The Stearns letter was in response to inquiries from "Cornish" about a young man named A. A. Harpster, who had been a clerk in the Knickerbocker Athletic Club and friend of both Cornish and Molineux. Harpster had worked for the Stearns Company and so had Cornish. The Von Muhl letter replied to a request for a sample of pills which were advertised "for men only."

Telegraphic requests to these two concerns brought us the original letters received by them from "Cornish." Both were written on the robin's egg blue note paper with the embossed crescents; both were in the familiar writing on the Cornish wrapper with an obvious, and unsuccessful, attempt to make the writing appear different. They had not been written by the real Cornish.

These letters, together with all other handwriting specimens thus far gathered, and some admitted specimens of Molineux's handwriting, were turned over to Handwriting Expert William J. Kinsley.

N. A. Heckman, who also operated a private mail box agency at No. 257 West Forty-second Street, read of the discovery in Koch's place and recalled that on May 27, 1898 (five months before Barnet fell ill), he had rented

Box 217 to a man who gave the name of H. C. Barnet. "Barnet" had called for his mail about twenty times since renting the box and had received shipments of patent medicine.

For some reason "Barnet" like "Cornish" had failed recently to call for mail and, as had happened at Koch's a letter lay unclaimed in Box 217. It was addressed to H. C. Barnet and was from the Marston Remedy Company, 15 Park Place, New York City. This firm also specialized in remedies exploited as "for men only." The context of this letter indicated that "Barnet" had recently filled out an application blank for a sample and, in this blank, gave a self-diagnosis of his ailment.

I obtained this application and startling developments followed. It was written in the familiar handwriting. In blank spaces provided for answers to diagnostic inquiries "Barnet" had written his age as 31, his chest measurement as 37, his waist circumference as 32. To the question "Has any relative ever died from consumption or scrofula?" the answer was indicated by underlining the word "consumption." A few days later I learned that Molineux's maternal grandmother had died of consumption some years before in East Hartford, Connecticut.

The measurements of the real Henry C. Barnet were far from fitting those given in the diagnostic application. But inquiry at a tailor shop patronized by Molineux disclosed his chest measurement was 37, his waist 32, and his age, according to a birth certificate in the files of the Board of Health, was 31!

These additional handwriting specimens were turned over to Kinsley. He reported that one man had written them all—Molineux. A battery of well-known handwriting experts from various large cities were summoned to New York City and they studied the handwriting specimens each at a different time and unaware that other experts were also working on the case.

The inquest was still under way. From questions Molineux's lawyer asked at this inquiry, and Molineux's tactics, it was obvious that they were trying to throw suspicion upon Cornish. Remarks dropped by Molineux about Cornish's activities convinced me that he was having the physical director shadowed. I determined to find out whether this was true. I arranged to have McCafferty and Cornish leave the clubhouse together one afternoon. They went out the front door; I out a side door. As they gained the sidewalk a man across the street also moved slowly in the same direction. I followed at some distance. McCafferty and Cornish turned a corner. Their shadow ran to the corner. I went up to him and learned he was a private detective in the employ of an agency hired by Molineux.

When I communicated this to Assistant District Attorney James W. Osborne he announced that since Molineux was so eager to aid the police he would be given an opportunity. So, when the chemist again offered to do anything McClusky wanted, he was directed to present himself at Osborne's office. He walked into Osborne's office with his lawyer.

He took a chair at a long table. He was asked to write whatever Kinsley, who was also at the table, dictated. Molineux's lawyer looked on. His client wrote words, sentences and figures which appeared in all the handwriting specimens we had collected.

The word "forty" he repeatedly spelled with a "u"!

Pleased and confident, he arose and left the room.

This accumulation of admitted handwriting was passed on to the experts. I resumed the hunt for more patent-medicine correspondence. It was the practice of companies in this field to sell letters they had received asking for samples. This accounted for the fact that in Barnet's office desk after his death patent medicine samples he had

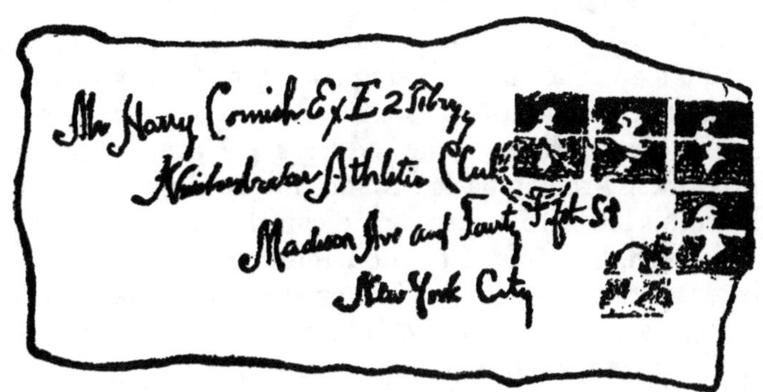

Mr Harry Cornish
Knickerbocker Athletic Club
Madison Ave and Forty Fifth St
New York City

Writing on the wrapper in which Cornish received the poisonous Bromo Seltzer.

Mr Harry Cornish
Knickerbocker Athletic Club
Madison Ave and Forty Fifth St.
New York City

Admitted handwriting of Roland Molineux which he penned at the dictation of handwriting expert.

never sent for were found. His name had gotten on a suckers' list.

I found a letter in possession of the Fowler Remedy Company, Modus, Connecticut, asking for a sample of Rudolph's Specific and inclosing twenty-five cents with the request that the sample be sent to No. 6–8 Jersey Street, Newark, New Jersey, the address of the Herrmann color works. Tracing back I found that Molineux had first written this letter to a patent-medicine dealer named Burns who, in turn, had sold it to the Modus company.

It was written on the robin's egg blue note paper with the interclasped crescents! Molineux at the inquest conceded it to be his handwriting.

Then events came with a crash.

The handwriting experts were unanimous in the conclusion that the Cornish and Barnet letters, the Cornish wrapper, and the diagnosis application were in the handwriting of one person—Molineux.

Dr. Witthaus reported that he had found crystals of cyanide of mercury in the Kutnow powder found on Barnet's sickroom table, and that the bottle from which Mrs. Adams had drunk also contained the same deadly crystals.

The coroner's jury accused Molineux of murdering Mrs. Adams.

McCafferty and I stepped up to Molineux as he was leaving the inquest room.

"I've got to put you under arrest," I announced.

He grinned, turned to his lawyer, and then came along. He was nonchalant, confident. He was silent on the way to prison, but his lawyer, a genial man, talked freely, commenting upon the outrage committed upon his client.

Molineux did not return to his bride that night, or for many days and nights that followed.

The day this happened was February 27, 1899. The following day Barnet's body was exhumed and analysis showed that he had died of poisoning by cyanide of mercury. The picture of the Barnet murder, however, was still a little dim and ragged. It lacked substantial proof of motive; that is, strong, legal proof. I was given the job to finish this part of the picture.

Barnet, I learned, had never quarreled with Molineux. On the contrary, they were, to all appearances, the best of friends. Indeed, both were interested in Miss Chesebrough. Molineux had met her in 1897 during a summer vacation in Portland, Maine. They met again in 1898 in New York City, where Molineux introduced the woman to Barnet. Thereafter she was oftener in Barnet's company, dining, riding, and theatergoing.

A suggestive thing entered the picture at this point. In the fall of 1897 Molineux was a guest aboard the yacht of a rich young man known as "Sapolio" Morgan, who had also been seen in Miss Chesebrough's company, and there was talk of their engagement. Also there was a guest, Walter S. Baldwin, aboard the yacht. Immediately after breakfast aboard the boat one day Baldwin fell violently ill and Morgan also complained of terrible stomach pains. Baldwin died; Morgan recovered. Molineux was not ill, although he had eaten at the same table.

Suddenly in the late fall of 1898 Molineux asked Miss Chesebrough to marry him. She declined. Then Barnet fell ill and took to his bed in October. Molineux again pressed the woman to marry him. She agreed. But even after accepting Molineux she continued to call upon Barnet. During his illness she sent him flowers and visited him. While he was on his deathbed this note reached him:

> I am distressed to learn of your illness. I arrived home Saturday and am exceedingly sorry to know you have been so indisposed. Won't you let me know when you are able to be about? I want *so much* to see you. Is it that you do not believe in me? If you would but let me prove to you my sincerity. Do not be cross any more. And accept, I pray, my best wishes.
>
> BLANCHE.

A few days later, on November 10th, Barnet died.

Nineteen days later Molineux married the writer of the note. It is not within my power to determine whether Roland Molineux saw that letter written or knew that it would be written. Nor did Barnet, his friend, ostensibly, live to know that the writer within a few weeks would be the bride of Molineux. Nor has anyone ever been able to say what happened between Barnet and Blanche that led her to plead "not to be cross any more." These are unfinished parts of the picture.

My task was not complete, however. Loose ends were still to be gathered up and put in their place in the larger picture, that a jury might read its story and act accordingly. At the Herrmann color works we found young Robert Zeller, who had been Molineux's assistant in the laboratory. He was fond of the chemist. In an unguarded moment he let slip the fact that Miss Mary Melando, who also worked in the factory, was fond of Molineux and often tidied an apartment which the chemist maintained in quarters above the laboratory.

Mary liked fine stationery, and so one morning while in the apartment she picked up from Molineux's desk several sheets that caught her eye. It was the robin's egg blue note paper with the interclasped crescents! She admitted the fact to me, but when it came time for her to testify at the trial of the man she silently admired she refused to leave New Jersey. She was within her legal rights, but a very vital witness for the State of New York. She could by her testimony put the robin's egg blue paper in the hands of the accused man. No way existed by which she could be compelled to obey the mandates of New York courts, and eminent lawyers saw that the poor working girl's rights were carefully maintained.

But she did testify, and in New York City. How she came to do this I shall not detail. Suffice it to say that she was fond of the theater. She attended one in Paterson,

New Jersey, one evening. She left the theater after the performance in a great hurry and went to the railroad station. Two trains going in opposite directions pulled in. A man cried, "This train for Newark." Mary stepped aboard it. She discovered it was not going toward Newark but toward Suffern, New York. But the train had started. She got off at Suffern and stepped into the arms of McCafferty, who was waiting at the depot. Most unwillingly she testified at Molineux's trial.

Molineux was convicted and sentenced to die for the murder of Mrs. Adams. An appeal was taken, and for twenty months he occupied a condemned man's cell in Sing Sing Prison. Finally the Court of Appeals reversed the verdict and ordered a new trial on the ground that the trial court had erred in admitting into evidence at the Adams trial testimony and documents pertaining to the Barnet case.

A second trial was had, but Mary Melando and other New Jersey witnesses were beyond the reach of New York courts. Mary's testimony at the first trial was not permitted in evidence at the second. An acquittal resulted.

Molineux was never indicted for the murder of Barnet. While the motive was stronger in the Barnet case, no man like Fineran had been present to suggest to Barnet that he save the wrapper in which he received the Kutnow powder. Thus evidence was lacking to implicate by legal proof the man accused of Mrs. Adams's murder.

And it was after Barnet's death that the letter signed H. Cornish was sent to Kutnow Brothers, asking that samples be sent to the mail box at No. 1620 Broadway. Whether the murderer had intended to send Cornish Kutnow powders and then switched to Bromo Seltzer is uncertain unless he knew, through chemical knowledge, that cyanide of mercury, mixed with bromide of potassium (the base of Bromo Seltzer) would tend to disintegrate and form cyanide of potassium, which is the deadlier of the two cyanides. Or he may have discovered also that cyanide of mercury mixed with stomach-regulating salts like the Kutnow preparation would remain cyanide of mercury and that its action upon the membranes of the throat would produce diphtheric symptoms and fool physicians, which, in fact, had happened!

An extended inquiry into the circumstances surrounding the death of Baldwin on the Morgan yacht was made. No conclusive evidence was found that his death had resulted from poisoning. His remains were not exhumed. Time had laid an obliterating hand upon whatever evidence of poisoning there once may have been.

In 1903 Blanche Chesebrough divorced Molineux and married a lawyer and went to live in South Dakota.

Molineux wrote a play, *The Man Inside,* in 1914. It purported to show the terrors of the death house as seen by a former inmate. It was taken from his own experience, but he studiously avoided references to the mooted issues that arose in his trials. The play was produced on Broadway and failed. After its failure he married the young woman who had helped him write the piece.

A few months later Molineux, dressed in a gay-colored bathrobe and a sorry-looking straw hat, ran through the streets of a small Long Island town shouting and capering like a clown. The chief of police locked him up, and the following day he was taken to a state institution, hopelessly insane.

There he died not many years back.

I might add in passing that after Molineux's last trial I found that the little dark blue bottle from which Mrs. Adams drank her death potion originally had contained cyanide of mercury; that it was such a bottle that Roland Molineux often had received in his laboratory from wholesalers. He used the contents to blend beautiful colors—Prussian blue and English vermilion.

My opinion as to Molineux's guilt? I prefer not to

express it and, if I did, what would it avail, now? Briefs are not required wherever he has gone, nor do I believe that a murder man's opinions are sought there, either.

Many New Yorkers who remember the trials of Molineux still consider he was innocent. How strange is public opinion, sometimes. As I was finishing this chapter a friend told me that for the first time since Molineux was tried the house where he honeymooned on West End Avenue had been rented. For years it had no tenant. Now I wonder why, if so many considered him innocent, that place was never sold or rented. Surely it wasn't haunted. No murders were committed there. At least none I ever heard about.

CHAPTER IX

FIN DE SIECLE

AMONG epigrams that rolled from the tongue of Inspector Byrnes was "the smarter they are the harder they fall." I don't imagine this was original with him, but the truth of it was glaringly apparent in the Harris, Buchanan, and Molineux cases. These men were educated and in varying degrees possessed special knowledge of poisons.

In September, 1900, there came upon the murder scene a man thoroughly versed in the processes of the law who tried his hand, via a proxy, at poisoning, and the cycle of murders by lethal dosages whirled again and then came to a stop in so far as New York City was concerned.

Captain McClusky, with his usual economy of details, handed me an assignment on September 24th. It was at night after quitting hours. He instructed me to go to the apartment of a Mr. Rice at No. 500 Madison Avenue. There I would find the remains of Mr. Rice, who had died the day before. I was to hold up funeral arrangements and see that the body was removed to the morgue. I was to question whoever I found in the apartment about the death of Rice and about his estate.

A thin-faced man admitted me to the apartment along with several fellow-detectives. He said he was Jones, valet to the dead man. We advanced into the apartment, and in the living room at ease sat a short, thin man of about forty, with a close-cropped Vandyke beard. He introduced himself as Albert T. Patrick, attorney for Rice. He was suave, cool, and self-possessed, but Jones moved nervously about the room as we addressed our inquiries to Patrick.

Rice, the lawyer explained, had died in the apartment the day before, Sunday, September 23rd. Patrick said he was not present at the deathbed, but Jones was. Death, the doctor's certificate explained, was due to natural causes. The lawyer's answers seemed evasive, and when we asked for details of Rice's illness and his death he kept referring us to the valet. Jones spoke in a low, quavering voice and made a poor impression.

The coroner's physician entered the apartment. We went into the bedroom and viewed the body. I saw the face of a well-preserved old gentleman about eighty-three, with white hair. There were signs of conflict and anguish on the still features.

"The remains will go to the morgue," said the coroner's physician.

"But arrangements have been made to cremate the body," Patrick spoke up. "It was Mr. Rice's wish. He left such a request with me."

"Regardless," said the physician, "the body must go to the morgue."

"But death was natural," said Patrick.

Jones looked in through the door and quickly withdrew when the lawyer looked at him. It struck me then that the valet was fearful, or under the domination of the little lawyer.

Patrick made one more effort to keep the remains from the morgue. He said he had written orders from Rice directing cremation. It was in the form of a letter. The undertaker spoke up. He said that the crematorium was being prepared to receive the body. Patrick left.

Little was learned on this visit, but the impression created by Jones and Patrick was far from satisfactory.

At headquarters McClusky enlarged the picture, giving us details which had come in since we left.

David L. Short, a friend of Patrick's that morning had presented a check for twenty-five thousand dollars to a teller named Wallace in Swenson & Company's downtown bank. This check was payable to Abert T. Patrick, signed by William M. Rice, and endorsed by Albert T. Patrick. Short asked to have it certified. The teller studied the check and noted the discrepancy in the spelling of Albert. He compared the writing and signatures with other checks made by Rice, who was a depositor, then handed the check back to Short, advising that before it could be certified the spellings of the name of endorser and payee must agree.

Short left but returned quickly with the check reëndorsed Abert T. Patrick. Wallace 'phoned to the Rice apartment. Jones answered and said that the check was genuine because he himself had made it out for Rice, who had signed it. The teller stamped the bank's certification upon the instrument and was making an entry of the transaction in a book when Eric Swenson, one of the bank partners, looked at the check and directed that Rice be gotten on the 'phone.

Wallace again called the apartment and insisted upon speaking with Rice. Reluctantly the valet informed him that Rice was dead—had just passed away. Wallace told Swenson of this, and the latter drew a pen through the certification, canceling it. He handed it back to Short, who left. Presently Patrick appeared at the teller's window and insisted that the check be certified in view of the fact that since Rice was dead payment might be held up by the probate court. Swenson refused to comply and Patrick left. The banker consulted his lawyer, James W. Gerard (later ambassador to Germany), who conveyed the story of the check and Rice's death to the district attorney and McClusky.

Information had been received from two elderly women, McClusky said, that on Sunday evening they had called at Rice's apartment with cakes and wine for the old gentleman, whom they knew well. They rang the apartment doorbell several times but received no response, although, at the time, Rice must have been dying, with his valet at hand. On the heels of this came news that three checks signed by Rice for $25,000, $135,000, and $65,000, and payable to Patrick, had turned up at the Fifth Avenue Trust Company, where Rice also had accounts. A man named Potts, who shared an office with Patrick, had deposited the check for $25,000 to Patrick's credit in another bank and asked that the other two checks be certified.

We had come into possession of the checks and a letter signed by Rice directing cremation of his body. I held the checks up to a light, one check over the other, and found the Rice signatures to be precisely the same to the slightest flourish. I held the cremation letter before the light with a check under it. The two signatures agreed perfectly. They fitted over each other as though they had been made by the same stamp. Now no matter how often a man may write his own name there are always variances in his signatures. A little while later David Carvalho, handwriting expert, was called in and denounced the signatures as forgeries which had been traced over a genuine signature thus accounting for their similarity.

While the forgeries became apparent there was yet no indication that Rice had come to his death under suspicious circumstances. The nervous actions of Jones, the evasive replies of Patrick to our questions, and the hurry about cremating the body of Rice suggested a motive for his death, but the checks might have been forged after his death from natural causes.

"In the meantime," McClusky directed, "pick up Patrick and Jones and hold them for forgery."

Patrick was coming out of a safe-deposit vault, where he had unsuccessfully attempted to get possession of a large block of Rice's securities, when I accosted him. Potts was with him and shrank back when he saw me. He, too, was under Patrick's domination.

"You're under arrest for forgery," I announced. Patrick grinned at me, then at Potts, and said to the latter, "Call up that lawyer." Potts scampered off. Patrick went with me to headquarters, silent all the way. He asked one question: "Has Jones been arrested?"

The valet was picked up in the Rice apartment by Detective Vallely. Vallely told me that Jones went white when he was arrested and seemed for a time to be unable to talk.

"Where's Mr. Patrick?" he finally asked the detective in a faltering voice.

"He's being arrested, too," said the detective. Jones braced up.

The two men were placed in adjoining cells and held for forgery on an affidavit which I signed. McClusky talked with the prisoners, and their conduct increased his suspicions.

Rice left relatives and friends in Texas and one of the latter came on to New York. This man, James A. Baker, brought with him a telegram which had been received from Jones on Monday, the day after Rice's death. It read:

MR. RICE DIED EIGHT O'CLOCK LAST NIGHT UNDER CARE PHYSICIAN DEATH CERTIFICATE OLD AGE WEAK HEART DIARAHUE LEFT INSTRUCTIONS TO BE INTERRED IN MILWAUKEE WITH REMAINS OF WIFE FUNERAL 10 AM TOMORROW AT 500 MADISON AVENUE. WHEN WILL YOU COME?

C. F. JONES.

The cremation letter attested to the falsity of this telegram and explained the hurry about disposing of Rice's remains by means of fire. Texas relatives on Sept. 24 replied to Jones's wire as follows:

PLEASE MAKE NO DISPOSITION OF RICE'S REMAINS UNTIL WE ARRIVE WE LEAVE TONIGHT REACH NEW YORK THURSDAY MORNING.

In spite of this Patrick had gone ahead with the arrangements for cremation, but had been careful to make it appear that the order for cremation had come from Rice himself. Apparently there had been a collusive arrangement between the lawyer and valet. And there was. It came to light in a dramatic way.

A jail guard on duty near the cells occupied by Patrick and Jones heard groans and, looking into Jones's cell, saw him writhing on the hard floor. His throat had been gashed. A penknife, the property of Patrick, lay close by. A few hours before Jones had been in the district attorney's office. He had made conflicting but not damaging admissions. He was unable to explain how it had happened that the two elderly women who had called with cakes and wine had not been admitted to the Rice apartment on Sunday evening.

Returning to his cell he had whispered to the lawyer, explaining what had happened at the interview with the prosecutor. The lawyer had remarked: "The jig's up. No use. We're done. You go first and I'll follow." He then passed Jones his penknife and the valet hacked at his throat. Patrick had no idea of killing himself, for he must have known that the shock felt by Jones when he cut his throat would have made it impossible for him to pass back the knife so that the lawyer might "follow." It was apparent that Jones was under the complete domination of the lawyer, even to taking his own life at Patrick's suggestion.

The valet, near to death, was removed to the prison ward in Bellevue Hospital. When Jones was fully recovered I took him to the House of Detention, where he was no longer near the lawyer. High bail was fixed so that he would not be liberated. I called on him one morning. We shook hands. There was an icy, lifeless touch to his fingers. He could hardly speak.

"How do you feel?" I asked him.

"Terrible. Terrible. Like a man smothering."

He was in great distress. He had reached the point known in police circles as "the break." His body was limp. I advised Assistant District Attorney Osborne that it looked to me as if Jones was ready to talk, and he asked me to bring the valet to his office.

To Osborne he unfolded the complete story. In my time no murder conspiracy had ever attained the length to which Patrick went to encompass the death of Rice. It was the story of Patrick, a failure as a lawyer, but a super-egotist, working with his subservient tool Jones, the trusted manservant of a kind master and benefactor. Dickens should have known Patrick, and Jones, too.

The story came from Jones's lips in a torrent.

In 1897 Jones was a storekeeper in the Capitol Hotel in Houston, Texas, which Rice owned and operated. The old man took a liking to Jones, who showed signs of an education, and engaged him as his valet, companion, and secretary. Rice was a childless widower and a recluse. He was possessed of a large fortune and gave generously to philanthropies. When Rice left for New York City he took Jones along and the two became the sole occupants of the apartment at No. 500 Madison Avenue. They had few callers.

In November, 1899, Jones asserted, a man giving the name of Smith appeared at the Rice apartment. The valet met him at the door and, upon being told that the old gentleman was in another room, entered. Smith told the valet that he was seeking evidence to prove that Rice's residence in Texas was not bona fide. There was pending at the time a litigation in Texas courts over the estate of the late Mrs. Rice to which Rice was a party. Smith flattered Jones; told him he was underpaid and unappreciated and promised if he would furnish the evidence he was seeking the valet would be rewarded. Jones said that he could not think of doing a thing like that against a man who had always befriended him.

Smith left.

A second visit followed in a few days. Smith revealed that his right name was Albert T. Patrick and that he was a lawyer hired by the side opposing Rice. He offered the servant a bribe. For a time Jones demurred, but finally Patrick put him under his thumb and boldly asked him to write a letter to which Rice's signature would be forged and in which it would be made to appear that Rice had given up hope of winning the lawsuit because proof had been found of his illegal residence in Texas. Jones wrote this letter and signed Rice's signature to it. Patrick promised him two hundred and fifty dollars.

The lawyer was deeply interested in Rice's affairs and questioned Jones at length about them. He learned that Rice had made a will in 1896 in which he left little to his natural heirs and nearly all of his wealth to the William Rice Institute, an educational organization in Texas which the capitalist had founded. The lawyer was solicitous about the old man's health. Jones told him that while his employer was past eighty-four he confidently expected to live many years. His health was good.

In December, 1899, Jones and Patrick, while running through Rice's papers in the apartment, came upon the 1896 will. The lawyer read it and remarked that he thought it unjust to Rice's natural heirs.

On a later visit Patrick produced a will he had prepared in which Rice was to leave him, Patrick, half the estate, the remainder to be divided among the heirs with little set aside for the Rice Institute. Jones, at Patrick's direction, copied the will on a typewriter in the apartment. For this Patrick promised the valet whatever he asked for and assured him that he would be well taken care of in the will. For a time, Jones said, he reflected upon what he was doing and was about to tear up the will when Patrick won him over again.

When Jones asked the lawyer what he intended to do with the 1896 will he replied that he would leave this in existence so that the heirs of Rice might see how much better they fared in the latter will and thus refrain from a contest!

The forged will, in its final form, did not suit Patrick. He had the valet write several substitutes until finally, on June 30, 1900, a document was produced which made Patrick the sole executor in place of the Rice Institute.

In this will Jones was not mentioned as a beneficiary, although in the previous drafts he had been remembered. Now the valet was out in the cold. Patrick apparently had him under the most complete domination. Patrick was quick to say that he would take generous care of the valet when the Rice estate came into his control.

Witnesses to the will were secured by Patrick. One was Short, and the other a clerk who worked in the lawyer's office.

At this point the lawyer's plot took a sudden turn. The appearance of his name in the forged will as residuary legatee might arouse suspicion when the fact leaked out that there had always been a deep hostility between Rice and the lawyer as a result of the will litigation. The rich widower hated the man, but Patrick took care to keep out of his sight. Patrick had tried to get around this situation by appearing as a friendly intermediary in negotiations to settle the litigation, but Rice rebuffed him.

The lawyer set about to build up an elaborate background by forgery. In August, 1900, he manufactured a document purporting to name himself as the agent who had settled litigation in a way that had pleased Rice. To carry this picture farther Patrick persuaded Jones to write a series of thirty letters purporting to be from Rice to Patrick in which Rice's business affairs were intimately discussed and in which it was made to appear that the capitalist reposed the greatest confidence in the lawyer. One letter gave Patrick explicit instructions as to how Rice desired the terms of the forged will executed. Carbon copies of these faked documents were inserted in the Rice files by the valet.

To insure against slip-up in his plan to gain control of all Rice's estate Patrick made a bold move. He caused the valet to prepare a forged instrument giving him, Patrick, detailed instructions from Rice to take full possession and control of his securities valued at several million dollars.

His legalistic mind went farther. From Jones he obtained three genuine Rice checks which the old man had signed but which had not yet gone out to the payees. Forged checks from a master tracing were made out in their stead and forwarded to the payees. Thus were placed in circulation three forged instruments which, in the event that any of Rice's forged signatures on other documents were questioned, the check signatures (forged) could be used as exemplars to sustain the forgeries!

Now Patrick's legalistic mind ran to possible litigation that might arise over Rice's property after he was dead. So he forged the checks later offered at Swenson's bank and the Fifth Avenue Trust Company. The money from these was to be used to defray the expense of suits to sustain the forged documents. Patrick was penniless. Now it appeared clear why he had hurried to have bank certifications placed upon the checks before Rice's body had been disposed of. He needed ready cash for expenses.

The stage was set. Within the lawyer's grasp was all of Rice's property amounting to more than $3,000,000 which would come into his control when the capitalist died.

How soon would he die? Jones had told the lawyer that the old man was robust and had many years before him. He suffered slightly from indigestion and cooked his own meals, which consisted chiefly of cereals.

In March, 1900, Jones related, he himself had suffered from an attack of indigestion, and Patrick had prevailed upon him to send for a Dr. Curry, who had been the lawyer's physician. Patrick told Jones to caution the doctor not to mention the name of Patrick in Rice's hearing.

When an attack of indigestion fell upon Rice later, Jones suggested calling in Curry and the physician came. Since the physician had given Jones some mercury pills which had helped him, the valet suggested to his master that he, too, try them. But they served to improve Rice's condition, whereupon Patrick gave Jones mercury pills of such strength that when Jones swallowed one he fell ill. The lawyer told the valet to try these on Rice.

Rice took some of them and grew worse. Suddenly Patrick suggested the cremation letter, realizing that mercury left traces in the human body!

About this time Rice spoke to his valet about reading a magazine article touching upon the risks to be encountered in handling anæsthetics, particularly chloroform, in a sickroom. Jones relayed his master's comments to Patrick. Later the lawyer asked Dr. Curry about chloroform and whether it would leave traces that an autospy would reveal. Dr. Curry advised that it would leave only slight traces if given in small doses to a man with a weak heart. Rice was in a weak condition. The strong mercury pills were weakening him.

Patrick suggested that Jones send to his brother in Texas for chloroform. He obeyed. The chloroform arrived.

On September 16th a violent attack of acute indigestion seized Rice. On the same day a telegram reached him with the news that an oil plant in Texas in which he was heavily interested had been destroyed by fire. He was asked for funds to rebuild the plant. Rice decided to supply $250,000—all the cash he had available in New York banks. Jones and Patrick intercepted the telegram in which Rice was notifying the plant managers of his decision to furnish funds. Already Patrick had sufficient forged checks to put his hands on all the capitalist's cash, but if it were sent to Texas the bank accounts would be gone.

Subsequently Rice was advised by telegram that a draft on him for $250,000 would arrive in New York on September 22nd.

"I showed the telegram about the draft to Patrick," said Jones. "He said the old man must be put out of the way at once."

The draft arrived at the Rice apartment on Saturday, September 22nd, by bank messenger. Jones met the messenger at the door and told him to carry the news back to the bank that Mr. Rice was too ill to attend to business, but would take care of the draft on Monday, September 24th.

At five o'clock Saturday afternoon Patrick hurried into the apartment and learned of the draft's arrival. He asked Dr. Curry if Rice would be able to leave the house on Monday to attend to business. Dr. Curry said he thought he would.

Patrick left.

Rice enjoyed a comfortable night. He awoke at eight o'clock Sunday morning and ate a hearty breakfast.

At 11 A. M. Jones rushed out to tell Patrick how improved the old man was. Patrick suggested that it was the time to do away with Rice, for if the draft were met the whole plot would fall through. He told the valet to chloroform his master. Jones demurred, pleading that he could never stand by and see his old employer die at his hands. Patrick suggested giving Rice a mixture of ammonia, water, and oxalic acid, explaining that the administration of this would not require the valet's presence at the moment of death.

Jones tried the mixture. Rice refused to take it. He told Patrick of this failure, and the lawyer gave him the chloroform and instructed him in its use. Jones returned to the apartment. It was six P. M. Rice was fast asleep. The valet saturated a sponge with chloroform and inserted it into a cone made with a twisted towel. He laid this upon the old man's face and ran from the room.

The doorbell rang repeatedly. The two elderly women were there. The valet did not answer it.

At the end of an hour Jones entered the sickroom and found his employer dead. He burned the sponge and the towel, opened the windows, and tidied up the room. He called the elevator man to get Dr. Curry. Then he 'phoned the news to Patrick.

The lawyer rushed breathlessly into the apartment and took charge of affairs. The man who hated him was dead. Presently the chain of forged documents would come to light. Patrick would be in possession of his enemy's fortune. He gave orders to have the body cremated and had the forged letter to back him up.

Here the elaborate plot went to pieces. Patrick had neglected to ascertain important fact about cremation. Twenty-four hours were required to heat the furnace and in the meantime Rice's body had gone to the morgue. A delay of four hours in the arrival of the coroner's physician would have wiped out all evidence of the felonious cause of the capitalist's death.

An autopsy revealed the presence of chloroform in Rice's body, thus contradicting Dr. Curry's certificate of death, which gave old age and weak heart as the cause. And while I was in Rice's apartment Patrick's tools were running frantically from bank to bank to get possession of the murdered man's cash to defray the expenses of possible litigation over his estate!

Patrick was tried and convicted for the murder of Rice. He introduced a novel defense, contending that there was no legal evidence to prove that Rice's death had been caused feloniously and that the congestion of lungs described by the State's experts as having been caused by choloroform had, in fact, been caused by embalming fluid. He attacked Jones as the murderer if there had been a murder.

He was sentenced to death. Much sympathy was aroused for Patrick. While in the death house he won the only important legal battle in his career. He saved a fellow prisoner from the electric chair.

The convicted lawyer spent twelve years in jail. He was sentenced to die in 1902 and resentenced twice to die, and in 1906 the death penalty was commuted to life imprisonment by Governor Higgins. In 1909 he sought an appeal on unprecedented grounds. Having been sentenced three times to die, he contended, and not having been electrocuted, he raised the unique issue that he was legally dead and should be given his freedom. The courts refused to grant this plea. He was pardoned in 1912 by Governor Dix after his brother-in-law had spent half a million dollars in his behalf. Not long after he was given his freedom he publicly announced that he was going to sue for his share of the fortune of Rice! Friends dissuaded him from this step.

He disappeared into obscurity. At the time this was written he was believed to be alive somewhere in the far West.

Jones, who turned state's evidence, was released and also vanished, a hopeless derelict.

Patrick struck me as a peculiar type. He had two personalities—Patrick the lawyer and Patrick the man. He made no attempt at flight. Perhaps this is explained by the possibility that Patrick the man entrusted his conscience to Patrick the lawyer. The actual slaying was left to his vassal and proxy, Jones, who was even willing to die at Patrick's suggestion.

In New York City at least, the Patrick case ended the cycle of murders by poison. Over this cycle one thing looms. All the plotters were educated persons. This may explain why the cycle ended. Educated persons can be convinced that murder does not pay no matter how skilled the mind that builds the plot. The best of them, even a skilled lawyer, will overreach, overpaint and overdo the picture.

Speaking of patterns that form in a murder man's mind the reader may recall that in the murder of Mrs. Anna Kronman she herself had suggested the axe which her slayer used to kill her. Rice, when he spoke to Jones of chloroform, suggested also the means by which his end was encompassed.

CHAPTER X

MURDER WHILE YOU WAIT

ITALIANS who came to this country at the beginning of this century had a penchant for grouping into small colonies. They came in great numbers to New York City and settled in districts which became known as Little Italys. The colonization laid them open to attacks by various criminal organizations from the Old World who brought with them much experience in murder and blackmail.

In 1902 and 1903 members of these colonies were terrorized by a series of outrages and murders. Bodies were found in sacks, boxes, and barrels in various sections of the city. In a good many cases the victims' tongues were slit, thus advertising to the colonists that the work was that of imported, professional villains.

The eighteen-year-old stepson of Giuseppi Morello, counterfeiter and leader of a Sicilian gang, was kidnaped, tortured, and murdered. His tongue, too, had been slit. He had betrayed secrets of his stepfather's society. Morello senior was the known associate of notorious bad men—Ignacio, Lupo the Wolf and Tomasso, Petto the Ox. When the names of these men were mentioned in the presence of Little Italy residents they crossed themselves and frequently appealed to parish priests for protection.

During these years counterfeit United States bills and coins made abroad flooded the United States.

One of the shrewdest murders that ever engaged my attention was one of these Italian terroristic killings. It was shrewd because it showed the perpetrators' long experience with murder. They did one little thing that marked them as professionals.

In April, 1903, the United States Secret Service Division set operatives to watch suspected sources of counterfeit money in the Italian section of the lower East Side. Three of these operatives were Laurence Richey, now one of President Hoover's secretaries, Captain John J. Henry, and George L. Burns.

They took up their stations near a butcher shop at No. 16 Stanton Street, operated by one Sarconi. Frequent visitors to this place were Lupo the Wolf, Petto the Ox, a hulk of a bull-necked man a little past twenty-four, and Morello. The plan of the secret service was to watch these men and all others who came into the butcher shop to join them, and when all their connections were established to swoop down and corral the entire band.

They were especially eager to locate a man about thirty who was suspected of being the gang's traveling agent and who distributed the counterfeit bills to dealers throughout the United States. Our Detective Bureau at the same time was trying to run down the slayers of a number of Italians. We suspected several of Morello's gang, but no one could be found who would testify against the suspects. Those who might have proved good witnesses were terrorized.

On the night of April 12th a man answering the description of the traveling agent walked into Sarconi's butcher shop, remained a little while talking to the Wolf and the Ox, and then left. His name and identity being unknown to the secret service men they called him the Newcomer. On the next night he reappeared, saw the Wolf and the Ox again, and came out. One of the secret service operatives followed him to an Italian pastry shop in Elizabeth

Street which was run by Pietro Inzarillo. After a few minutes the Newcomer came out of the pastry shop, walked gingerly down the street, turned into Prince Street, and entered an Italian saloon in the rear of which Morello operated a small restaurant that was a blind for his counterfeiting operations.

The secret service operative waited until the lights went out in the place. The Newcomer did not come out. The operative discontinued his watch and went home.

The next morning Mrs. Frances Connors, an elderly woman, appeared upon the street in front of her home in the lower East Side. She was shrieking frantically. Two patrolmen rushed up to her. Incoherently she told them that she had just looked upon the body of a man jammed into a barrel standing in the shadow of a lumber pile in the east end of the Italian section. She took them to the barrel, and they reported the finding of the body.

Inspector McClusky assigned McCafferty, Detective Sergeant Joseph Petrosini, the Detective Bureau's expert on Italian matters, and myself to the case. In addition twelve other detectives, including Italian-American plainclothes men, were detailed to circulate in the Italian colonies to learn what they could.

The man's body had been jammed into the barrel, over the top of which had been thrown an overcoat. Around his throat, tightly wound, was a coarse burlap sack of foreign manufacture. The dead man was young and fairly well dressed. His left hand and right leg protruded from the barrel, making it obvious that his murderers had intended that the body should be discovered so that it might be a warning to others. The body was still warm. The head was almost severed by an ugly wound running from ear to ear. A razor-sharp knife had been used. A watch chain dangled from his vest; the watch was gone. Both ears had been pierced for earrings, the mark of a native of Sicily. In one of his pockets I found a crumpled note in the handwriting of a woman. Petrosini translated it:

> Come in a hurry. You understand that it is most urgent.

It was unsigned. This letter had probably lured the man to his death. He was killed indoors. The presence of the gunny sack around his neck indicated that it had been placed there to prevent blood from spattering or falling.

There was not a scrap upon the body to establish identification. It was taken to the morgue and a photograph of the man's face appeared in the newspapers next morning.

In the bottom of the barrel I found a thick layer of sawdust thrown in apparently to prevent blood from leaking out. This sawdust had been walked upon and in it were chawed ends of black Italian stogies and onion skins. This sawdust, I concluded, had come from some cheap Italian restaurant where floors usually are covered with it.

The barrel had contained sugar. There were particles of it caught between the staves. On the bottom of the barrel, outside, was a stenciled mark: W. & T.—233. On the Long Island side of the East River were a number of large sugar refineries. I visited these until I found a manufacturer who identified the barrel as his and explained that W. & T. were the initials of grocers, Wallace & Thompson, No. 365 Washington Street, Manhattan. The figures designated the shipping lot number.

Employees of Wallace & Thompson told me that they had received six barrels of sugar in the 233 lot, but could not tell where they had shipped these barrels. No record was kept of buyers of this lot.

"Have you got any Italian customers?" I asked.

"Only one," was the reply. "Pietro Inzarillo, who has a pastry shop in Elizabeth Street."

An examination of the victim's stomach revealed that immediately before death he had eaten a heavy meal of potatoes, beans, beets, spaghetti, and salad. Petrosini described it as a typical Sicilian meal. Morello's restaurant served only Sicilian food. Thus the dead man was placed in this restaurant a short time before he was killed. The barrel came from Inzarillo's. But it was useless to question frequenters of these places. They would just arch their shaggy eyebrows and say nothing.

On his way from Brooklyn Secret Service Operative Henry came upon the photograph of the dead man's face in a morning newspaper and visited the morgue. He viewed the body and felt quite sure it was the suspect known as the Newcomer. Operative Richey came in later and made a positive identification. The dead man was the Newcomer whom he had shadowed to Inzarillo's and then to Morello's on the night of April 13th and who never came out of the latter place.

But who and what was he?

Petrosini, fearless and therefore respected in Italian quarters, circulated among the slain man's countrymen and heard hints that if an unnamed convict in Sing Sing Prison was approached he might establish the identity of the slain man. I knew of a convict, Giuseppi de Priemo, who was serving a four-year term in Sing Sing for counterfeiting. He was reputed to have been one of Morello's gang.

When Petrosini approached de Priemo he found the convict as dumb as a wooden Indian. They chatted about this and that; then the detective produced a photograph of the dead man. De Priemo's huge body trembled. His lips set tight.

"Him dead?" said the convict. "He's my brother-in-law, Beneditto Madonia. Who kill him?" The prisoner fainted and was revived. Petrosini told of the killing. De Priemo said that a week back Madonia had visited him in prison and then went on to his home in Buffalo to meet Mrs. de Priemo and arrange to have the counterfeiter transferred to Erie County Jail, which would place De Priemo closer to his home. Madonia had promised to return to New York City and demand property which Morello and the Wolf had taken from De Priemo and refused to give to Mrs. Madonia.

Petrosini wanted to know more about this property and the inside details of Madonia's connection with Morello and his gang.

"I say nothing," said De Priemo, scowling. His heavy jaw snapped. "Never minda," he said. "Bimeby I go down to New York and see those fella. Bimeby I meeta him. Alla him."

He said no more.

Mrs. Madonia was found in Buffalo. She had last seen her husband on April 3rd when he left for Sing Sing to see De Priemo. A few days later she had a letter from him in New York City saying he surely would be back on the twentieth.

He never came.

The woman identified the body of her husband, also the watch chain found on his vest, and described the case of the watch, which had a locomotive stamped into it. Madonia, she said, was a stone mason, but had given up this work to "go on the road for Morello." Just what he did on the road no amount of persuasion could get Mrs. Madonia to say. Her stepson identified the body as that of his father and said the chain was his, but he was as silent as his stepmother about the dead man's activities. Fear had seized both of them.

It was useless to attempt to build up the picture further with these frightened sources to work with. The best we could hope for would be to forge a strong chain of circumstantial evidence around the murderers. Circumstantial evidence is often the best in this type of case, for it is not easily fabricated, whereas human testimony from fear-stricken persons is faulty and governed by motives and foreign traditions not always ascertainable or understood.

The barrel was a pretty good mute witness if it could be placed in any of the rendezvous frequented by Madonia and the gang. I visited Inzarillo's pastry shop. In the rear room I found an empty sugar barrel marked "W. & T.—233" which Inzarillo had received a few days prior to the slaying of Madonia. But there were no signs of foul play in the little shop, and it was concluded that the murder had not been committed here.

A visit was paid to Morello's little restaurant in the rear of the saloon. Here I scooped up several handfuls of sawdust from the floor. It contained onion skins and the chawed ends of black Italian stogies. The place was thoroughly examined for bloodstains, but not a speck was found. The sawdust was sifted for signs of blood but none was found. Then information seeped through to us from Petrosini's private sources, indicating that the murder had been committed here. One man had held Madonia's hands behind his back while the other cut his throat.

Moreover, we knew that Madonia had last been seen in this restaurant. The secret service man had seen him enter but not come out. He was murdered while the place was under watch. Old hands had done this murder. It was shrewdly planned and brazenly executed. Only professional murderers with long experience back of them would so skillfully and thoughtfully employ an absorbent gunny sack to prevent even a drop or speck of their victim's blood from falling on the floor or walls.

Inzarillo was mute when I questioned him about the sugar barrels. I arrested him. Petrosini had gathered information that on the day Madonia's body was found Petto the Ox had spent money recklessly in Inzarillo's and in a wine shop which Lupo the Wolf operated as a blind for counterfeiting operations. Morello had joined the Wolf on the spree, and as they went about from place to place, growing more hilarious, acquaintances congratulated them for some unexplained achievement. Also on this day Petto's dark-eyed sweetheart blossomed forth in expensive raiment.

At midnight of the day I arrested Inzarillo, Petrosini and Detective Foye closed in on Lupo's wine shop. The Ox was there. When Foye stepped up to handcuff the bull-necked man he coiled a hairy arm about the detective's neck and drew a long stiletto. He was about to plunge it into Foye's throat when Detective McCafferty arrived. Throwing himself on the Ox he knocked the stiletto from his hand and floored him, relieving him of a .45 caliber revolver and a second stiletto which was hidden in a secret pocket in his trousers.

That night the Tombs Prison held Lupo the Wolf, Petto the Ox, Morello, Pecoraro, Laduca, an employee of Sarconi the butcher, Inzarillo, and three other suspects. All were doubly armed with guns and razor-sharp stilettos made of files.

In the Ox's pocket we found a pawn ticket for a watch which had been pledged the day Madonia's body was found in a Bowery pawnshop. A clerk in this shop, which was not far from the Wolf's haunts, described the man who had pawned it as a stocky young man with a bull neck. But when we confronted him with the Ox the clerk could not positively identify him. The watch was Madonia's. It had a locomotive stamped on the case.

Petto claimed that the watch had been given to him by a stranger he met in an East Side boarding house on the night of April 14th, where he had slept that night. This story was proved false. Petto had not been near the boarding house.

The suspects were arraigned in the Magistrate's Court and held for further action. Eminent counsel appeared to defend them.

In the meantime, information had been gathered showing that the Ox and the Wolf were Morello's spies who went about Italian colonies selecting victims for Black Hand levies and reporting on members of Morello's gang whose disloyalty he suspected. Lupo's wine shop, it was learned, was the receiving station for cans of olive oil imported from Italy. These had false bottoms which carried the imported counterfeit money. In Lupo's, Inzarillo's, or Morello's back-room eating house the gang met, held their secret conclaves, and plotted their activities.

The motive for Madonia's killing was partly revealed by a letter he had written to Morello. While Madonia was in Pittsburgh, whither he had gone at Morello's direction, three of the latter's gang were arrested for passing counterfeit money. One of these men were Laduca, the butcher-shop employee. He was released. The others were sent to prison. Madonia wrote to plead with Morello that he had done everything in his power to save the other two and that he was through with that kind of business and was returning to his home in Buffalo. Morello feared that Madonia, out from under his domination, was a dangerous man to have about. It was after Laduca returned to New York that Madonia was killed.

Finally the prisoners were discharged by the police magistrate but were immediately rearrested by order of the coroner. McCafferty and I thought that Morello seemed to be weakening; that he might talk. It had not been unusual to find that gang leaders like him would talk, for the tradition prevails among this type of criminal organization that the king can do no wrong and Morello was a king; hence, if he talked it was his privilege which none dared dispute. We took Morello to the morgue. Madonia's body was brought out. I asked Morello if he knew the dead man. For a moment he swayed. Then his thick, flowing mustache twitched, and shaking his head ruefully he said softly:

"Poora feller. I never seena him before. I no know him."

This, of course, was a lie. The letter from Madonia proved their relationship. Morello's denial of this was a strong link on our chain. But the gang chieftain knew his own people, and his power, better than we did.

An inquest was begun May 1, 1903. Madonia's son was called as a witness to identify the watch found in the pawnshop as his father's property. The watch was handed to the lad. He looked at it and was about to speak when there was a shuffling of feet and hissing in the court room, which was filled with swarthy-faced men. One of these jumped up and put his fingers to his lips. Young Madonia was now not sure it was his father's timepiece.

Mrs. Madonia took the stand. The watch was handed to her for identification. There was the same shuffling of feet in the court room; the same dark-skinned man arose and crossed his lips with his fingers. Mrs. Madonia, positive the day before that the watch was her husband's, now suffered a lapse of memory. She couldn't tell. The one positive link in our chain connecting Petto the Ox with the murder, by legal proof weakened. The Madonias perhaps should not be blamed. There was the fate of young Morello to think of and a dozen more murders where talkative victims' tongues had been slit.

Inzarillo had shown signs of aiding the State. He was prepared, among other things, to admit the presence of the sugar barrels in the rear room of his shop. But when he appeared upon the witness stand he paled and became mute as the same sinister shuffling of feet occurred in the court room. Morello told conflicting stories upon the witness stand; and, to cap the climax, De Priemo, brought down from Sing Sing Prison to testify, laughed upon the stand and said that Petto was his very good friend and surely would not have killed his brother-in-law. Yet we knew he hated the bull-necked man.

Petto was indicted as the actual assassin, and the others were not held. Later the indictment against him was dismissed. Some time later Morello and the Wolf were arrested by secret service men for counterfeiting. At the trial of Morello an Italian physician testified that the day Morello was supposed to have been working in his spurious money plant he was in bed, ill. However, men who had been shadowing the gang leader testified that on the day he was supposed to be ill he was about the streets and in the plant.

Morello and the Wolf were convicted of counterfeiting and sent to Atlanta Federal Penitentiary for twenty-five and thirty years, respectively.

Inzarillo was convicted of altering his citizenship papers and sent to prison.

De Priemo suddenly became an exemplary prisoner in Sing Sing. His sentence was reduced and he was released from prison. He went quietly to New York City.

Shortly afterward Petto the Ox moved to Brownton, Pennsylvania. On the night of October 25, 1905, the bull-necked man stepped into the back-yard of his home and five shotgun blasts did to him what orderly justice had not been able to do.

Inzarillo, after coming out of prison, opened another little pastry shop, but hardly had time to get a fair start. He was shot and killed.

Laduca, the butcher, was slain in Connecticut.

Three other members of the gang met the same fate.

A most tragic sequel robbed the New York Police Department of one of its bravest men. In 1908 Petrosini, then a lieutenant, was sent to Palermo on a secret mission to gather the prison records of many notorious Sicilian criminals in the United States. The federal government had agreed to deport them when proof of their criminal pasts were available. Petrosini was to return with the records. He was walking through a park in Palermo on his way to his hotel when an assassin shot and killed him.

Not long afterward Congress, stirred by this tragedy, sent a commission to Europe to investigate immigration matters. In Palermo a member of the commission was surprised to learn that Sicily was practically crimeless.

"How is it that you have so little crime here?" he asked a Palermo police official.

"My dear sir," he replied. "Our criminals have gone to America."

Black Hand terrorism suffered a setback with the disposition of Morello and his gang. My impression is that the processes of Americanization and tighter immigration laws were largely responsible. The old Italian gangs were lawless killers. We have successors to them to-day who are even more lawless and ruthless, and they are made up largely of native born. And a good many of them wriggle through the machinery of the law, but as a rule they reach about the same end that befell the Ox and some of his confederates.

CHAPTER XI

THE MURDER CLINIC GETS A START

MY EXPERIENCE with murder gradually forced the conviction upon me that it was a subject which required the attention of detectives who not only were interested in this special field of investigation but who were equipped for the job by special training and a natural bent. It was vastly different from running down professional thieves and solving other crimes where the victims were alive and from whom the crime picture could be built up. In murder victims were dead; and, moreover, courts and jurors required far stronger evidence where a man's life was at stake.

This situation was brought home to me on many occasions. In particular I recall a case which clearly indicated the need for homicide specialists. It was a cyanide of potassium mystery.

A man of middle age was found dead in a chair in a room on the Bowery. His trouser pockets and the pockets of clothing hanging in the room were pulled out stiff, as though they had been rifled. A patrolman had been to the room ahead of me, and later two detectives took up the case. They reported to McClusky that it looked like murder, yet no wounds or evidences of a struggle were found.

A quick glance at the pockets made me skeptical of robbery. They were pulled out too far to have been the work of a professional thief. I moved the body and detected the familiar odor like that of bitter almond. On a mantelpiece, about ten feet from the body, was a bottle. It was empty but had contained cyanide of potassium.

From my knowledge of this deadly, quick-killing poison I knew that if the man had drunk it from the bottle at the mantelpiece it would have been impossible for him to reach the chair ten feet away, or, had he drunk it while sitting in the chair he would have been unable to reach the mantelpiece, place the bottle there, then go back to the chair. The victim of this poison drops in his tracks.

It looked like a real mystery.

Every place in the vicinity where cyanide of potassium was available was visited, but the man had not purchased any. Then I found there was a photographer in the building. Cyanide of potassium is used in photographic dark rooms. I called on the photographer and put this question to him:

"Why did you give that man upstairs that poison?"

"He said he wanted to kill some rats," the photographer stammered.

Perhaps I should explain that the abrupt directness with which I put this question was more or less habit, or instinct, with me, for persons dislike being drawn into police investigations, and unless directly and boldly approached will evade questions, especially when a suspicious death is involved.

The photographer's answer convinced me that it was a case of suicide, yet how did the bottle get on the mantelpiece?

A short time later I found the patrolman who had been the first on the scene. I told him that I had been unable to figure out how the bottle got on the mantelpiece while the dead man had passed out in a chair ten feet away.

"Oh," said the patrolman, "I found the bottle on the floor at the side of the chair. It smelled rotten and I dumped out the stuff that was in it and put it on the mantelpiece."

This man was not murder trained. His error was not deliberate, but he was unaware that the first step in a homicide inquiry is to leave things as they are. The first picture that a murder man gets of the scene is often the best. Had the bottle not been touched the suicide would have been obvious. The pulling out of the pockets was merely an effort on the man's part to remove the stigma of self-destruction. Scores of suicides resort to the same device.

I had often commented to my superiors and associates on the need for trained murder investigators. Some thought it would be a good thing; others were indifferent. The idea in the back of my head was a special bureau within the Detective Bureau which would train men for murder inquiry and, at the same time, function like a research clinic in a hospital or medical college. I believed that men could be found in the ranks who could be trained. That was the way I had come up.

In 1906 General Theodore A. Bingham, a man of military training, became Commissioner of Police. In looking about for likely timber for deputy commissionerships his attention was called to a young man who had been doing efficient work for the Citizens' Police Committee, an unofficial body which kept its eye upon police administration. Previous to this work he had been a newspaper reporter in New York City and had caught a pretty fair glimpse of the picture of crime and police affairs. Before taking up newspaper work he had been an instructor in English at a well-known private school for boys. He was a Harvard graduate. His name is Arthur Woods.

Bingham offered a deputy commissionership to Woods, but before he would accept he felt he would like to add to his qualifications by making a study of police systems in Europe. He was sent abroad to do this. Just before he left the legislature created a fourth deputy commissionership, and the occupant of this portfolio was to be given command of the Detective Bureau. At this time I was a detective sergeant working on general investigations and handling most of the homicides. By act of legislature detective sergeants were raised to the rank of lieutenants, and I automatically was elevated to this position. My old partner McCafferty was made inspector in command of the Detective Bureau. Some time later I was promoted to a captaincy.

Woods returned from his European trip late in 1906 and accepted the fourth deputy commissionership. The idea of a Harvard graduate and former English instructor in a fashionable private school coming in from the outside to run the Detective Bureau was received with various reactions by members of the force. Woods soon convinced the men by his democratic manner and his practical knowledge of police methods that he was fitted for the job. He put on a workingman's shirt and went out on jobs; lay all night on important plants with the men. One of his first public statements was that the door of his office would be open at all times to the men and that merit, and merit alone, would determine a detective's fitness for promotion.

In Europe he had studied the work and organization of the Metropolitan Police of London and its famous detective arm, the Department of Criminal Investigation in Scotland Yard. He liked the Yard system under which trained detectives were assigned to special investigations in any part of the British realm upon request from the local police authorities. He thought well also of the Paris detective system which employed detective specialists in squads that were assigned to crimes by classes. The Highway Squad or Brigade of the Paris police took care of all offenses committed on the highways.

He suggested that a special squad might be built up in our bureau to handle all homicides and another squad organized to hunt pickpockets. I told him I thought that would be the only way to cope with the homicide situation which had grown to some proportions in New York City owing to the prevalence of organized gangs. We agreed that criminals and criminal activities had undergone vast changes in a decade; that old methods of fighting them were sufficient unto their time, but New York City now had a greater and faster-increasing population and was spreading itself over a wider territory. Moreover, the newer criminals were younger, more wanton, and were killing either for pay or as a preliminary to robbery. What Woods hoped for was a completely reorganized system of crime control to cope with the changing conditions.

His picture of an efficient policeman was a man who, in addition to other duties, reported dirty back yards, over-congested districts, rendezvous for habitual criminals, saloons which fattened on the trade of habitual drunkards and dissolute persons, receivers of stolen goods, gambling resorts, and other conditions conducive to crime and the making of criminals. He saw the uniformed force as a crime preventive arm. Yet he did not want policemen to be arrogant toward the citizenry. He wanted them to concentrate their attention upon known criminals and conditions which bred them and not harass law-abiding citizens.

In this connection Raymond B. Fosdick, a noted expert on European police systems, told a story while addressing executives of our department at Woods's invitation. He had been present at a suffragette outbreak in London when mobs of women stormed the House of Parliament.

A bobby halted one of the suffragettes at the door, and

she promptly knocked off his helmet with a bottle. He picked it up and said:

"My dear madam, if you do that again I shall be compelled to take you into custody."

Whether that amount of reserve would work with New York policemen thrown suddenly into the thick of a gang feud was a topic laid upon the table for future discussion. It was generally agreed, however, that the situations in London and New York City were vastly different, for in the former city the police had to contend mainly with members of their own race, while the influx of aliens to New York City gave the police a problem not encountered in European cities. And especially was this true of homicides where racial characteristics govern the motives and methods of murderers.

Finally Woods announced that a special body of detectives to be known as the Homicide Squad would be organized and placed under my command. I believe this was the first organization of its kind in the world. It was to function not only as a special unit to detect and apprehend slayers but to train men in all branches of murder inquiry. In the meantime, detectives were to be assigned to special branches in each precinct to work on crime independently of the uniformed force but with their coöperation. The idea back of this was to place a mobile force of trained investigators at strategic points where no time would be lost in getting to the scene of murder and taking up the hunt. I was assigned to open and command two branches and at the same time instruct men assigned to me in the handling of murder investigations. Other men in these branches were detailed to handle other classes of crime, pocket picking, house breaking, safe and loft robberies, and gangster activities.

In July, 1908, I was called back to headquarters by Woods to take command of Squad Number One, which designated the Homicide Squad. Men were picked for this who had especially good records as patrolmen and some experience as plain-clothes men or detectives. Lieutenant William Jones, the Department's firearms expert, was assigned to instruct the men in the models and calibers of revolvers and pistols, ammunition, powder burns, scorches, smudges, and the effect of fire from different distances and angles. It was my idea that first of all a field man should possess sufficient information about the weapons most used in murder together with a knowledge of wounds, for very often the picture is built up with only these two factors available.

The first class of students in this pioneer murder clinic was assembled on the rifle range in a National Guard armory. The shaved heads of hogs were used to demonstrate the effect of gunfire. Dr. Arthur T. Gorham, a police surgeon of many years' experience with wounds, and myself measured the wounds for the benefit of the class and instructed the members in their classification, indicating to them what could be determined by minute examination of the point of entry and exit of a bullet.

Most important, from my point of view, was the process of training the men to "get the picture" as I had been trained to get it, and to understand how each homicide case, when completed, would form a pattern from which might be worked subsequent inquiries, using the pattern as a mold into which available facts might be poured, mentally, of course, to form the complete picture.

We were making progress, with now and then a murder to furnish an exemplar for discussion in the clinic. We were pioneering in a new field. The men we had selected liked their new assignments, and all had taken up murder inquiry as a lifetime career.

Then the old cry. Shake-up! The public reading about shake-ups may relish the excitement they cause, but men who have settled down to a serious study of murder in the hope that their work will be of benefit to human society see no thrill in a shake-up. Bingham left the Department in 1909. His deputies, including Woods, resigned. A new commissioner came in. I drew a transfer. No reasons for it were supplied to me, nor could I figure them out except to surmise that a new man with his own ideas was now in charge. I found myself again on uniformed duty in command of a precinct in Brooklyn. The usual thing happened to the Detective Bureau. It was completely reorganized. The branch detective system was abolished.

I spent four years in the uniform meditating upon the vicissitudes of life in a police department, the largest in the country, where a man would just get settled down to building an effective machine to control homicides (when they were increasing) and then be transferred to a totally different job.

It may have been well that I put in four years on precinct duty at this time, for it placed me in contact again with life as it moves along. I witnessed changing conditions and their influence upon the lives, hopes, ambitions, habits, and activities of rising generations, all of which come to bear upon new causes of crime, new ways of committing crime, and new factors that rule human motives.

Interesting things happened in the precinct, some of which may show the reader how a policeman may be an effective single unit in the control of crime.

Making my regular tours of the precinct I came upon a saloon conducted by a woman of ill repute. Upon watching the place I saw that many known thieves congregated there. It was a breeding place for criminals. My job was to curb crime.

One afternoon I walked into the place and found it filled with professional criminals whose records I knew.

"Madam," I addressed the woman, "what kind of a place is this?"

"Very respectable." She smiled.

"Respectable nothing," I exclaimed. "It is a rendezvous

for nothing but thieves." My voice rose. The hangers-on began to move.

"But, Captain, what can I do? They will——"

"Then you *do* want to get rid of them, do you?"

No reply was necessary from the woman. Quietly the place had emptied. Within a few weeks the saloon changed hands.

Shortly thereafter I was advised that a notorious man had taken over the place, and that when someone had spoken to him about me being in the precinct he had said:

"Oh! Arthur Carey in charge here? Why, I know Carey."

The inference to be drawn from this statement was that he was my dear friend. Well, we did know each other, in a professional way. Naturally I went to see him. I found him to be Al Jacobs, a notorious pickpocket. At the bar when I entered stood Chris Mulrooney, who also had crossed my path before. I asked Jacobs who owned the saloon now. He said his wife did.

"But," said Jacobs, "we're running a high-class, respectable place here now."

"So I see," I remarked, eying Mulrooney. "But listen, Jacobs, if you let thieves hang out here I'll come and kick in the place." I observed that Mulrooney had gone. He had vanished in a flash.

"I can't do nothing about these fellers coming in here," Jacobs whined.

"You do something about it or I will," I said, and left the place.

In a way Jacobs was right. He was a marked man and a magnet for thieves. Thieves would follow him wherever he went because he was one himself. In spite of my warning they would come into his place. So he adopted a tricky system of crime control all his own. The saloon was in a busy section. Hundreds of thirsty men to and from work stopped in. Sometimes they were robbed while drinking.

When this happened Jacobs, mindful of my warning, dispatched Mulrooney to find the thieves who had pulled the jobs in his saloon and force them to return their loot. Mulrooney carried the booty to Jacobs, who gave it back to the rightful owners. In this way he hoped to forestall receipt by me of complaints victims might have made.

Jacobs's system worked for a short time. Then a young thief named Dinny Meehan objected to Mulrooney's activities and complained that the latter held out on some of the stuff given to him. One morning Meehan appeared at the saloon and called Mulrooney out to the sidewalk. Pickens Laydon, one of the shrewdest little crooks I ever met, was with Meehan. Just as Mulrooney poked his head out the side door of the saloon a bullet hit him between the eyes and he fell dead.

This ended Jacobs's saloon. Its doors and windows were boarded. Some years later Meehan was killed in about the same way he had dealt death to Mulrooney. Thieves are strong for self-determination and also strong for self-extermination.

We had less crime in the precinct after Jacobs closed shop. There was no place else for thieves to congregate and be welcome.

Within a short time I was transferred to another and quieter precinct. Why? I never asked and never learned. I was here for only a month or so when business men in my former precinct, without my knowledge, appealed to the commissioner to have me sent back. They complained that crime was on the increase. They said I had stopped crime. But I never was sent back. Nor did it cause me any great concern. The station house which had been my headquarters in the former precinct was old and depressing. The one I now commanded was new and spotless. Sunlight streamed in through the windows. The air was fresh and invigorating. My men were on their toes, as always they have been with me. I was quite contented.

But I was not engaged in my favorite pursuit—murder inquiry.

An uprising of criminal elements in New York City in 1913 brought on a reform wave. Organized gangs had increased both in numbers and defiance. Gamblers began fighting among themselves—they never fail to do this. A scandal involving a high police official with gamblers had broken out. John Purroy Mitchel was elected on a Fusion reform ticket whose platform was largely a demand for a clean-up of criminals. Mitchel took office as mayor in January, 1914. Arthur Woods became his secretary. Mitchel appointed him Police Commissioner on April 3, 1914, while I was still in command of a precinct. Mitchel gave Woods *carte blanche* to run the department in his own way.

Woods sent for me, and presently I was again in command of the Homicide Squad and we started afresh. Woods reduced seventeen inspection districts of the Detective Bureau to nine branch offices, going back to the branch detective system which his predecessor had abandoned. More than six hundred detectives in the inspection districts were distributed among the branches. He brought experienced detectives back from precincts where they had been scattered by the previous administration's shake-up. He restored the line-up, which had been abolished, and in July, 1914, established a school for detectives serving in all branches of the Detective Bureau which was now called a division.

There was talk about putting the men attending this school through a course in applied psychology. I argued against it, insisting that the psychology most needed by detectives was not to be taught out of books or by lectures; that they developed a psychology of their own from their experience, and any attempt to impress a stated psychology upon their minds would only confuse them. Training them to get the right picture at the scene of murder, developing the faculty of quick and accurate observation, and building up an unusually good memory were, and still are, the foundations for a workable detective psychology. This formula had worked in my case. Years of experience have confirmed its efficacy. Let me have a man who has been a good policeman on post, who is gifted with natural common sense, initiative, honesty, bravery, and a never-failing memory; let me put him to work with an older detective who has made good; add to this a course of training in the examination of wounds, weapons, and other murder clues, and he will develop his own psychology and put it to effective use. He may not be able to pick clues out of thin air, but the clues he does find he'll know what to do with.

In my own way, using experience as the guide, I gave the men assigned to the Homicide Squad my ideas on murder inquiry. It's pretty hard now to detail what I told them. It was even difficult then to tap my mental resources and transfer to their minds what was in my own. The reader will glimpse the knowledge I imparted to them as he goes from chapter to chapter of these memoirs. I did emphasize what I consider the most vital requirement in modern murder investigation. There are two phases to it: first, establishing that murder has been done; and, secondly, hunting the murderer. These two phases must be joined, that is to say, the work of establishing the crime in a legal manner and tracking the slayer must go on concurrently. It is not always possible to do this, nor have I always found the murderer in every case where murder has been established, but it has afforded me a modest measure of satisfaction to find that experts outside of the Police Department who are in a position to know assert on the basis of nation-wide statistics that New York City for some years has had next to the lowest homicide record in the large American cities.

It is a temptation to young detectives to concentrate

their efforts at first upon the fascinating enterprise of unraveling the mystery without working at the same time to find the slayer. Criminals are deterred not by reading how clever murderers are but by the specter of a trained machine that finds them, fastens crime upon them, and turns them over to the prosecuting and punitive agencies of organized society. This is the substance of murder control.

Nor are young detectives the only ones subject to this temptation. I recall having listened attentively to an address delivered to a group of detectives by an eminent police official from Continental Europe, widely known for his scientific and psychological methods of detection. He told of a burned paper match that had been found in a room where murder had been committed; of the finding later of a packet of paper matches at a point remote from the crime. The burned match fitted precisely into a stub in the packet. Weeks were consumed in establishing this fact. The lecture had all the interesting high-lights of a good mystery fiction story.

My opinion was that it was not good stuff to lay before practical detectives as an exemplar because the criminal apparently had not been apprehended as a result of the discovery. After the lecture I met the speaker in the hallway.

"By the way, Doctor," I asked, "did you find the murderer? I mean through the burned match and the packet?"

"I believe I heard some time later that the murderer was reported to have been picked up some place or another for some other crime."

"Through the medium of the match?"

"No, unfortunately, no," the doctor smiled sadly.

I quote this bit of dialogue not to show that I was sharp or captious but because it goes to the very heart of efficient, practical murder inquiry. It shows the futility of spending weeks, perhaps months, developing a clue which lacked directness, while during the period spent on such fascinating research the slayer had ample opportunity to put time and distance between himself and his pursuers. It is quite all right for the fiction mystery writer to indulge the fancy of his readers in a long-drawn-out analysis of this or that clue, but not many murderers would be caught by the practical detectives of real life if they followed the same practice. It's good amusement for readers, but then they are not required to build up evidence for hard-headed and sometimes inscrutable American juries.

The personnel of the Homicide Squad represented a cross section of the Police Department whose qualifications were, first, that they had been good policemen on post. One outstanding man had studied dentistry before joining the force; another had been a silversmith, while others had been plumbers, chauffeurs, locomotive firemen, and one had been a horseshoer. A former bank clerk, whose father was a police surgeon, proved to have a mind with an amazing aptitude for the finest and most intricate detail while also possessing a certain amount of inherited medical skill. They were all quick-witted, painstaking men. The only detective science they picked up was what came to them on post or in the clinic.

Before our original plan could be carried out to the fullest extent certain practices in homicide matters had to be adjusted. Under an old rule the borough coroner was the only official who could first touch the remains of a homicide victim. This put us at a disadvantage in getting the picture and made it impossible to photograph the body in various positions. The rule finally was changed so that men from the Squad were empowered to search the body and scene before the arrival of the coroner or his physician. Later the office of coroner was abolished, and in its place came the modern auxiliary of crime detection—the Medical Examiner.

This brought to our aid Dr. Charles G. Norris, chief medical examiner, and his staff. Dr. Norris is an eminent pathologist who has spent a lifetime in the study of homicide. He had taken a post-graduate course at the University of Vienna and had the advantage of courses established by Kraft-Ebing, noted authority on medical and nervous diseases. On Dr. Norris's staff were pathologists, chemists, bacteriologists, and toxicologists to work hand in hand with our squad. Thus we had available experts capable of giving us analyses of poisons, human hair, dusts, and other articles, and making examinations of stains and important clues where the scientist could penetrate and we could not.

With these resources at our command we needed little of a scientific nature in the clinic. Our men were provided with kits consisting of measuring instruments, wood- and glass-cutting tools, electric flash lights, and magnifying glasses. They didn't carry them around in little black bags with an air of mystery. This type of detective exists only between the covers of an exciting mystery yarn or upon the musical-comedy stage.

The clinic's technical equipment consisted of a large portable searchlight, rubber gloves with which to handle wounds and bodies, a jimmy, saw, metal tape measure, magnifying glasses, and test tubes in which to seal specimens of importance to our investigations. Cameras, fingerprinting apparatus, microscopes, and scales were not necessary. The Bureau of Criminal Identification in headquarters had cameras and fingerprint experts; microscopes and scales were available at the Medical Examiner's office to be used by experts. Here there were microscopes and photo-microscopic devices, and scales of all descriptions so fine in adjustment that they could weigh and find the difference between two human hairs or determine the ingredients and history of specks of dust. In addition the city contained a number of universities and medical colleges where expert counsel also was available if needed.

The Clinic's library was made up largely of my own books which I had studied for years—Phelps on Wounds, Brundage on Toxicology, Tanner's Memorandum on Poisons, and volumes of medical jurisprudence, homicide laws, firearms, explosives, metallurgy, and a large dictionary.

A more comprehensive library was unnecessary, for we had at our call an unofficial consulting faculty. The staffs of three universities, experts on almost every subject under the sun; noted men in great hospitals and research foundations were available when we needed them. And within the confines of this mammoth city of six million persons were experts in every line of endeavor, from the makers of pins to the builders of skyscrapers, whose advice could be sought—and was always generously given—on any special technical problem that presented itself during our investigations. And why should this talent go unused? Perhaps no city in the world offers such a galaxy of experts. How they were employed from time to time is explained in various chapters. An incident which brought to my mind the idea of falling back upon these unofficial experts might not be amiss here.

In the course of my investigation into the killing of Elsie Sigel, granddaughter of General Franz Sigel, famous Civil War hero, I had occasion to turn to an unusual expert. In a trunk in the apartment of Leon Ling, a Chinese, who slayed Elsie, I found a batch of letters in Chinese. It was necessary to have them translated by someone who knew the language and who also could be trusted to give me an accurate translation. Columbia University officials referred me to a young Chinese who was editing a publication in his native tongue and who was taking a post-graduate course in the university. I found him to be an affable and highly intelligent Chinese. While I stood by he translated the letters aloud and from their contents much was learned about Ling, who fled after the murder and has never been found.

Later the young man who served me as translator became secretary to the first president of the Chinese Republic. The last time I heard of him he was Chinese minister at Washington, D. C. One could never tell who might serve on the consulting faculty of the clinic. Hundreds of New Yorkers have, some quite unconscious of the fact that they were advisers to murder men. Others who were aware of our objects were more than pleased to get an opportunity to view a murder inquiry from the inside. I never found what is commonly known as a lay crime analyst. There may be such experts. I never had need for one.

The office in which the Clinic held forth at headquarters was a square room with the usual quota of chairs and desks to be found in a public office. Partitioned off was my private office. It was about twenty-nine feet long and narrow and contained a desk and two chairs. Its walls were bare, but there was a large window at one end overlooking a busy street below. It contained none of the pictures that Inspector Byrnes had in his private office and museum. Nor was there mystery or uncanniness about the place.

It was just a refuge where I could step in and have a quiet talk with a suspect without distracting interruptions. I usually sat at the desk, the suspect occupying the chair at the side. There was one picture he might see. This was outside the big window and he could look upon it at will. It might be raining or shining, a bright day or a gloomy one. But whatever kind of a day it might be the picture was tempting. It was freedom. It served its purpose. I had long since concluded that murderers when caught and subjected to examination look back not at their crimes but think only of getting out, getting free, returning to that outside seen through the window. Few honest, law-abiding citizens ever had occasion to visit this room, but a good many murderers talked their way to doom while sitting at the desk looking out the window or scowling at me. Finally when the break came they cast their eyes at the floor and told their story.

Later I improved upon the method of examining suspects by inviting them to accompany me in a police automobile to the scene or scenes of their crimes. More than once on such trips I have had suspects point out the most damaging circumstances against themselves, and in many cases they uncovered crimes they had committed which we had not associated with them. Funny that a little motor trip should lead men and women to purge themselves of all their crimes, including some we had not known about.

In this office, however, I had my headquarters for many years, working exclusively upon homicides. For nearly twenty years I worked with only seventeen days of vacation, but it was my own fault. I could have taken a rest but there was an unfortunate feature to a job like mine. It couldn't be left while a case was on. And in a city of six million persons there is almost a fresh case daily, and sometimes as many as a hundred, old ones and new ones, flaring up or hanging fire. If a man stepped out for a few days' rest his train of thought was broken. A thread slipped from his fingers. The picture might be spoiled. I imagine a painter of pictures has a job like that. He gets busy on his canvas, makes a fine start, and then is afraid to take time out, fearing that the touch he's been cudgeling his brain to find might take wings and fly.

The great difference, however, between an artist of that sort and a murder man is that the artist can throw away an unfinished canvas, whereas murder never outlaws. The murder man has to keep the unfinished pictures in the back of his head. I've had tips come in on murder cases that were thirty, forty, and fifty years old.

CHAPTER XII

THE WAY GANGS GO

FROM the previous administration Commissioner Woods inherited a number of unsolved gang murders. Between 1911 and 1914 powerful groups of thieves, gamblers, and gunmen were organized in various sections of the city. They were brazen and reckless. On the day Woods was installed four of the most notorious professional gunmen, Dago Frank, Lefty Louie, Gyp the Blood, and Whitey Lewis, were doomed to the electric chair by the refusal of Governor Glynn to grant them a respite.

In spite of this gang brazenness continued. A placard hung upon a lamp-post in what was known as the Car Barn District, which lay along the East River from Ninety-sixth Street north, indicated the defiance with which the gangs operated. It read:

NOTICE

COPS KEEP OUT

No policemen will hereafter be allowed
in this block.

By order of

THE CAR BARN GANG

Policemen sent out to break up this gang were beaten and slugged. Two leaders were finally arrested and convicted of murder and the Car Barn Gang ceased to exist. There were other gangs which had not been broken up, and perhaps ten murders known to have been committed by these gangs, but which could not legally be traced to their doors. Woods was determined to end gang rule. One of his first moves was to show them that the old murders were not forgotten. He directed me to begin an investigation into the slaying of a well-known and respected citizen, Frederick Strauss, a court clerk, who had been shot and killed in St. Mark's Place while on his way to attend a lodge meeting. A bullet fired during a gang war had slain him. In many of the other unsolved gang killings the victims had been gangsters killed by their own kind.

The Strauss slaying occurred in January, 1913. Several arrests had been made, but the suspects were released in Magistrate's Court. Nothing more had been done with the case.

Upon reopening it I learned that two rival gangs had engaged in a long-drawn-out contest for East Side supremacy. The feud had started on November 13, 1912, when a notorious pickpocket and gang leader, Dopey Benny Fein, had sent his aide-de-camp, Jew Murphy, to look into labor troubles among East Side clothing manufacturers and striking workers. A number of employees had refused to strike at command of their leaders. Fein was hired to persuade these recalcitrant workers to obey orders. Murphy looked over the situation and reported that the bosses, as the manufacturers were known, had hired protectors to fight off gangs. These protectors were Tommy Dyke, an East Side character, and Harry Lenny an ex-prize fighter who furnished guards to protect the bosses against the raids of "entertainment committees" that not only molested workers who took the places of strikers but smashed up the workshops.

Dopey Benny had many followers. Among those who admired him was Jack the Dropper, a younger man, who specialized in protecting East Side gambling places against holdup men and blackmailers. Also in the picture was a thug known as Little Orgie, whose real name was Jacob Orgen. Fein sent Jew Murphy out to warn Dyke and Lenny that unless they withdrew their protection from the bosses war would follow. One of the Dyke and Lenny men punched Jew Murphy whose right name was Joe Miller, in the face. This amounted to lese majesty. Fein took it as a personal insult. A month passed. The six-day bicycle races, an annual sporting event, began in old Madison Square Garden. Fein scattered his gunmen among the crowds attending this affair, and when they were emerging from the Garden shooting began. A formidable Dyke and Lenny man called Tony Cheese was wounded. This picturesque sobriquet he gained through marriage. His wife's father was a cheese dealer on the East Side.

Later that same night Dyke and Lenny men sought reprisals. They shot Little Augie del Grasso, a Fein henchman, while he was zigzagging from shadow to shadow under the elevated railroad structure along the Bowery. Del Grasso was not killed.

Fein brought his forces together and directed that the next attack be made against Dyke and Lenny themselves. These two men, both Italians, had a large following on the East Side. It was customary for them to bring their friends together once each year at a ball and reception given in Arlington Hall under the auspices of the Dyke and Lenny Association. Invitations had been sent out for this affair; all the big and little bad men of gangland were bidden, among them dance-hall habitués who knew Dyke when he was bouncer, or sheriff, for Chick Tricker's notorious Bowery dive.

The night of the ball arrived. Togged out in rented dress suits Dyke and Lenny started up St. Mark's Place for Arlington Hall, which is in the center of the most thickly populated section of New York's ghetto. Following them a pace behind was a chubby-faced youngster carrying a box of lurid silk badges which were to be distributed to the honored guests and members of the floor committee. The entrance of Dyke and Lenny into the hall was to be the signal for the commencement of festivities. The band stood ready to begin with "East Side, West Side."

As the trio approached the stairway leading up into the hall pistols cracked suddenly and blazed from a dozen hallways across the street. The badges went into the air like a fountain of many colors. The young man carrying them took to his heels. Dyke and Lenny went up the stairs four at a time. The shooting continued for several minutes.

When it ceased Strauss was found upon the sidewalk just outside the hall. He was dead.

The Dyke and Lenny ball was postponed. Its guests scrambled out of the hall through rear windows.

The case was cold when I got it. It puzzled me how Dopey Benny's gunmen had gotten their pistols. It was not likely that they would walk the streets with them in their pockets, for they were being hunted at the time. A new figure in gangland had entered the picture—the "independent" gun carrier. For two years I sought to find who had carried the guns of the Fein crowd. I finally learned that Annie Britt, a chunky blonde, had toted seven guns into St. Mark's Place in a handbag "just to do the boys a favor." As each man found a point of vantage in a hallway she stepped up and handed him a gun. She waited until Dyke and Lenny appeared, then, gayly swinging her empty handbag, vanished. The shooting began.

With this information as a wedge I split open the story and named as the gang that had killed Strauss the following crew of Dopey Benny cohorts: Irving Wexler, alias Waxey Gordon; Little Orgie, who had a special grudge against Dyke and Lenny; Jew Murphy, who never forgot the punch in the face; Shorty Gordon and Abie Beckerman, a holdup man. Miss Britt, too, was indicted.

A father and son who were passing just before the shooting began described a man they had seen looking on from the corner and who appeared to know what was about to happen. From descriptions given by them I picked up Joe the Greaser, who admitted that he had stood by while preparations for the battle were being made. The generalissimo, Joe said, was Shorty Gordon, who placed the gunmen in the hallways. Gordon confessed to me in the privacy of my inner office, revealing the entire conspiracy but reluctantly admitting that a woman had been employed as gun carrier. He told me where the guns had been thrown after the battle and we found them. He was not aware that Strauss, an innocent passer-by, had been killed until he read about it in the newspapers.

Gordon and Murphy were tried but acquitted. The testimony we were forced to rely upon came mostly from gangsters and was involved in many conflicts. Other members of the gang were not tried. A legal issue was raised when the gang's lawyers contended that their clients did not have a felony in mind when Strauss was shot. Beckerman was later killed.

Dopey Benny ceased to be a figure in New York City gang affairs. His mob broke up.

Woods continued a relentless war against gangs. More than a hundred of the most notorious gangsters were arrested, and most of them sent away for long terms. There was a cessation of gang homicides in the sections of the city that had been under gang rule. When Woods took office the number of murders for the year previous had been 244. In 1916 he had reduced the year's slayings to 186. During the first quarter of 1915 arrests in the city numbered 48,013, with 10,636 men on the force. This was a twenty per cent. increase over the number of arrests for the same quarter in the preceding year. There was also a twenty-five per cent. increase in the number of convictions. These figures form a quick index to what can be done by a commissioner who means business as Woods did, and who did his best to run the Department for the public's interest and not the politicians'.

There was little gang activity during his administration. Dopey Benny, Jew Murphy, Joe the Greaser, Punk Madden, Jack Sirroco, Owney Madden, Little Doffie, Skush Thomas, and dozens of other notorious gang leaders found police resistance too stiff and dispersed their gangs. Nor was any more heard of the Car Barn, Slaughter House, and Pansy gangs, the Hudson Dusters and Pearl Buttons who had given rise to a reign of terror before Woods came in. Not all of their leaders were jailed. A good many of them disappeared the way such crooked potentates usually go—killed by usurpers or slain in inter-gang battles.

I have already observed how this lawless policy of self-determination leads to self-extermination even among cutthroat gangs of the imported variety whose organizations had centuries of experience back of them. Let me trace briefly how these two factors work out with the newer type of gang.

Benjamin Levinsky had a long criminal record. He had associated with thieves as a boy, trained under older gang leaders, and became ambitious to head a gang of his own. He gathered together a group of thieves and gunmen and hired out their services in strike work. He set up opposition to one William Lipshitz, alias Levine, a nineteen-year-old gang leader who saw his lucrative business going into Levinsky's hand. Lipshitz, too, had a criminal record and was a lob (handy man) for Jack the Dropper who worked for the bosses in many strikes that occurred in the East Side needle trades. Levinsky was a follower of Little Orgie, who hated the Dropper because the latter had once slashed him across the cheek. Little Orgie had a monopoly on work for the strikers.

On December 5, 1922, Levinsky stepped out of a taxicab in front of No. 715 Broadway, and as he entered the place he was shot and killed by Lipshitz. The latter had been sent by Jack the Dropper to take Levinsky out of the field and kill two birds with one stone, remove an enemy and weaken the forces working for the strikers. Lipshitz pleaded guilty to murder in the second degree and was sentenced to life imprisonment. We were certain he had killed others but could not legally fasten the crimes upon him.

Various attempts had been made to convict the Dropper of crimes. In his time he had done four "bits" in prison and knew the tricks by which prisons could be avoided. He became a great hero among gangsters. He was a treacherous operator. He shifted from one side to another, and his gunmen had a hard time telling which cause they were supposed to espouse. Whoever offered the most money got the Dropper's services.

Finally on August 27, 1924, the Dropper was arrested in a Broadway office. An arsenal of side arms was found in the place. It was the concentration point for the Dropper's killers. When a job was to be done they met in this office: the guns were passed out with directions for the attack.

Detectives took the Dropper into the Essex Market Magistrate's Court for arraignment on the gun-carrying charge. He was discharged on the morning of August 28th. Anticipating gun-play among gangsters who crowded the court room, patrolmen and detectives began to search spectators for revolvers. A thin, pale-faced gunman, Louis Kushner, a sniper for Little Orgie, stepped out of the court room when he saw the search going on.

Upon discharge the Dropper wheeled round in the

court room and smiled benignly. He walked out of the courthouse with Lieutenant Cornelius Willemse, a member of the Homicide Squad. The Dropper entered a taxicab and closed the door. Willemse stood talking to him through an open window in the taxicab.

"It's about time you were beating it out of town," said Willemse. "A man can go so far in your game and——"

"Aw, they're afraid to take me," the Dropper barked in a raw, pompous voice. "I——"

The Dropper never finished the sentence. Five shots poured in through the open window. One passed through the crown of Willemse's straw hat; another hit the taxi driver in the shoulder. Three lodged in the Dropper's pudgy form. He toppled over dead.

At the side of the taxi, with a smoking gun in his hand, stood Kushner, grinning. Willemse seized him.

"Well, I got that guy," said Kushner. "Now gimme a cigarette."

Little Orgie and another of his henchmen, Sammy Weiss, were arrested for instigating the killing of the Dropper, but Kushner protested that the assassination was his own pet scheme. Little Orgie and Weiss were released. Kushner went to prison for life.

The Dropper's gang empire broke apart, leaving the field to Little Orgie. But this gang leader quit his strike activities and went into another and more profitable field. He transfered his theater of operations to the Broadway white-light center and went into bootlegging and hijacking. He flourished and planned to retire with a fortune.

He prospered until October 15, 1927. On this day he went back to the East Side to display his wealth before old friends. He took along a bodyguard—Legs Diamond. The two stood chatting in front of No. 103 Norfolk Street. A touring car drove up to the curb. A man in the car called out, "Hey, Orgie." Little Orgie looked around, smiling, and got a bullet in the back of his head.

Legs was wounded. Orgie died on the spot; his bodyguard recovered.

Nearly all gang murders fall into the same pattern, and their authors usually come to the same ends meted out to Jack the Dropper and Little Orgie. For a long time they beat the courts and laws set up by organized society for its protection. But their own form of justice, of which they are very proud, disposes of them without trial or hearing or benefit of counsel. They are anxious in a court of law to take full advantage of every technicality which the law builds around men accused of murder. Their lawyers rail against the death penalty and impress juries with the severity of capital punishment, but their clients resort to it in their own lawless world on the slightest provocation.

The most glowering, outraged look a gangster ever gave me came from Waxey Gordon, whose arrest for the murder of Strauss I had caused. Waxey was picked up on a minor charge and stood in the office of Chief Inspector John D. Coughlin. It was some years after Gordon's acquittal.

I stepped into the office.

"You know this man, don't you, Gordon?" Coughlin asked the gangster, indicating me.

Gordon's face screwed itself into a hideous frown.

"Where are you living now?" I asked Gordon.

"On Riverside Drive," he said. The Drive is one of New York's finest boulevards. Rents are high there.

"Riverside Drive, huh?" I said. "Up in the world. You never earned an honest dollar in your life, Gordon.

"Wha's 'at?" he snapped. "You're sore because you tried to burn me once, and I beat it."

"And you deserved to burn," I said.

"What d'yuh mean I ought to burn?" His voice had risen to a screech. No wrongly outraged citizen ever showed more deeply aggrieved feelings than Gordon. His lynxlike eyes followed me out of the room.

Of all murder cases gang-feud killings are the most difficult to establish from a legal standpoint. The motives are obscure. They may have been planted in the minds of the slayers years back, while in the meantime the feuds that result have taken a thousand ramifications. And evidence that will meet the tests in a court of law is hard to get. Witnesses the State must rely upon to establish the motives, conspiracy, and the actual killing are men and women of the underworld, ex-convicts for the most part, whose testimony even under oath must be taken with a big grain of salt under prevailing rules of evidence. Even though it may be the truth, and substantiated by circumstantial and documentary evidence, the known criminal records and activities of such witnesses detract from their credibility.

Persons on the outside imagine that gunmen and gangsters live in a world of romance, dark romance, and that among them exists a code of honor. It is a popular belief that a seasoned crook never squeals on his associates. It's a myth. Of the hundreds of crooks I have examined few, when cornered, fail to squeal. If they don't it's not because they are bound to silence by a code of honor. They're afraid to squeal, fearing death at the hands of their own kind. Alone and cornered they are most abject cowards. The very fact that they operate in bands is an indication of this cowardice. They are afraid to work single handed.

Confessions from professional gangsters are not difficult to get, but the trouble is they usually are full of lies uttered in a cowardly attempt to fasten their crimes upon others. Frequently in my career gangs of killers have been brought before me. Together they display a cool, cocksure bravado, but alone they wilt. Separate them and each man races to be the first to confess, always throwing the blame on another or the rest of the gang. In this way they hope to pave the road to a bargain with the State and save their own skins. They are so inherently distrustful of one another that a bare hint to one of a remark which a pal has dropped brings on the race to see who can tell the most soonest.

The dying gunman, shot by one of his own, who refuses to confess or make a deathbed statement naming his slayer is supposed to be a tragic, sympathy-arousing figure, if you look at crime through romance-colored glasses. He may be a killer himself, the most vicious type of criminal, but, the romancer says, he lives up to the code of honor of his class. Code of honor? There's no such thing among these misfits of life. Fear stops them from talking, fear of death to relatives or pals, or certain death for themselves if they should happen to recover.

If they do talk upon their deathbeds their statements are usually worthless. It is the practice in cases where the victim of attack appears to be dying to send detectives and a police stenographer to the bedside to procure a dying statement from the victim and record it for future use at a trial if the slayer is apprehended. The law requires that before such a statement may be admitted into evidence before a jury in a murder trial it must be shown that the maker knew he was about to die and had no hope of recovery.

Human beings, including gunmen that I have encountered on the brink of death, alike display most hopeful qualities.

"Do you believe you are about to die?" I have asked many of them who later died. This question meets the law's requirements.

"Why, how do I know!" had been the usual reply, or a positive "No" or, "Ask the doctor about that." In any case the reply, even if the dying victim did make a statement, would bar it from a jury's consideration.

"Have you given up all hope of recovery?" I have inquired.

"I should say not!" is invariably the hopeful reply, although at the very moment life was being sustained only by artificial means. This reply also nullifies whatever statement the victim may make.

In this one respect honest persons and gunmen are alike—in the face of certain death they cling to hope when there is no hope. Gunmen, it is said, show great fortitude and an easy willingness to die. More myth. They like life as all of us do. Sometimes they do talk and name slayers. But the presence of death makes them no more truthful or trustworthy than they were in the heyday of their illicit power. The slayers they name in many instances are not the real slayers but old enemies against whom they were working out an old grudge with their dying breath.

The old saying that a professional crook will stick to his friends through the last ditch belongs also in the realm of the mythical. I'll cite a case in proof:

Fat Joe Bintel was a pompous easy-money figure on the lower East Side (nearly all professionals originate on the East Side, not because the people there are worse than others but because poverty is still intrenched). He was an ex-convict with a long record. He was the much-vaunted friend of every crook that crossed his path. He had a gurgling laugh and a buoyant spirit. Crooks swore by him. Knowing his underworld very thoroughly and possessing intimate inside connections that kept him in touch with crook activities, he went into the bail-bond business, but dealt only with professionals, killers, thieves, and holdup men. He had advance information on crimes that were committed; knew who committed them, and this gave him a jump on his competitors in the bail-bond business. He was like the proverbial early worm.

He opened headquarters in a shabby little office at

No. 52 Second Street, adjoining the Essex Market Magistrate's Court, which, by reason of its location in the center of the populous East Side, handled most gangster and gunmen cases. To outdo his competitors he offered his customers an inducement. He would also supply lawyers, not the type learned in law, but the shyster or mouthpiece type who know the loopholes in the law. Fat Joe also held himself out to be a great power with the courts. He boasted he could fix cases.

His reputation for never turning down a crook—that is, a crook with an established criminal record—ran far and wide. His rates were high, but when he bailed out a man that left the crooks free to go back to work at crime and earn money to pay Bintel and his lawyers. Fat Joe worked a profitable endless-chain proposition. He became a sort of demigod in the underworld. He had a way of making strange crooks new to the city see him first before beginning operations. He had a thousand friends singing his praise on every occasion as the best friend a fellow could have. Anyone who ventured to dispute his standing found himself in a rough-and-tumble mix-up with Joe's defenders.

At one time he had so many professional crooks out on bail that he couldn't keep track of all of them, but he depended upon the so-called code of honor that was supposed to keep crooks in bail from fleeing with Fat Joe compelled to forfeit the bail.

Suddenly, while Fat Joe was enjoying great prosperity with scores of felons out on bail, the State of New York passed a new crime law imposing life imprisonment upon habitual criminals who were convicted a fourth time of felony.

All of Fat Joe's customers had long records, three, four, and five previous convictions for felonies, and were out on bail pending trial for additional felonies. Conviction would mean isolation in prison for the rest of their natural lives.

One by one some of these men who were out on bail put up by Fat Joe disappeared.

Fat Joe, the great, undisputed friend of the underworld, saw ruin ahead when out of his pocket he would have to make good the forfeited bail bonds.

So quietly he began to "turn in" his customers, tipping off the fact that they had committed fresh crimes. He could not afford to ask openly to be released from the bail bonds. That would be an unfriendly act. But there was a crowding of jails by felons whom Joe had "turned in"—secretly, of course.

Consternation prevailed among his customers. For a while they couldn't figure who was tipping them off.

A week passed. Late one afternoon two men stepped into Fat Joe's little office. One shot was fired. It hit Fat Joe in the back of the head. He fell forward in his swivel chair, dead. The great, good friend was gone; the bullet was a protest against his idea of honor among thieves.

His slayers could not be identified and consequently never were found. Fat Joe was given a cheap burial. The fortune he had built up "chiseling," as his occupation is called, was swept away meeting forfeited bail bonds.

Self-extermination among gangs is a recognized law in their shadowy world. Many a gangster and gunman has beaten apparently fool-proof cases we built up against them. Months were spent getting the evidence, but in court they wormed their way through the law's meshes, boasting of their ability to beat any case the police worked up against them. We failed frequently to get them in life, but time and again they came into our hands sooner or later as victims of just another homicide to be looked up.

In view of this situation it is not surprising to hear opinions expressed that it might be good police policy, where gang-feud killings are involved, not to turn loose a large staff of detectives to run down the slayers and work for months trying to build up a case when in the end it will be beaten in court by trickery. Better, some of these opinions hold, to concentrate the detective energy which taxpayers pay for on running down the slayers of honest men and women, for in the end self-extermination takes care of the professional killers. To me, however, homicide is homicide whether the victim is a murderer or an honest man. The law makes no distinctions. Murder is murder, and it is the duty of the police to seek the slayer.

Looking back on the gang murders that occurred in my time, I recall one fact that seems sufficient to destroy the myth about the underworld's code of honor. Most of the gangster victims slain by their own kind were killed from the rear, usually shot in the back of the head. A code of honor in gangland? There isn't even a semblance of sportsmanship, or the sign of an even break, when gangland sets out to kill.

The fact that New York does not suffer from gang activities to the extent that other large cities do is largely the result of Woods's work and the efficient administration of Commissioner George V. McLaughlin, who came later. Woods spent almost four years at the head of the Department. The mayor gave him a free hand. The men liked him. He got results. But in 1918 a change in administrations produced the usual reorganization at headquarters. Woods resigned. There was genuine regret at his going. He had built up the morale of the Department through the trying period of the Great War. His successor held office for exactly twenty-two days. The job was too onerous for him. Finally Richard E. Enright was elevated to the commissionership from a lieutenancy. He made many changes. The Homicide Squad became the Homicide Bureau and went on functioning with about eighteen trained men to handle homicides in a city of six million persons and covering more than 350 square miles.

CHAPTER XIII

DABBLERS IN CRIME ANALYSIS

SHAKE-UPS are not the only disturbances that come along to interrupt a murder man. The Homicide Bureau was not molested in the change of administrations, but other sources of discomfort opened up. However, life always offers a compensating influence. For every dark moment there is a bright one; for every disquieting incident in my work there was a chance to laugh and thus relieve the heavy atmosphere that sometimes pervaded the Murder Clinic.

From time to time men and women with startling new ideas, discoveries, and inventions in the field of criminal investigation came to see me. I had always been skeptical about new ideas in this field. I inherited it, I believe, from my early experience. When Francis V. Greene was Commissioner of Police under Roosevelt he sent a man to London to study Scotland Yard's fingerprinting system. The Yard had just installed it.

A very favorable report on the system, then in its infancy, was brought back to Greene. He thought it would be a good thing to try out. His chief inspector of detectives was noncommittal on the subject, but a very practical man. He decided to subject the Yard system to a severe test. There was in prison in New York at the time a noted English thief whom we all knew. His fingerprints were taken and then sent to the Yard's fingerprinting expert. No name, description, or other indication of the thief's identity accompanied the prints.

"Now we'll see how good this finger-tip business is," said the chief inspector. "If London identifies this man I'm for the system."

In a month Scotland Yard sent back word that the fingerprints were those of English Harry, house breaker and sneak thief. He was the man we had in prison.

The fingerprinting system was installed at headquarters. To-day it contains more than six hundred thousand prints of known criminals. It is a sort of an index to crookdom's population, and these are not, by any means, all the crooks in the United States.

Whether or not it is because I have a loud laugh when my funny bone is tickled, visitors with queer devices who called at headquarters were always sent in to me. Now it was a man with a mechanical lie detector guaranteed to tell when crooks were prevaricating. Or someone would turn up with a divining rod to locate missing weapons and clues, while others offered psychic powers capable, so they said, of finding any murderer. They were all anxious to get the Homicide Bureau's approval of their devices.

One afternoon I was called into the assembly room where a thin, dark-featured woman was sitting with two men. She would pass her hand over her face, then gaze at the ceiling and whisper in a ghostlike voice. She was on a psychic hunt for crooks, they said.

The two men at her side followed her movements, jumping up when she pointed, sitting down when she lapsed into a dreamy mood. They wanted to know what I thought about her powers. I asked the two men who she was and who they were. She was about to go on the vaudeville stage, they said, and they were her agents. If the Homicide Bureau would approve of her methods she would get a booking and much publicity.

I laughed and walked out. Three days later the young woman was arrested for shoplifting. Well, she should have known crooks, but not through any gift of divination. She could "feel" them all right, and so could our men. They caught her in the act.

Others who called were too far gone to offer any hope. And the usual number of mentally unbalanced persons came in to confess crimes they had never committed, or to solve crimes we had never heard of. Yet their stories had to be listened to. They were permitted to tell them up to the point when the ambulance arrived from Bellevue Hospital to carry them off to the psycopathic ward for observation and treatment.

There were also self-appointed crime analyists who dabbled in criminology without training or talent for it. Occasionally they arose to plague us, and some hung on with bulldog tenacity. Such a person was my friend, whom I shall disguise as Mr. Holmes. He was not a bad sort, just a putterer indulging a habit or conceit. He had a flair for murder inquiry and a predilection for taking issue with me on cases which looked like mysteries but were not. He lent a willing ear to anyone who could dig up a mystery. It had to be murder. He was not concerned with lesser crimes. He bobbed up with regularity.

One night at ten o'clock the telephone in my home jangled, as often it did at that and later hours. I answered it. My office was calling to advise that a body had been found in a motor boat in Flushing Bay, Long Island. By a circuitous route, the only one available at that hour, I reached the bay and, by still more circuitous travel on water in the pitch dark, reached the motor boat.

In the cabin lay a form in woman's clothing. But the face was that of a young man. It was peaceful and contented, as is almost always true of suicides. I set it down for a case of self-destruction after my first look. A man who has been viewing death nearly all of his adult life reaches the point where he instinctively differentiates between homicide, suicide, and accidental death. A good tailor usually can tell at one quick glance whether the suit a man wears is ready made or built to order or whether buttonholes are machine or hand sewn. Men with long experience in any line, if they are observant, can do the same thing.

The fact that the young man was dressed in feminine attire did not point to murder, for experience and certain studies I had made of the works of Kraft-Ebing explained this aberration.

The body was cold. Rigor mortis had set in. It must have lain in the cabin for some hours.

A voice sounded from an opening in the cabin. "Hello. Is that you, Carey?" It was the friendly, familiar address of my fellow worker in homicide, Dr. Norris, chief medical examiner. "Well, where did he hang?" he next asked. Dr. Norris, too, had gotten the same picture from the first glance, even looking at the picture from the darkness above. His inquiry was induced by the sight of a rope around the dead youth's neck.

"He didn't hang," I explained. And so he hadn't. The rope was a hangman's noose which, once drawn tight, is almost impossible to slacken without untying. He had pulled it tight about his neck.

"Plain case of long-studied suicide," said Norris.

"I agree with that," said I.

Further inquiry disclosed that the youth had been taken to the launch in a rowboat at two P. M. the afternoon before. Men at work on a boat near by saw him enter the cabin. He did not emerge. I reported it as a clear case of suicide and so did Dr. Norris. The verdict was met with doubt by the youth's father, who gave his version or theory to my friend Mr. Holmes. Instantly Mr. Holmes, sitting in his office, figured it as murder. He hung his theory upon the fact that the young man was dressed in woman's clothing and that he had employed a hangman's noose. And, moreover, he opined, no motive existed for self-destruction. Indeed, these circumstances might appear mysterious to a layman. I hardly blamed Holmes for getting excited about it. The circumstances were unusual to a man on the outside, and, moreover, the angle from which he looked at it made good newspaper reading. But Holmes was more than excited. He was incensed to think that I would not countenance his theory.

There was a lull. Holmes may have gone into a séance. Presently I heard from him. He asked me to meet the father of the dead youth. I did. The old gentleman protested that I was all wrong. His son could not have killed himself.

"Now, sir," I said to him, "I have all the sympathy in the world for you, but your boy killed himself."

No, the father insisted, I was wrong. I had not intended to prolong the family grief, so had made no extended investigation into motive. Now, however, my conclusions were challenged. I resumed my investigation. Just one short trip was necessary. I found that the young man had taken out life insurance less than a year before his death. There was the usual clause in the policy that rendered it null and void if the insured killed himself before the policy had been in effect a year.

The life-insurance policy was never paid. No more was heard from Holmes on this case.

But he bobbed up again on another matter that intrigued his penchant for murder inquiry. A young woman was found dead on the steps in front of her home, shot through the temple on the right side, a contact wound. She was standing on the steps when the shot was fired and fell backward. The pistol was found beside her body. These circumstances all pointed, and invariably point, to a self-inflicted death. I so reported. I had made a few inquiries about motive and found that the young woman had fallen into fast ways, but about this her family knew nothing. I wanted to spare them the details and not blacken her memory and had quickly closed the inquiry.

But Mr. Holmes, viewing things at a distance between puffs of his pipe, saw murder in the picture. He could not understand how the young woman, happy, prepossessing, of good family, and with everything to live for, possibly could have killed herself. He sent men (he never went out on his own missions) to examine the body and they returned with theories which fitted into his picture —his long shot.

Newspapers flared with a new mystery. It was summer time, and a good mystery story is relished by the best of papers during the dog days. The young woman had been murdered in spite of what the Homicide Bureau said. I did not care to answer this publicly and thus awaken unpleasant memories. But I put in a long-distance call for a certain dentist in Philadelphia. He answered.

"Is this Dr.——?" I asked.

"Yes."

"Do you know a girl named Frances——?"

"I do."

"Have you seen her lately?"

"Last Saturday night. She stayed here in my apartment with ah-h-h-h friends."

"Doctor, do you own a revolver?"

"Yes, I have one. I keep it here."

"What's the make and caliber and color of it?"

"Smith and Wesson, .32, nickel plated."

It was the description of the gun found on the steps.

"You've got the gun now?"

"Of course. It's in my bureau drawer. I'll see."

He stepped away from the 'phone. I could hear him say to himself in a loud, surprised tone, "My God. It's gone."

He came back to the 'phone. "The revolver's gone," he said.

"Now, Doctor," I said, "could you come over to my office at police headquarters?"

"When?" he asked eagerly.

"Oh, in a couple of days," I replied.

I hung up.

Scarcely four hours later he rushed breathless into my office and told me a version of the young woman's life which her family and Holmes had not heard. And the dentist was in Philadelphia when she killed herself. She had taken the revolver without his knowledge. But the most convincing indications of his innocence was his outcry when he went to the drawer in his apartment and the rush he made to get to my office when I had told him a couple of days would be all right.

Holmes was deeply chagrined. A newspaper sensation died. And in so far as I was concerned Holmes was through. My official connection with murder inquiry ended a few years later. During my time in the Detective Bureau I might have devoted all my time to running down theories propounded by self-styled and self-appointed crime analysts like Holmes. For almost every suicide and many accidental deaths may be conjured into murder mysteries by an over-active imagination. A thousand letters pouring weekly into the Detective Bureau of a large city from experts, cranks, and revengeful persons voicing theories, tips, and ideas on murder indicate the throng of potential sleuths that are at large and unknown but willing to stick a finger in the pie. In more recent years there has been a drop in the number of amateur crime analysts. Possibly they satisfy their imaginations in the detective story books. If so I thank the writers of these, for they have done their part in relieving homicide men of one source of annoyance.

Holmes would have found fertile ground for his talent in the tragic case of Barbara Reig. It was a sensation while it lasted, but a little case from a murder man's standpoint. For a time it was wrapped up in mystery.

Barbara was twenty, good looking and well thought of by girls she worked with. One July evening her body was found on top of a tool box in a shelter house in Irving Park, Brooklyn. There was a pistol wound in the right side of her head, again a contact wound, which showed that the pistol had been held against her temple. Her legs were crossed, which is a frequent thing in suicides. Blood had run down back of her right ear and around her neck. Had she been murdered this would have taken different courses.

There was no pistol in the place! I offer the reader an opportunity to guess whether it was murder or not. From the facts just described I said at once that it was suicide. The solution follows.

A summer thunderstorm had come up which drove the girl into the shelter house. Her skirt was wet. She took it off and hung it upon a hook to dry. Presently Patrolman Shillard, on duty in the park with a probationary patrolman, entered the house. Barbara was infatuated with him. The night was hot; the shelter house had one light over which Shillard put his cap to dry. He took out his revolver in its holster and laid it on the tool box. For three hours they sat talking, Shillard trying to convince the girl that she should be courting someone her own age. The girl, in a huff, arose and was drawing her dress down over her head when she shot herself with the officer's pistol which she had picked up in the dark unseen by him.

He picked up the pistol and ran from the place. He encountered another patrolman who, having heard the shot, was rapping the sidewalk with his nightstick.

"Did you hear that shot?" the officer asked Shillard.

"No," said Shillard, "but I heard you rap. Where did the shot come from?"

"I don't know. Let's look in here," said the officer,

advancing toward the shelter house. The two entered, and with feigned surprise Shillard looked again upon the body. He said he did not know the girl, but later admitted having flirted with her and finally described what had gone on in the place. He claimed that he had left the shelter house more than an hour before. He was indicted, tried, and the jury disagreed. The case was dismissed. It was plainly suicide.

The trouble with Officer Shillard was that he was married, for one thing; that he was afraid if he admitted being in the shelter house three hours the punishment for being off post that length of time would be greater than if he admitted having been gone only an hour. So he only admitted the hour, tangled himself up in all kinds of trouble, and created mystery where there should have been none.

What Analyst Holmes might have made out of that case!

In story books and in some newspapers, and frequently on the stage, one hears and sees much that would tend to support the belief that policemen fasten crimes upon the wrong persons to satisfy revenge or to gain glory. The story that known criminals are hounded by the police and convicted of crimes they have never committed has gained a good deal of currency. My experience has been to the contrary.

Back in my early years in the Bureau Sergeant Goldenhammer was shot and killed by a bartender named Byrnes, who was an associate of crooks, though not one himself. Goldenhammer was on plain-clothes duty, hunting for a thief. He had been informed that his man was sharing a room with Byrnes. He went to the room. Byrnes admitted him, and a few minutes later Goldenhammer dropped to the floor, shot through the head.

Byrnes was arrested and admitted shooting the sergeant. He said that the officer had come to his door dressed in a dark blue shirt and working clothes. He demanded admittance without saying that he was an officer. Byrnes objected. Goldenhammer pressed in. Byrnes ran to a bureau drawer, got out his revolver and, thinking Goldenhammer was an intruder bent on robbery, tussled with him. Goldenhammer seized Byrnes's right arm. The pistol went off, the bullet entering the side of Goldenhammer's head and going almost straight upward through the skull. The sergeant died almost instantly.

In view of Byrnes's association with thieves it might easily have been possible to fasten murder upon him. But my conclusions did not run that way. The course of the bullet upward plainly indicated the truth of Byrnes's version of the shooting—that it was accidental. Moreover, Goldenhammer was known as a man who plunged into things without due judgment. His life would have been spared had he announced that he was an officer, for it was soon determined that, although Byrnes knew crooks, he was on friendly terms with many policemen and had helped them on various occasions. He was not tried.

To have fastened that crime on Byrnes not only would have been a grave injustice but a professional error of the worst kind. It would have been like cheating at solitaire, fooling yourself. Only by playing the game square do you learn its niceties, the winning plays. The same is true in murder inquiry. You become adept at it only when you strive to get at the truth, for in the processes thus employed is the knack of real detection acquired. At threescore and three years I am inclined to believe that it's true of the whole game of life.

One more little humorous incident before I close this chapter. I don't want every word I write to be about murder.

Not many years ago a stout little man came into my office. I was first attracted to his presence by the squishy sound of his feet as he sauntered in. I looked at his feet.

They were what a policeman calls boloney butcher's feet, long and round like an inflated inner tire of a motor car.

"Inspector," he said very seriously, "I want to interest you in a great idea."

"Well, let's have it."

"I've done a lot of detective work up around Canada. I always found it hard to communicate with my brother detectives when there were people, maybe crooks, around. I got to thinking it over, and for two years I've been inventing an eye language for detectives."

"So?" I invited him to a chair.

"I've got a whole code arranged so that two detectives can talk to each other any time in secret. For instance, if you wanted to say 'Arrest him' you'd move your eyes this way." His eyelids fluttered and his eyeballs circled in their sockets. "Now, it won't take long for your men to learn this code. Wherever I go people are greatly interested in my invention. Think of what it would mean to the men on this force."

"I am thinking, thinking hard," I said. My caller smiled pleasantly. I looked out the window. There was a silence of about half a minute.

"How would it work if the detectives were out in a dark alley on a pitch black night?" I asked.

"Well, of course, you understand, Inspector, this system is for daytime detectives."

Very shortly he bowed himself out the door, backing out, his feet making the same squishy noise. I had to laugh loud and long. His feet were as funny as his eye language. Still I would not have barred him from my office. Not even a black subject like murder will make a man worry if he knows where to turn for comedy relief.

CHAPTER XIV

BUSHWHACKERS AND RIPPERS

THERE are two types of murderers whose identity and apprehension are difficult, almost impossible, to achieve. One is the bushwhacker, a chameleon-like criminal who slays wantonly as a prelude or aftermath to robbery, and the other is the ripper, author of the most atrocious crimes on the calendar. The crimes of both types grip the populace with profound terror, horror, and puzzlement. To a man of murder experience they are not the deep mysteries they seem to others, though their solution in a legal sense is rarely ever perfected.

The bushwhacker emerges at night out of a background of foliage in public parks and along lonely highways to prey upon couples carrying on clandestine flirtations. Police have given him this name because it aptly describes his modus operandi—out of the bushes and whack! Blackmail is one of his assistants in crime. Let me furnish a typical case.

Patrolmen on post in Van Cortland Park, a wooded playground at the northern edge of New York City, heard pistol shots on the night of September 3, 1916. They hurried in the direction of the firing and came upon a touring car at the side of a tree-bordered lane known as Golf Links Road. The night was unusually dark. In the front seat at the wheel slumped the form of a well-dressed, distinguished-looking man about forty. Beside him sat an attractive woman about two years his junior. He was dead. The woman had fainted.

When revived the woman gave her name and said that the dead man was Dwight Dilworth, a lawyer, who lived in Montclair, New Jersey, a fashionable suburb of New York City. An examination of his body showed that three bullets had been fired into the region of his heart. No revolver was found in or near the car. The young woman was gravely concerned and confused.

She told her story. At about six o'clock that evening Dilworth, who, she said, was her family's lawyer, asked her to accompany him on a motor ride and she agreed. They dined at a popular roadhouse, got back into the automobile, and started through Van Cortland Park. It was a warm, pleasant night in Indian summer, and hundreds of persons were on park benches and lawns. Dilworth drove beyond into the more heavily wooded section and entered Golf Links Road. The car stalled. He pulled to the side of the road and stopped. He was about to arise and alight from the car to look at his engine when two men jumped from a clump of bushes.

"Hands up!" commanded one of the men.

"I won't," Dilworth shot back. He was a tall, robust man. He lunged at the robbers. Three pistol shots were fired at him. He fell back dead. The woman fainted. The slayers disappeared into the woods and were never found. The woman could not give a description of them. In the darkness she could see only the bulk of their forms and not their faces. She reconstructed the murder scene as best she could for the benefit of detectives. There was little that she could reconstruct. All had occurred in the flash of a minute in the black night.

In spite of the apparent simplicity that attended the crime, newspapers, with an elaborate background available, made a sensational mystery of the killing. It was hinted by unnamed sources, who are always valuable in building backgrounds, but worthless in a court of law where every accused person must be confronted by the witnesses against him, that a jealous woman had plotted to kill Dilworth. It was known, by rumor, that Dilworth had a wide acquaintance among women, although he lived in respectability with his wife and small son, who at the time of the killing were visiting relatives in Kansas City. Likewise it was hinted that his slayers were gunmen hired by a woman to kill him.

The Great War, too, crept into the background. It was intimated that a firm with which the lawyer was associated was making ammunition for foreign armies, and that it had been blacklisted by the British government. The inference was that his death was caused by secret agents of one of the nations at war. Nothing was ever uncovered to support this theory.

Had Dilworth not attempted to fight back at his slayers the probability is that he would have lived, but more than likely the story of the attack in that case never would have reached the police. Therein lies the secret of the bushwhacker's method. He is first of all a professional thief equipped and ready to kill on the slightest provocation. Prowling about parks and highways with his eyes and ears alert he discovers couples whose conduct and conversation indicate a clandestine relationship. He swoops down upon them and robs. If they fight back he wounds or kills, usually the latter, for it is the certain way of eliminating a witness against him. He figures that owing to the clandestine relationship the victim will submit to robbery and not reveal the crime, for revealing it to the police or others involves admitting the relationship. If the victim submits to the robbery, as most do, that is the last of it. Reports of these crimes scarcely ever reach the police unless, of course, the victim is slain, in which case the identity of the killers is seldom established. When the victim submits and makes no report of the robbery to the police the thieves are left to repeat the operation on other trysting couples. Men have been wounded by robbing bushwhackers, but the report of the crime often has reached the police only by accident, and then invariably the victim shies away from prosecution of his assailants.

Bushwhacker cases are quite numerous in large cities. The Homicide Bureau has had its share of them. Now and again a criminal of this type is caught and confesses, and the murder man gets a complete pattern. In 1907 we had a case which fully revealed the bushwhacker's secrets. A young tea taster, married and apparently happy, was promenading one summer's night with a pretty manicurist. They got off a car in a sparsely settled section of the city and walked arm in arm in the shadow of a stone viaduct. Suddenly a man sprang out and ordered the couple to throw up their hands. The tea taster offered resistance. He was struck over the head and killed. His companion ran screaming. The assailant was captured some blocks away, and in his possession was identifiable property of the slain man.

This bushwhacker was a Negro and a seasoned hand at this nefarious specialty. He confessed that he had followed the couple along in the shadows; had overheard enough of their talk to tell him that the tea taster was married and that the young woman on his arm was not his wife. Thereupon he struck, as he had done on other occasions in the same vicinity. These earlier victims had willingly submitted to robbery and made no report to the police. The Negro was executed.

Some time later a young man was sitting with a girl on a bench in Central Park when a man came out of the darkness and ordered them to throw up their hands. Being too slow in obeying the man was shot. He recovered and told his story. His assailant too was a Negro who was never caught.

Bushwhacking is a crime to which the criminally inclined Negro is peculiarly adapted. He is like a chameleon. His black skin makes concealment and escape easy. He melts into his background of heavy shadows and underbrush. Grouping the few crimes of this type which have reached the police, one thing stands out in most all of them—about all the victims ever saw of their assailant were two rows of pearly teeth and the whites of eyes. These are high lights which the Negro bushwhacker cannot conceal, but they are not enough to identify an assailant by, for nearly every Negro possesses the two characteristics.

With a famous double murder case which occurred near New York City in 1922 I had no official connection, but watched developments only as an interested professional observer. A clergyman, who was married to a highly respected woman, and an attractive woman who was a member of his church choir, and also married, were found murdered in a dark and unfrequented spot on the outskirts of a small city where both lived. The minister was shot through the head; the woman was shot three times and her throat cut. The murder was committed about 10:30 P. M. Two days later the bodies were found.

A sensational background was provided for the case. The minister's widow and her two brothers were tried for the crime and acquitted. In this case the colorful, insinuating background was followed. I can only express an observer's opinion about it. This fact I consider of utmost importance: the minister's watch, chain, and wallet were missing indicating robbery. And the woman's throat was cut. The Negro bushwhacker frequently wields a knife. I am inclined to think that the woman, true to her sex, screamed, and her assailant cut her throat to silence her; that the minister charged at her attacker and was killed. The bullets fired into her body were to make death doubly certain and instantaneous, for there were houses near by with occupants in them.

The background of gossip, suspicion, theory, and illicit relationships, and the wealth and social position of the murdered minister's widow, made sensational reading. The murder still remains a mystery, one of the most talked-about mysteries of recent times.

Backgrounds are diverting and interesting. To the public a good mystery with new fresh developments each day is like a three-ringed circus. The spectator finds it difficult to concentrate his eyes and mind on one ring at a time while the other rings are alive with performers, and clowns are cavorting, and the air is being plowed by hurtling aërialists. The murder man is like one of these aërialists. He's got to keep his mind on the business in hand and not on the large and diverting background all about him.

Ripper murders, like poison slayings, occur in cycles and are directed against women and small children. The perpetrators are hard to find. Patterns explain why to the murder man.

In March, 1915, the mother of Leonora Cohn, aged six, sent the child to a grocery store for a pail of milk. She did not return. The mother, hurrying frantically out of her apartment to look for the child, found her body in a dark corner of the hallway. A fiend had violated the child and had horribly mutilated her body, slashing the abdomen with a small knife which I concluded was a pocketknife. A pail of milk stood near the body, and near by was a piece of moist candy which the child had been eating. No one in the tenement had heard screams or a struggle, nor had anyone seen the child or her assailant enter or leave the tenement house.

We located the manufacturer of the candy, but since

his product was widely distributed to almost every small candy store in the East it was impossible to trace the piece the child had been eating. The presumption was that the fiend had lured the child with the sweet. Asylums were searched for a man with such a propensity who might have been released from the institution or had escaped just before the crime.

Three months later Charlie Murray, aged four and a half years, was slashed and killed in the same way. His body was found under a staircase in the tenement where his family lived. A small knife also had been used by the fiend. No clue ever was found to lead us to the slayer. Indications were that the same murderer committed both crimes. In the Murray case, as in the Cohn case, no one had seen the slayer enter or leave the tenement, so the most important thing necessary to start a search and vital to the process of fastening the crime upon a slayer was missing. The two ripper killings also occurred in approximately the same neighborhood. Parents throughout the city were terrorized. Small children were kept indoors for weeks. Plain-clothes police were concentrated in the sections of the city where the murders had occurred. They did not recur.

Great surprise and indignation are expressed when ripper murderers are not caught. Police departments come in for a lot of criticism. Yet the circumstances under which this type of crime is committed almost always preclude the possibility of finding the slayers. They are deliberately planned atrocities. The perpetrators purposely make certain that no one is around at the time, and they select dark and hidden recesses for their act. That such crimes are committed in cycles is explained by Kraft-Ebing, who says that the slayers are perverts. The lust to kill comes suddenly upon them. They appease it and the cycle ends. Very frequently the desire never occurs again in their lifetime or, if it does, long intervals elapse between their acts. In some cases, which have come under psychopathic observation, rippers have forgotten all about their crimes.

It is generally believed that the ripper murderer is a follower of the sea or a man who has long been out of touch with civilization. Scotland Yard invariably looks for a ripper in low dives in seaports. There are several patterns in my mind to support this. One is the Totterman case.

Totterman was a misfit of the sea. In a water-front rooming house the body of a young woman was found slashed in the ripper fashion. Her slayer left behind a clue to his luggage. We found it and then began a long search for Totterman. Being a sailor he had gone from ship to ship. McCafferty and I combed water-front resorts for trace of him and finally located him aboard a vessel in a New England port. He was arrested. Had it not been for the finding of an article which he had unwittingly dropped in the slain woman's room Totterman probably never would have been found. No one had seen him enter or leave the place. He had carefully studied his opportunity to visit the woman's room unobserved. Except for the age of the victim this crime varied little in its details from the killing of Leonora Cohn and Charlie Murray. Many years, however, elapsed between the crimes. Totterman was convicted and sentenced to die. He escaped from Auburn Prison and was recaptured, and later sentence of death was commuted to life imprisonment.

Men of this perverted type often are presumed to be mentally unsound. Notwithstanding, they display shrewdness in eluding arrest. It took us five years to locate a murderer of this species whose crime, while not a ripper case, falls into the same category.

In 1921 a young woman was found dead in a closet in a midtown tenement house. From articles found in the room it was ascertained that she shared the apartment with her brother. Both went under the name of Fay. The brother was missing. In Cambridge, Massachusetts, we learned that his real name was Harry Townsend and that relatives and friends had not heard from brother and sister for several years. Townsend had been born in Nova Scotia in a town near the sea. He had shown a desire in early youth to be a sailor. No deep-water vessels came into the small port where he was born, but a great many coastwise barges did.

Detective Oswald was sent to Nova Scotia to gather together the man's past and make a picture. He found that Townsend had become a bargeman. The last heard of him was many years back when he was employed aboard a barge running between Perth Amboy, New Jersey, and Boston, Massachusetts.

Barges are plentiful along the eastern coast and they are forever moving. I sent men to nearly every port along the seaboard with instructions to make inquiries for Townsend among barge workers. They left behind verbal descriptions of the man and asked those they interviewed to let us know if a man of that description ever turned up.

This process is known in detective circles as "laying the wires." It is a long-drawn-out operation involving the scattering of descriptions among thousands of persons. Years may elapse before the information required comes into the murder man's possession. Great patience is required; the detectives engaged in the task must keep in constant touch with their "wires."

For five years this process went on. Finally Detective Thomas J. Martin, a most patient member of the Bureau, heard from a "wire" in Philadelphia that a man answering the description of the man he was looking for had been seen on a coal barge in that city and quite strangely was going by the name of Collier. Martin went to Philadelphia, attired in the garb of a bargeman. Circulating among barge workers, he learned that his man had last been seen on South Street, which lies along the New York City river front.

The search was transferred to New York. Martin spent days on South Street, while other men were sent to interview wholesale coal dealers who operated barges. New York City uses more coal, perhaps, than any other city in the world. Most of it comes in by barge. Finally a dealer was found who had a man in his employ that answered Townsend's description, but was known as Collins. He was living on a stake boat moored at Whitestone Landing on Long Island Sound.

With Detective Joseph Donovan of the Bureau Martin visited the stake boat at five o'clock one morning and found Collins. He admitted he was Townsend and confessed. He pleaded guilty and was sent away for life. Five years, almost to the day, had elapsed since we first started the hunt for him. For two years he abandoned the sea and buried himself in a lumber camp. But the call of the sea was too much for him. He had to get back to a barge.

In a preceding chapter I spoke of the unofficial consulting faculty of experts which the Murder Clinic employed from time to time. Also, when occasion required, the Clinic had an unofficial army of scouts. In the Townsend case they were bargemen, hundreds of them, scattered along the seacoast, canals, rivers, and lakes, with eyes out for the man we wanted.

CHAPTER XV

A HORSESHOER JOINS THE CLINIC

AT FIFTY-SEVEN seconds past noon on September 16, 1920, the financial district in lower New York City was shaken by a tremendous explosion. Thirty-one persons were killed outright; one hundred and twenty-five were injured, some of whom died later. Most of those killed and injured were on their way to or from hasty lunches. The explosion seemed to have been timed for twelve o'clock, just when crowds on the street would be thickest.

As near as could be ascertained a bomb had exploded in Wall Street near Broad directly in front of the United States Assay Office which adjoined the Federal Sub-treasury Building. Across the street was the bank of J. P. Morgan & Company, one of the world's great banking institutions; to the west 205 feet, the Bankers' Trust Company, and to the southwest, 165 feet, the New York Stock Exchange.

The destructive charge thus had been set off in the very heart of the banking district. J. P. Morgan was in Europe at the time. His bank building and the Assay Office suffered the greatest damage. Windows were shattered and granite walls bitten into by myriads of metal missiles hurled in the explosion. The marks of these missiles still are to be seen in the outer walls of the Morgan bank. One Morgan employee was killed.

All available detectives at once were sent to the scene, where later appeared United States secret service operatives, Department of Justice agents, post-office inspectors, private detectives, and explosive experts.

The scene was a shambles when we reached it. It was at once apparent that an outrage was committed which far overshadowed the Haymarket assassinations in Chicago many years back and the I. W. W. killings in Seattle of more recent date. It was wholesale murder.

Dr. Norris was early upon the scene. In the body of a sixteen-year-old victim he found a section of smooth, curved sheet iron, apparently part of a metal jacket which held the explosive.

In the street pavement near the curb in front of the Assay Office was a shallow depression, about two feet in diameter, which looked like the mark which might have been made by the impact of a heavy barrel falling on hot asphalt. It was such a depression as the downward force of dynamite or T. N. T. would have made. A search of the immediate surroundings revealed bits of metal and two handfuls of cylindrical metal objects which might have been packed into a large bomb.

The process of building the picture of what had stood over this spot began. Herman Davis, a nineteen-year-old chauffeur, told us that he was standing beside his employer's motor car in front of No. 40 Wall Street looking west toward the Assay Office when the pavement seemed to give way and he heard a deafening thud. A wagon standing in front of the Assay Office burst into flames and vanished. Davis dived under the motor car to escape the rain of metal, glass and débris which flew in all directions.

A dying victim declared that immediately before the

explosion he saw a rickety old wagon tip over at the curb and go up in flames. A street cleaner said he had been sweeping in front of the Assay Office a few minutes before twelve when an old wagon with one horse rattled up from the west. A voice cried out to him: "Hurry up, beat it, get out of this." He looked up and on the driver's seat saw two poorly dressed, dark-skinned men. They looked like East Side peddlers. Within a few minutes the explosion took place. From the street cleaner's account it was reasoned that the drivers had not wanted to kill a laborer.

Others asserted that shortly before noon they had seen a red wagon carrying flags going east on Wall Street toward a building under construction. They thought it might have been an explosive wagon delivering dynamite to the building.

Dr. Norris reported that yellowish burns had been found on the bodies of victims which were found nearest the explosion. Trinitrotoluol (T. N. T.) burns on the human body are yellow.

All that was left of the wagon were two worn hubs, pieces of a single-horse shaft, a pair of damaged whiffletrees, two bent axles, several spokes, scraps of wagon iron, and torn harness. The horse had been torn apart. Examination of the spokes and the hubs disclosed that the wagon was old, for the spokes had come easily from the hubs. The wagon had long been in disuse and apparently the sun had loosened the spokes. The rear axle was bent downward, indicating that the explosion had occurred in the back of the wagon.

Confusing elements entered the picture at the very start. Theories without end and reason were offered. The statements of eyewitnesses that they had seen a red wagon carrying flags in the vicinity was one confusing factor. The theory that a gang of anarchists had set off the bomb was immediately proposed. Suspicion was at first directed against a group of Mother Earth Anarchists. In 1914 three members of this group had been killed by the premature explosion of a bomb they were making in a flat in Lexington Avenue. It was suggested that the survivors of this gang might have caused this explosion. But the anarchists who were killed were members of a group which had been annoying John D. Rockefeller at his country home in Tarrytown, New York, whereas this explosion, if directed against any particular person or group, was meant for the financial district. The theory that these anarchists were again busy seemed untenable for the simple reason that the disastrous consequences which had come to two of their members likely would deter other members of the group from handling bombs again.

A still more confusing element was the fact that a number of prominent Wall Street men had received warnings a few days before the explosion. One broker had received this letter:

> Greetings. Get out of Wall Street as the gong strikes at 3 o'clock, Wednesday the fifteenth.

It was signed "Ed Fischer." He was found and it was learned that he had been employed by the French Military Commission during and immediately after the war. He was in Canada at the time of the explosion and, moreover, he was mentally deranged.

On Friday, September 17th, Captain Cochran, chief post-office inspector, reported that his men had found a batch of circulars in a mail box at Cedar Street and Broadway, about a block away from the scene of the explosion. They had been dropped in the morning before. The postal authorities calculated that they had been put in the mail box between 11:30 and 11:58 A. M., *probably* while the rickety wagon was turning into Wall Street.

These circulars were printed with rubber type in red ink. They contained this message:

Remember

We Will Not Tolerate Any Longer
Free the political prisoners
or it will be death
for all of you

American Anarchists

Fighters!

Obviously these circulars had a direct bearing upon the crime. They tended to support the conclusion that the diabolical slaughter was the work of direct-action anarchists but of foreign, not American, origin. Several words in the circular were misspelled, and the use of the words "American Anarchists" apparently was intended to divert suspicion from a foreign group. Many groups of anarchists were active, and nearly all of them were engaged in campaigns to liberate men who were in prison for subversive activities in connection with our part in the Great War. To investigate all these groups would be an undertaking of months, with the possibility that in the end nothing would be found to legally fasten the crime upon its perpetrators. And while this work would be going on the criminals would be scurrying to cover.

The two most direct clues were the rubber-typed circulars and remnants of the horse and wagon. In the meantime detectives were sent out to circulate among anarchistic groups to gather such information as these sources might reveal.

The task of tracing the authorship of the American Anarchist circulars came to a blind end. It was apparent that the rubber type was new; the face of the type showed this. Probably the outfit had recently been purchased. A canvass was made of the manufacturers of rubber type, and here it was learned that such an outfit was carried in stock by stationery stores all over the country. It might also have been purchased in other English-speaking countries.

But the wagon and the horse presented possibilities that narrowed the search to New York City. The age of the wagon indicated that it probably had been in the city for a long time. Therefore we set out to build up a minutely accurate picture of the wagon and the horse. The remnants of both were taken to headquarters, and here we subjected them to an intensive study. We had before us the wagon shaft, whiffletrees, a bent axle, hubs, and spokes. We had torn bits of leather harness, the horse's four legs, and part of the jaw bone; also a pair of new shoes on the hind hoofs.

As I have pointed out in the chapter telling how the Murder Clinic was organized, a murder man in New York City has at his call an unofficial faculty of experts in almost every line of endeavor. It had been my aim to build up a wide acquaintance among men, and often women, who were experts in their own lines and upon whose expert opinions I could safely rely. Also I had within reach of my voice some fourteen thousand policemen that had entered the Department from various walks of life who would have, in addition to police experience, an expert knowledge of many trades in which they had been engaged before joining the force. A request for their services, sent through official channels, would bring them into the Homicide Bureau for special or permanent duty.

Accordingly I sent for wagon manufacturers and harness makers who would be willing to help us build up the picture of the wagon and the horse. Explosive experts were already on the job, but so little was left of the bomb that nothing was learned of its size, shape, or contents.

At my request Patrolman Spillane was assigned to the Homicide Bureau. Before coming into the Department

Spillane had been a horseshoer, and a very competent one.

With the aid of the wagon manufacturers we reconstructed the wagon. It was found to have been what is commonly known in the trade as a butter-and-egg wagon of one to one and one-half tons capacity. It was covered and had double tailboards which opened up and down. Its running gear was painted red, which accounted for the picture some witnesses had given of a red wagon. The spokes were black and striped with white. It had patented wheels. Originally it had been built for two horses, but the remnants of the single horse shaft showed that it did not belong to this wagon. The steel couplings were not an exact fit. The condition of the hubs and spokes which were covered with dry stable refuse indicated that the wagon had lain a long while in disuse, perhaps for years in the yard of a stable exposed to deteriorating elements.

Harness experts advised that the pieces of leather they had studied plainly indicated that more than one set of old harness had gone into the making of the outfit worn by the horse.

A newspaper artist rebuilt the wagon and horse in a wash drawing, which was published and broadcast.

Sufficient detail had been supplied up to this point to build quite a definite picture. It was this. Whoever had driven the wagon into Wall Street had gone to careful pains to use a horse and wagon which would be difficult to trace. The use of more than one old set of harness indicated this as did also the old, dilapidated wagon which might have been picked up anywhere in a vacant lot or stable yard. The premeditation with which this was done plainly showed that the crime was not the act of a madman, nor could it have been an accident. Days, if not weeks, had been spent in the creation and execution of the plot. Perhaps more than one mind was in it; indeed the presence of two men on the driver's seat pointed to this.

Publication of the wash drawing of the horse and

wagon brought no one to us who could identify them, nor did a canvass of stables reveal a missing butter-and-egg wagon or a horse.

We built up a picture of the horse from the jaw bone and four legs in our possession. The teeth showed the animal to have been about twenty years old, fifteen and one-half hands high, and a dark bay whose coat recently had been clipped. The shoes on his front hoofs were old and worn; those on the hind hoofs apparently had been put on the day of the explosion, so again evidence of premeditation appeared.

A horseshoer's union brand was stamped into the two hind shoes. Spillane studied them. The stamp told him that the shoes had been made and put on in a shop in a certain union jurisdiction. This territory took in all of New York City and three counties in New Jersey. Again the hunt narrowed down to our immediate vicinity.

Spillane had been abroad with the American army, and his natural interest in his former trade led him to observe the methods of foreign farriers. As in other trades so in horseshoeing; the artisan leaves his individual mark on the thing he makes. Spillane found that the heels of the hind shoes were drawn closer together and were thicker than shoes made by an American-trained horseshoer. He thought that a farrier of foreign training had made the shoes, and with him on this point other experts agreed.

Search for the farrier of foreign training began. The entire territory indicated by the union stamp was fine combed by sections. The hunt was most intensive in districts in the city that were frequented by peddlers with horses and wagons. Wherever the detectives called and showed the hind shoes the remark of the farrier was the same: "Made by a foreigner, probably an Italian." Finally one horseshoer of Italian extraction said that he thought the shoes might have been made by two Italian brothers who had a shop on Elizabeth Street. This man recognized the hammer marks on the heels made by a lighter, smaller-nosed hammer than American farriers use.

The detectives found the shop on Elizabeth Street run by two Italian brothers.

Here it should be explained that a detective of long experience with certain races uses the indirect, undercover approach when dealing with members of these races. The operation of Black Hand and anarchist groups is well known to the men of these races. They fear their vengeance, and not without good cause, as was shown in the Morello-Pupo-Petto murder cases. Death, I have reason to suspect, has more than once been the penalty for an honest man's conscientious effort to help the police in an endeavor to run down criminals in this racial group. Even native-born Americans now have reason to understand how gang power to enforce silence is built up in this, the freest nation in the world.

So, instead of approaching the two brothers openly and indirectly, Detectives Martin, Donohue, and Spillane entered their shop and had a horseshoe made. They took this away and upon comparing it with the hind shoes of the mutilated horse saw the same evidence of one horseshoer's handiwork. The two brothers had learned their trade in Italy.

The elder brother then was approached directly and asked if he recalled shoeing a horse of the description given by the detectives which was attached to a rickety butter-and-egg wagon. The Italian denied that he had. The detectives gave him the date upon which he might have shod such a horse. It was the day of the bomb explosion.

The man's eyes brightened. He shook his head. Oh, no, he hadn't shod such a horse.

They showed him the two hind shoes and asked him if he hadn't made them. He shook his head again.

They showed him the shoe they had made in the shop and indicated where the three shoes were alike. Now, he reluctantly recalled, on the day of the explosion, quite early in the morning, two dark men drove up to his shop in an old covered wagon. One man got down from the driver's seat and, addressing the horseshoer in Italian, arranged to have hind shoes made for the animal. The brother made the shoes and fitted them. The dark, squat man who was dressed like a peddler paid him and jumped back into his seat and drove off. The horseshoer had not observed the men closely. His description of the squat man he had talked with was meager, but what characteristics he had noticed about the man agreed with the also meager description given by the street sweeper who saw the drivers in Wall Street a few minutes before the explosion.

The horseshoer would say little. When his fears were quieted by the detectives, who told him he would be protected, and that neither his statements nor his identity would be made public, his tongue loosened. He said that he had seen the same squat man loitering about certain places in an Italian section of the city. He was certain it was the same man.

The detectives suggested that he accompany them through this section of the city in an effort to point out the man. The horseshoer balked. He was willing to go as far as he felt it was safe to go to aid the law, but he was unwilling to make a target of himself. The news that he was helping police detectives would spread fast.

The horseshoer was brought to my office. For hours I sat with the hard-headed, fearful little man, trying to get him in the frame of mind to do as we wanted him to. I impressed him with the seriousness of the crime; how he could aid the authorities; how we would arrange complete protection for him not only now but in the future. He was the only man who could help us. His part in the search would never be known. I had given orders that nothing be said of this development to the newspapers.

He sat in silence but restless for quite a time. Finally he spoke up and agreed, when all arrangements to protect him were made, to go with the detectives. He was convinced that the newspapers were not aware of his discovery, for nothing was printed about him.

He went home. He was to accompany our men next day to point out the suspect.

I arrived at my office early the next morning, quite certain that we were about to uncover one, if not both, of the men who had driven the wagon into Wall Street. The horseshoer's description of the squat man was definite. There was no "maybe" or "perhaps" or "I guess so" about it.

I picked up a morning newspaper and on its front page read of our discovery of the horseshoer. It was not credited to our department but to another investigating agency not a part of the city and county government. Moreover, the horseshoer's name and address was given and he was to be summoned before a federal grand jury!

An hour later the little horseshoer came rushing into my office. His face was white. He trembled and spoke incoherently. He was in terror of his life. He could not go on with our plan. He was publicly known now. No amount of persuasion or compulsion could change his mind.

And here the hunt for the driver of the wagon abruptly ceased.

I have no means of knowing how the information leaked out. I am certain none of my men passed it on. It was our duty and ours alone to find the murderers, for the prosecution would lie in our jurisdiction where the crimes were committed. Someone had butted in. Unfortunately some officials holding public office are overfond of publicity. They climb on the shoulders of others to get it. The official who gave this important information to the press was such a person. He was not connected with the Police Department. He loved to find his photograph on newspaper front pages.

Whether, if our plan had gone through, we would have found the suspect, and, if we had found him, he would have turned out to be one of the fiends who planted the bombs, I cannot say. The lead the horseshoer had given us, after days and nights of unrelenting toil on the part of our men, looked most promising, but we were robbed of the opportunity to develop it to a finality.

The Wall Street bomb case remains among the Homicide Bureau's pending matters. Some day it may be closed. My opinion is that the explosion was the work of legally sane men with some experience at handling bombs. The care with which the wagon and harness were put together to prevent detection indicates the working of a shrewd mind, probably more than one mind. Moreover, the outfit cost quite a sum which probably was shared by more than one person.

Will the perpetrators ever be found? I can only rely upon experience in answering this. The vagaries of human nature and time play tricks on even the shrewdest conspirators. For years they may go along, the best of friends bound together by the tie of guilt. Then one day they may quarrel. Interested ears will listen, memories will quicken, and tongues will wag. A tip may reach the police. Human nature is that way the world over. Conspiracies of this sort take time to build up and time to uncover.

Or the horseshoer may one day spot the man he was about to find for us and, having in the meantime lived down his fear, "turn him in," as the police saying goes. We went as far as we could with the horseshoes. They offered the only definite, direct clue, but our plan was nipped by a man who was trying to build up a synthetic fame for himself.

CHAPTER XVI

GLAMOROUS BACKGROUND

In this chapter I shall depart from the reminiscent form in which I have been writing and invite the reader to place himself at my side and imagine we were together on the morning of Friday, June 11, 1920. For the time being consider yourself attached to the Homicide Bureau as an unofficial observer looking on at one of New York City's most widely exploited murder mysteries.

It is a little after 10 A. M. An official report informs us that a man is at Bellevue Hospital, dying from a pistol wound. He was found unconscious but breathing in his home at No. 244 West Seventieth Street. The ambulance call was received at the hospital at 8:31 A. M. The supposition is that the man has attempted suicide. It is useless to visit the hospital and talk to him. The surgeons are certain he will expire in a short time.

The wounded man is Joseph Bowne Elwell. The name, particularly if you play bridge or follow horse racing, is instantly recognized as that of a famous sportsman and card expert, the author of many books on bridge and a familiar figure in the social life of the town. As an authority on bridge he is known the world over.

With Inspector John Cray of the Detective Division we proceed at once to the house in West Seventieth Street in a police flyer.

It is a three-story, gray stone building on the south side of the street. Not far to the west is the Hudson River. Just below on the south is San Juan Hill and below that Hell's Kitchen. These are districts which are known to experienced police officers as "busy spots." They are frequented by professional criminals. In earlier days they were the scenes of gang battles.

In the immediate vicinity of the house are scores of boarding places and small apartments, furnished, which are patronized largely by transients. This locality, by reason of the transitory character of many of its inhabitants, is a favorite hunting ground for sneak thieves, burglars, and other types of house breakers.

The Elwell house is of precisely the same pattern as the houses which adjoin it on both sides. Apparently all were built at the same time. We survey the exterior of the building. The window curtains are drawn; the panes are dusty. An iron gate opening into the basement is rusty and fallen apart. It is propped up from the inside by a stick of wood. The occupant of the house, judging by its exterior, may have gone away for the summer, for this is the time of the year when New Yorkers begin their trek to beach and mountain resorts. Down the block are houses whose doors and windows are boarded, indicating that their owners have gone for the season.

In the police-trained mind this suggestion arises instinctively: a professional housebreaker would very likely pick out the house before us as a target for attack, thinking it unoccupied. There is a type of burglar known as an unoccupied houseworker who specializes in this kind of robbery. He is a killer type of thief. What we have seen of the house from the outside may or may not figure in the picture built up on the inside, but it is well to place it in a handy recess in the memory.

We enter three doors. The first are swinging storm doors with large plate-glass centers. The second are heavy solid wooden doors which are thrown open against the vestibule wall. The third and last door is a single door with a panel of leaded glass. It has a snap lock and is shut by an automatic self-closing pressure device.

The house is well but not luxuriously furnished. We walk along a short hallway, which is quite dark, and enter a small reception room on the right. Just as we step into this room, not more than a pace, we see on our right a large, comfortable plush-upholstered chair with curved arm rests—a piece of period furniture. It faces west and stands out from the wall about a foot. In this wall, about a foot above the top of the back of the chair, plaster has been gouged out as though a bullet had struck it. There are spots of blood on the wall and on the chair. Less than an arm's reach from the chair, on its right, is a collapsible card table on which a telephone is standing.

On this table is a misshapen, metal-cased bullet covered with flecks of plaster evidently from the gouge in the wall. From the shape and condition of this bullet it appears to have passed through the head of the occupant of the chair, struck the wall, and bounded back upon the table. There are several pieces of mail on the floor in front of the chair. One letter lies open near its envelope. This and the other mail must have been dropped by the person who had sat in the chair.

The open letter is addressed to Elwell. It is signed by Lloyd Gentry, who has charge of a stable of Elwell's race horses quartered in Covington, Kentucky. It tells of the condition of the horses and the expenses of the week incurred in maintaining the stable. It was mailed in Covington the day before. Another letter which we open is from a private school which the bridge expert's fifteen-year-old son is attending. The remaining five pieces of mail are advertisements.

It is evident from these two letters that Elwell was more deeply interested in his stable of horses than in his son's schooling, for the trainer's letter was the first he opened.

A discharged brass cartridge shell is found upon the carpeted floor to the right some distance from the spot where the sitter's feet touched the floor. This cartridge is of .45 caliber and was made in 1917 for the United States army. The year is stamped upon the rim. It was fired from an army automatic pistol of that caliber.

On the shelf of a mantelpiece set into the westerly wall of the room a few paces from the chair is a vase of flowers, and near this, resting on the edge of the shelf, is the burned stub of a cheap cigarette.

There are two other chairs in the room, a wide, high-backed chair and an ordinary living-room chair, each in a corner of the south wall of the room. A man could conceal himself behind the large chair.

The only window in the room is in the front wall. It is locked and barred by iron gratings on the outside.

We now have the bare picture of the scene of the shoot-in of Elwell, all that the eye can give us up to this moment. It is the usual picture a murder man first encounters on a case. It is being recorded for future use by police photographers who are busy with various cameras getting the room from all angles. No opportunity is offered us to see the body as it sat in the chair. Inasmuch as Elwell was breathing he was rushed to the hospital. Other details, and perhaps very important ones, might have been furnished had we seen the body in the chair, when we could have noted the position of the arms, legs, and head.

A middle-aged woman appears, hatless and frightened. She is Mrs. Marie Larsen, Elwell's housekeeper. She tells us in somewhat disconnected sentences that it was her regular practice to enter the house in the morning, cook breakfast when her employer asked for it, and remain to arrange the house until he left, which usually was around noon. This morning she arrived at the outer door at about 8:10, opened it, picked up a quart bottle of milk standing in the vestibule, and unlocked the inner door with her key. She had this key; Elwell had the other. These were the only two keys to the door. And the lock on this door, she says, was recently changed by Elwell because he was suspicious that watchmen paid to observe the house were not doing so.

Mrs. Larsen closed the inner door, at least she let go of it, and permitted the self-closer to complete the operation. She walked into the living room. She thought she smelled powder smoke in the hall. In the plush-upholstered chair at the card table she saw Elwell sitting, his chin upon his chest, blood flowing from his forehead and breathing heavily. She called to him. No response. She stepped closer. Her employer was in his silk pajamas. The coat was unbuttoned. His feet were bare. His head was bald—a rather strange sight to the woman, for she had never known he was bald. His mouth was open, but no teeth were visible—another strange sight, for Mrs. Larsen had noticed that Elwell had two rows of fine teeth. A gaping wound in his forehead between but slightly above his eyebrows told Mrs. Larsen what had happened. She hurried out and called a policeman. The ambulance arrived shortly and took away the unconscious man.

We are told now that Elwell has just passed away.

Mrs. Larsen continues. She saw no pistol in the room, nor had she ever seen one in the house. The room is searched for a pistol. None is found. We may dismiss the suicide conjecture. Mrs. Larsen has told all that she can remember. Her story will be checked presently.

Dr. Charles Norris, the chief medical examiner, arrives and a few minutes later several assistant district attorneys. Detectives from the Homicide Bureau and precinct station house are on hand. The latter are at once detailed to find the milk man who left the quart bottle of milk in the vestibule, the letter carrier who must have brought the mail found on the floor, and to interview every person living in the block to determine whether anyone was seen entering or leaving the Elwell house and whether a shot was heard. All the tradesmen who might have had delivery wagons in the block are also to be questioned.

Mrs. Larsen is again questioned, this time about Elwell's entourage. It consists, she says, of William H. Barnes, a sort of a confidential business manager for Elwell, and Edward Rhodes, chauffeur. Detectives are dispatched to find and question them and to check up on their movements during the morning. Barnes and Rhodes do not sleep in the house. They had not been in the house during the morning or the night before. Mrs. Larsen lives uptown in her own apartment with her husband.

Elwell's bedroom is on the third floor, two flights up. We inspect the house. In the rear of the first floor is the kitchen and a storeroom which are not connected by door or window with the reception room. The second floor contains a den and card room in the front, a small reception hall and a dining room in the rear. These rooms have not been disturbed. The windows in them are locked and have not been tampered with.

In the front of the third floor is a guest bedchamber. The bed is made up. It had not been slept upon. The window in this room is locked and dust upon its sill indicates it has not been opened in some time. In a closet is found a number of women's garments—lingerie. From one of these garments an embroidered monogram or a manufacturer's label has been cut. This room is connected with Elwell's bedroom in the rear by an open passageway which was once a hall but is now furnished as a bar. Prohibition has been in effect not long. A sideboard contains a small but choice supply of liquors and fine glassware. The bar is handy to both front and rear rooms. There is no indication that it had been used in the last twenty-four hours.

Elwell's bedchamber in the rear contains a double bed

with a canopy over the head. A dark satin spread with lurid stripes covers the bed. One corner of this cover is turned back slightly, but the bedclothes under it have not been slept in. The night before and the early hours of the morning were muggy; the occupant of the bed probably sprawled out on top of the bed. An extension telephone stands upon a small bedside table.

On the floor beside the bed is a copy of the *Morning Telegraph,* a racing newspaper. Its pages are open to the entries for to-day's races at various tracks and tips on horses that will run. Several of Elwell's horses are among them. Piecing together what has been observed up to this point the picture is a little more complete. Elwell probably lay upon the bed in his pajamas with blouse open, reading the racing news. For some reason he arose, probably quite suddenly, for the newspaper was thrown upon the floor. He went downstairs in his bare feet, dressed in his pajamas, without his toupee and false teeth, for both are on a chiffonier in the room.

His dress clothes are hanging upon the back of a chair four or five feet from the foot of his bed. On a small table near by is a whisky flask. On a couch is about four hundred dollars in currency, a watch, pin, and other jewelry valued at seven thousand dollars. Elwell had been out the night before, apparently. Mrs. Larsen has been looking through the house and finds that nothing is missing. If robbery were the motive of the slayer it is evident that the plan miscarried. Yet robbery cannot be dismissed from consideration.

Again I refer to patterns in my mind. They tell me that housebreakers, especially those who rob unoccupied residences, are frequently surprised in the act and kill or wound their discoverers, hurrying from the house without carrying anything away, especially when the weapon they use is a pistol whose report may be heard throughout the house and on the outside. We proceed a little farther with the picture. What probably happened was this: Elwell, with his mind on his race horses and the races that were to be run as shown by the *Morning Telegraph,* learned that the morning mail had arrived. It was customary for him to receive weekly letters or reports from Gentry, his trainer. His mind therefore was on his horses as he lay upon the bed. He threw down the newspaper and went downstairs.

He did not expect to meet anyone, for as already mentioned he was in his pajamas with the blouse open and without his toupee and false teeth. Mrs. Larsen says that on other mornings she had encountered Elwell, but she had never noticed that his teeth or toupee were missing, and he was always attired in a bathrobe with slippers on his feet.

Mrs. Larsen, upon further questioning, says that she saw no one leaving the house when she arrived at 8:10. An intruder could not have entered or left by the basement, for the door in the basement has not been touched in a long while, nor have its windows been tampered with. Of Elwell's mode of life and habits we learn more from the housekeeper. He was separated from his wife, and in this house maintained bachelor quarters. Women frequently visited him. He led a gay but not dissolute life. He knew many women; he sent money to some of them; they called him up frequently or he called them. Mrs. Larsen says that no woman was in the house the day before or this morning when she arrived. She knows of no enemies, of either sex, that her employer might have had.

A list of names is found in an index in Elwell's private desk in the den on the second floor. They are the names, addresses, and telephone numbers of women. This is not strange when we learn that one source of the bridge expert's income was lessons in bridge playing which he had given to many prominent women whom he tutored either in small classes or alone.

Detectives are sent to find these women, obtain their statements, and check them up. The possibility that a woman may have killed him presents itself, but unless she was an expert with pistols she would not have chosen a .45 army automatic, which is a heavy weapon with a hefty kick.

There is much activity in front of the house. The stoop is crowded with young men questioning everyone who enters or leaves the house. They are newspaper reporters gleaning, as fast as they can from whatever sources are available, the details of the murder, Elwell's history, and theories concerning the crime. As I already have stated Elwell was a national figure. His wealth, associations, and the suddenness of his taking off conspire to make a great newspaper story. It will make a greater story than usual because women's names have become involved and the mystery will develop and deepen from day to day, giving each day's news fresh angles.

If Elwell was an ordinary man, unknown, and lived in this same house, there would be no reporters on the stoop. The case would flare and die down the same day. But there is background in this case. The newspapers are building it up. Their business is to present the news, and news may be anything, while our search is for legal proof that a murder *has been* committed and for clues that will lead us to the slayer and then fasten the crime upon him. In this case it will be difficult to do this. Nothing having been stolen from the house, there will be nothing by which to trace the slayer and connect him with the crime by finding Elwell's property in his possession. And no one saw anyone enter or leave the house or heard the shot. You may be sure that the newspapers, supplying a popular demand for news of the tragedy, will stir up suspicions and here and there point to more or less prominent persons—the more prominent the greater will be the "play" given to them. But newspaper readers are not juries, courts, or presecutors. In considering the newspaper background it is well to remind the reader that the greater the prominence of the persons named in the newspapers and the closer their association with Elwell, the less possibility exists that they are involved in the crime.

The body of Elwell is next examined. The wound is between the eyes, just above the nose, as Mrs. Larsen said. About the point of entrance are ingrained particles of smokeless powder. These particles are close together. From this fact we may be certain that the gun was fired at close range or the ingrained powder would have been scattered over a great area, and the imbedded particles would have been wider apart. The slayer probably was not more than three feet away when he fired.

The range of the bullet through the head is slightly upward. Its point of exit in the back of the head is about an inch above the point of entry. From Dr. Norris it is learned that the muzzle of the pistol was held not more and probably less than three feet away from Elwell's face. The narrowness of the little reception room makes it improbable that the murderer could have stood and fired at a greater distance. There are no powder burns about the wound, only the particles of ingrained powder. The pistol was held so near that the bones of the forehead were broken inward by the explosion of powder gases. From the course of the bullet it would now appear that Elwell's head at the moment he was shot was tilted back and he was looking up; or he might have half arisen from the chair in surprise with his head tilted in this position, which would account for the bullet gouge in the wall back of the chair about a foot above the back of the chair. An examination of the bare soles of his feet shows them to be clean. He could not have walked much before he was shot.

The picture grows. We have the approximate position of the slayer and the attitude of Elwell when he was shot.

His assailant might have come from behind the large high-backed chair in the corner and made for the hallway when Elwell looked up from the letter he was reading, saw him, and made a move for him, whereupon the slayer halted and killed him. Elwell was a shrewd man, a card player, a man who had studied moves and strategy most of his life. Moreover, he was robust and quick on his feet. Or the slayer may have recognized Elwell as a man who knew him. The card expert and horse owner was a public figure known to thousands in the sporting world and he knew thousands. Surprise, fear of identification, is a motive which impels the cornered house thief to kill.

The cheap cigarette, whose stub is on the mantelpiece, may have a bearing upon the situation, although there is no evidence that it was the intruder's cigarette. None of the same brand was found in the house and Elwell never smoked them. Its cheapness attests to the possibility that if it were the slayer's he came from a low, perhaps criminal class. But it is hardly likely that the intruder was smoking if he were concealing himself.

The position of the exploded cartridge shell is a little confusing. Since the automatic pistol would have ejected the shell to the right of the slayer it seems strange that it would be lying on the floor to the left of the position which the murderer must have held when he fired. We make a test in the pistol range at headquarters and find that it is quite an easy matter for an ejected cartridge to strike an object like a chandelier and bound back off its normal course. There is such a chandelier in the Elwell reception room which the ejected shell might have hit and been thrown to the left where it was found on the floor. Or in the confusion of finding the wounded man and rushing him to the hospital Mrs. Larsen or the ambulance attendants might have kicked this shell across the floor. At any rate, the shell has served a useful, definite purpose. It has given us the make and caliber of the pistol.

Henry Otter has been found by the detectives. He is the driver of the milk wagon who left the quart of milk in the vestibule where Mrs. Larsen found it. He fixes the time he did this at about 6:15 A. M. He saw no one about the house or activity within. The two outer doors were unlocked, and he put the bottle in its accustomed place. He went on about his deliveries.

Charles G. Torrey is located. He is the letter carrier who brought the mail to the door. At about 7:25 A. M. he walked up the Elwell stoop, found the outer storm door unlocked, which he thought unusual because it was usually locked, entered the vestibule, and dropped the letters on the tiled floor. He pressed the doorbell twice —two short rings. He had been giving this signal for years. People on his route knew this signal. He saw no one near the house or in it and went on making his deliveries.

Mrs. Larsen had already told us that she arrived about 8:10 A. M. and not later than 8:15. We knew that Elwell had the letters dropped by Torrey at about 7:25, that the milk was left at about 6: 15, and that the telephone company's record discloses that the ambulance call was sent in at 8:31. Thus we have a pretty complete picture. Elwell was killed between 7:25 and 8:15 and possibly nearer the latter time, for Mrs. Larsen detected pistol smoke upon entering the hall and Elwell was breathing.

A better picture of Elwell's movements is available. He was lying on his bed upstairs with his mind upon racing and his horses. Two short taps on the bell by Torrey announced that mail had arrived . . . Gentry's letter about the stable. . . . He arose in his pajamas . . . no one was in the house . . . he went downstairs barefooted. He opened the inner door and picked up the mail Torrey had left. He spotted the Gentry letter. He was eager to read it. He may have taken his hand from the doorknob to pick this letter out of the seven. He stepped back into the hall, started to open the envelope and, not looking back to see whether the door closed, left that operation to the self-closer. He stepped into the reception room to read the letter, sat down, and before he had finished the letter was shot. For the letter lay open upon his lap when Mrs. Larsen first saw him.

Now the vital, focal center of mysterious killings of this type enters into the picture. How did the slayer enter the house? There are several possibilities. He may already have been concealed in the reception room behind the big chair, or he may have entered as Elwell turned his back on the door and went into the reception room. The self-closer may not have fully closed the door. The action of self-closers is often slow. Moreover, there are patterns in my mind too numerous to mention where skilled house thieves have stolen into a house past butlers, maids and even owners without being seen.

I can picture another, but perhaps more remote, possibility. There is a type of thief who trails letter carriers. Such a criminal might have followed Torrey, the mail man, up the block—saw him enter the Elwell vestibule with mail in his hand. He may have waited until the postman came out and was busy at another door and stepped into the Elwell vestibule. The letters were gone, but the door had not yet been closed! Elwell had gotten the letters and had gone into the reception room. The thief may have pressed in and suddenly come upon Elwell in his chair. There may have been mutual recognition with killing resorted to to remove the risk of identification by Elwell. This type of professional thief, invariably a killer, is primarily interested in robbing hall letter boxes. He operates in the early morning hours when the bulk of the day's mail is being delivered. If he sees an opportunity to sneak into a house through an open or unlocked door he does so. He is one of the most skilled operators. He makes a special study of screening his entry and exit.

We will turn to the elaborate system of robbery records kept at police headquarters. In these we find that in the winter of the year before three thieves entered the Elwell home via the basement. The card expert was in Palm Beach, Florida, at the time. His home was closed. A neighbor saw the thieves enter, notified the police, and detectives caught the intruders. Two were hiding behind the chairs in the reception room—the same chairs that are now in the room. The third man was crouched behind a door. They had loot, but dropped it when they heard the detectives enter. The three had come up out of the San Juan Hill section just south of the Elwell house.

But this trio are now in prison, have been there for almost a year. They are eliminated as suspects, but their attempted robbery furnishes a pattern. It supports the conclusion that the Elwell house would be, indeed has been, picked as a target, and that the thieves were found in the same reception room, about to leave the house with their loot. Moreover, they had entered the place shortly after 7 A. M. The trio were men who made a specialty of entering unoccupied houses. They didn't kill when cornered because they were confronted by detectives with guns drawn.

As yet we know nothing of Elwell's movements the night before his death. Mrs. Larsen, Barnes, the confidential business manager, and Rhodes, the chauffeur, know nothing of their employer's social affairs. Their statements have been taken, their movements checked. Mrs. Larsen's husband has been seen. Only the woman has relevant information which she already has given. But in Elwell's bedroom his dress clothes were found on the back of the chair.

The bell of the telephone on the table in the reception room rings.

"Get that call!" A detective steps to the telephone.

"Yes, this is Mr. Elwell's home," says the detective.

"Who is calling him?" The detective jots down the name and address of Walter Lewisohn, who is the speaker at the other end of the telephone. He is a member of one of New York City's most prominent and wealthy families. He advises the detective that Elwell had an engagement with him to go motoring with Mr. and Mrs. Lewisohn and friends at 1 P. M. to-day. It is past that time. They have not heard from Elwell. They were out with him the night before and at that time to-day's engagement was agreed upon.

The detective states that Elwell cannot be seen. The telephone receiver is replaced upon its hook. And that detective hurries to talk with Mr. Lewisohn.

An intensive search of Elwell's effects takes place. Letters, notes, memoranda, scribblings, are found. Some of the letters are from women, some friendly, others importuning the card expert for funds, while others speak of bridge, parties, horses, money, and social affairs. One letter in girlish handwriting, and of old date, speaks of the writer's approaching trouble and seeks Elwell's help. It was written in Kentucky and is signed "Annie." A detective is sent to find Annie and interview her.

The glamorous background which is built up by newspapers in all cases where the persons involved are prominent unrolls like a lurid panorama. The bare facts surrounding the killing have dropped into the distance. Now there are names, hints, gossip, women friends, blackmailers, jealous lovers and angry husbands, enemies, racetrack plots. A score of motives are intimated. In it all there is not one legal clue which would justify police action, nothing that would stand up before the tests applied to evidence.

The detective returns with Mr. and Mrs. Lewisohn. They are greatly upset. Elwell was a close friend. They had dined with him on the evening of June 10th in the main dining room of the fashionable Ritz-Carlton Hotel.

A fourth member of the party was Viola Kraus, the attractive sister of Mrs. Lewisohn. Elwell had been in high spirits. Just as the party was about to enter the dining room at 7:30 P. M. they encountered Victor von Schlegell and a young woman, Emily Hope Anderson, a singer from Minneapolis attending voice school in New York City. The two are said to be engaged.

Von Schlegell is well known to the Lewisohn party, for earlier that very day Viola Kraus was divorced from him and was already using her maiden name. Miss Kraus was Elwell's dinner partner. Pleasantries were exchanged between the former husband and wife and Elwell. The Lewisohns and their guests enter the dining room; Von Schlegell and his fiancée go elsewhere. The newspapers are saying that Von Schlegell was cool toward Elwell; the facts are that they were on the best of terms, and, moreover, the divorce was welcomed by Von Schlegell, for it will make possible his marriage to Miss Anderson. Elwell is not divorced from his wife. He is ineligible thereforce to wed Miss Kraus. The divorce offers no motive for the killing of Elwell.

About 9 P. M. in the roof garden of the New Amsterdam Theatre the Lewisohns and their guests again encountered Von Schlegell and Miss Anderson. Here a young South American, Octavia Figueroa, joined the Lewisohn party. Von Schlegell, sitting with Miss Anderson at a table two rows away from his former wife, laughed and remarked to his companion how odd that he should again so soon meet his former wife. He smiled repeatedly at Miss Kraus and at Elwell.

At 2 A. M. the Lewisohns and their guests left the roof garden, descended in the elevator, and reaching the sidewalk hailed a taxicab. All save Elwell got into it. He said something in an undertone about it being too crowded. The taxicab departed. Elwell started west toward Eighth Avenue. This would be the direction he would take to get a taxicab, for Eighth Avenue was not as crowded as other thoroughfares and it would be a direct route to his home.

Detectives are detailed to find a taxicab which might have taken him home.

The taxicab which took the Lewisohns and Miss Kraus to the home of the former and dropped Figueroa at his apartment is found. The driver's story agrees with that told by the Lewisohns and Miss Kraus. They made no stops except at the Figueroa apartment.

Miss Kraus is interviewed. She can throw no light upon the murder. She was well acquainted with Elwell. At the time he was slain she was in her bedchamber in the Lewisohn home, asleep. Shortly after coming from the roof garden she called Elwell on the telephone. She was wondering whether he was put out by not having ridden home with her in the Lewisohn machine. He was not in the least upset, he told her.

Von Schlegell and Miss Anderson were interviewed at great length. Miss Anderson knew Elwell. Von Schlegell not only knew him but admired the man. Both establish irrefutable proof that they were not near the Elwell home.

The taxicab driver who took Elwell home is found. He drives us over the route he took, up Eighth Avenue as I had reasoned Elwell would go. Ten blocks south of his home the card expert directed the driver to stop. He bought the *Morning Telegraph* at a corner newsstand. The taxi went on. At 2:30 A. M. Elwell got out in front of his home, paid his fare, tipped the driver, then entered his home, alone. No one was following or watching Elwell as far as the driver could see. The driver's whereabouts from the time Elwell got out of his car until long after the body was found are established by verbal and documentary evidence.

We turn for a moment to see what has happened in the newspaper background. They are still suggesting various motives and hinting that a disgruntled race-track follower slew him. Elwell's racing stable partner is brought into the picture, but that angle already has been investigated by our men and it offers no solution.

A lurid touch is added by the naming in the newspapers of the Countess Sonia Szinswaska, a Polish noblewoman, and Princess Hassan el Hammel. Both are friends of Elwell. There is gossip that the countess's husband once had threatened Elwell's life. A still more lurid touch is the gossip that Elwell, during the war, was a voluntary spy hunter and in this capacity made unfavorable reports to the government about the countess's war opinions. The countess and the princess, the former's husband, their friends, all are interviewed, and this phase, delectable reading from a newspaper standpoint, fades into nothingness. The two women establish unshatterable alibis.

So we have only one definite picture of Elwell's movements from 7:30 P.M., the night before his death, to the next morning at about 8:10 or 8:15, when Mrs. Larsen found him in the chair. And we have the other picture, the colorful, interesting background built up by the newspapers—possibilities, suggestive situations, suspicions, gossip, and rumors which are always possible to find or to be suggested in the life of almost any active, prominent man. We have, too, that interesting gentleman, the anonymous crime analyst, who wonders why we haven't worked the case like the Paris Sûreté would have worked it. He does not appear in person, however, but it is apparent that he would have relished the arrest of anyone or all of the figures who have been mentioned in the case.

One more figure appears in the background. It is that of Helen Derby Elwell, wife of the slain man. She informs us that about three weeks before his death Elwell had asked her to divorce him and she had agreed to visit Reno, Nevada, for this purpose. She was already legally separated from him, receiving alimony which he never failed to remit, and she was charged by the court with the custody of her fifteen-year-old son. She is bitter against Elwell. She had helped him write his first book on bridge, which brought him a small fortune and started him on his way to fame. But he sought the company of other women. Mrs. Elwell's movements on the morning of the murder are carefully checked. It was impossible for her to have been anywhere near the house at the time of the shooting.

Annie, writer of the note appealing to Elwell for help and hinting at trouble she anticipated, is found in Kentucky living with her parents. Elwell had met the girl and her father while he was in Kentucky looking over his stable. The girl knew him to be a man of wealth and appealed to him for funds. Neither she nor her father had been in or near New York in months. Scores of others known to Elwell, scattered from Palm Beach to Canada, have been seen and absolved. The elaborate background in the newspapers slowly dissolves. After a careful sifting the bare picture, built up at the scene of the murder, remains.

In as concise a form as it is possible to tell the story I have given the details of the Elwell mystery. No clue has been found to this day to establish the identity of the killer or to supply motive for the act.

I have a conclusion drawn from the facts, but before stating it I might add one fact not hitherto related. During the course of my investigation I learned that a maid, Miss Kane, who had worked for Elwell some time before his death, had spoken to a friend about having seen a young man dressed in a soldier's olive drab uniform talking to the card expert sometime before he was slain. The soldier's clothes were unkempt and wrinkled as though he had slept in them. His hair was disheveled. Others who knew Elwell had seen the same man talking to him.

In the meantime Miss Kane had left the employ of Elwell and went back to Ireland. We asked the Irish police to find and interview her for us. Miss Kane told them that the man in the soldier's uniform lived in New York City and gave us the name of the street where he was supposed to reside. This street was searched from end to end for a trace of the man, but the inquiry was fruitless.

The information she gave to the Irish officers was meager. She was reluctant to talk freely. I hoped that she would return to the United States before I left the Homicide Bureau, but she did not do so. Only her incomplete story was in my possession.

This man suggests interesting possibilities. The pistol which killed Elwell was, as will be recalled, an army automatic and the discharged shell found on the floor was army ammunition. This man may know something.

My conclusion, or opinion, as to who killed Elwell will be found at the head of a subsequent chapter, "The Man with Five Hundred Names." In that chapter I offer the reader a master pattern which explains much that is missing in the Elwell picture and also missing in the two cases which follow this chapter.

I call it a master pattern because the killer in the case was found and convicted. On the mooted issue of how Elwell's slayer entered and left his home this master pattern throws much light. It is about as complete a pattern as the murder man ever gets.

CHAPTER XVII

MAGNETIC BUTTERFLIES

IN THE same pattern with the Elwell case belong the murders of Dorothy King and Louise Lawson. To be sure, they were young women, and they were not shot to death. In these respects they differed from the Elwell slaying, but their youth, good looks, and the sudden exposure of their amours which involved prominent figures furnished glamorous backgrounds. And the focal point around which the mystery of their killing revolved, the means of entrance and exit employed by their slayers, parallels the mystifying elements in the Elwell case.

They were also Broadway figures, which always furnishes a gilded frame for murders in the big city.

Dorothy King was found dead on a bed in her studio apartment on the top floor of a five-story building at No. 144 West Fifty-seventh Street at 11:30 o'clock on the morning of Thursday, March 15, 1923. A colored maid, known as Billy, found the body and reported it to a policeman on post. An ambulance attendant who came to take the body away saw burns about the mouth of the young woman, and an empty bottle on the bed, and concluded it was a case of suicide by poison.

It was not until a medical examiner, many hours later, expressed the opinion to me that "it did not look right," that I went to the apartment and began to piece together the picture. It was plainly murder. The apartment consisted of a living room, bedroom and bath, and a cubbyhole kitchen with a window opening on a court.

The usual search for fingerprint patterns was made, but revealed nothing from which the experts could work. Police photographs were made of the room. At the foot of the bed was an empty bottle which had contained chloroform and pieces of absorbent cotton. Near the bottle was a vest pocket comb such as a man might carry and which apparently had fallen out of the pocket of a man as he leaned over the bed to apply the chloroform. In a rack in the entrance hall was an umbrella of the size usually carried by a man. A shred of cotton like that found on the bed was caught upon the folds of the umbrella.

A pair of man's pajamas was tucked under a couch in the living room. They were yellow silk and of large size. They had been hurriedly stuffed under the couch. Two medium-priced cloth coats belonging to the dead woman were found on the floor near the door of the living room which opened into the outer hallway. There was a Yale lock on this door. It had not been tampered with, nor were there signs that the door had been forced. There were windows in each room. The one in the bedroom was opened from the bottom. The thief might have entered through this, the door, or might possibly have been admitted by the young woman.

The motive for the murder clearly was robbery.

The face of the victim was burned about the mouth by chloroform and there was a slight abrasion inside her lower lip, while the rumpled condition of the bed indicated that the young woman had struggled with her assailant.

From the maid, Billy, a clearer picture of what probably had happened was obtained. Billy had arrived in the apartment at 11:30 A. M., admitting herself with a key. The two cloth coats lying on the floor first alarmed her. She walked through the living room into the bed-chamber and found the body. It lay on its right side, Miss King's head half buried under a pillow. Her left arm was twisted under her body and her right hand hung over the edge of the bed. The maid had touched the young woman's bare feet. They were cold but the bosom was warm, which gave the approximate time of death, which we fixed at between 7 and 7:30 A. M.

The maid next observed that the telephone, which always stood upon the table at the head of the bed, was upon the floor in the adjoining living room, but still connected. This indicated the probability that the murder was the act of a professional thief who had administered the chloroform to render the victim insensible and not to murder her. Had the intent been to murder it is improbable that the telephone would have been touched. The use of chloroform and the displacement of the telephone were circumstances pointing to the fact that the thief or thieves anticipated that the woman might regain her consciousness. It is reasonable to assume that he or they were strangers to her; otherwise they would not have risked the possibility of her recovering and thus revealing their identities.

A patent-leather suitcase was missing, the maid reported. Jewelry valued at fifteen thousand dollars, money, and wearing apparel also were gone. A light summer ermine fur coat and an expensive wrap were missing. The two cloth coats on the floor were the cheapest garments Miss King had in her wardrobe. From this it was reasoned that a professional thief, of the type known as a "flat worker," had committed the crime. He had been careful to select the most expensive coats and leave the cheaper coats behind, a trick in taste which is common to an experienced flat worker. Many criminals of this type are colored and run strongly to the theft of clothing, which after a crime is frequently found adorning their women friends. Moreover, the position of the cloth coats on the floor showed that the thief had intended taking them, too, but found the suitcase too small to accommodate them.

Two moves were made as a result of this reasoning. A thorough investigation among the friends and acquaintances of Billy was started, but she was soon cleared of even an unwitting part in the affair. Also every drug store in the city eventually was visited in a search for the place where the bottle of chloroform had been purchased, but no trace was ever found.

One other article was missing. I purposely have avoided naming or describing it in the interest of public policy. It is the one clue that may lead eventually to the slayer or slayers.

The maid spoke of many letters that Miss King had received from male admirers. Billy produced a packet of them. They were couched in affectionate terms and signed by a masculine hand. They were all of an amorous nature. One, which I quote in part, will serve as an index to all the others:

DARLING DOTTIE:

Only two days before I will be in your arms. I want to see you, O so much! and to kiss your pretty pink toes . . .

The handwriting, I might add, had about it a slight waver, but yet was done slowly and meticulously as if by an older person of some dignity.

The yellow silk pajamas found stuffed under the couch came in for further consideration at this point. I was about to examine the maid about them when a rather pompous woman entered the apartment. I questioned her. She was the mother of the dead woman. She was highly incensed and spoke in angry gusts about a man named Guimares. She said she hated him because he had been cruel to her daughter. His first name was Albert and he was a frequenter, she said, of night clubs.

Detectives were immediately detailed to find Guimares and take him to headquarters.

I resumed questioning the colored maid. She declared that the pajamas were not those of Guimares, whom she knew, but had been left in the room by her mistress's rich friend, a Mr. Marshall, of Boston. Mrs. Keenan, the mother of Dorothy, spoke up at this point and said that a friend of Mr. Marshall had called up at noon and was shocked to learn that Dorothy was dead. When the mother went on to supply the man with details he hung up the telephone receiver.

Billy was evasive about the pajamas. Finally she admitted that she had stuffed them under the couch when she had entered the apartment that morning because she had not wanted the police to see them. Mr. Marshall, she added, was "such a nice man." She was under the impression that Marshall must have been in the apartment the night before.

The letters found in the apartment, the maid said, were from Marshall while he was in Palm Beach, Florida. A few days after the last "Darling Dottie" letter arrived Marshall 'phoned the apartment from New York City and said he would be up to have luncheon with Miss King. He arrived with a Mr. Wilson, whom the maid described as Marshall's secretary, about noon on Wednesday, March 14. The two men dined with Miss King and Wilson left. Marshall also departed an hour or so later, promising Miss King that he would return at 7:30 P. M. and take her to dinner.

Marshall, the maid said, had not been gone long when Miss King called Guimares on the telephone and told him of jewels and money her luncheon caller had brought her. Apparently, the maid declared, Miss King quarreled with Guimares, for her voice rose as she spoke, and when she hung up she was in tears.

Marshall and Wilson returned at 7:30. A few minutes later they left with Miss King. They were taken to the street floor in an elevator by the colored hallboy and elevator operator, John Thomas. About midnight, Thomas said, the three returned to the apartment, and later he took Wilson down. He denied that he had taken Marshall down, but finally, under extended questioning, he admitted that at 2:30 A. M. on Thursday morning, March 15th, he had taken Marshall down in the elevator and that he had given him a two-dollar tip.

This placed Marshall in the King apartment about five hours before the young woman was slain. Both the elevator man and Billy described Marshall as a man of middle age, tall, dignified and white haired.

Detectives were detailed to find Marshall.

While this search was on Guimares was brought in. He proved to be a young Porto Rican who had met Miss King in a night club about a year before and she had become enamored of him. He admitted that he had once been indicted for dealing in worthless stocks and bonds, but before the indictment had been returned had fled. He was apprehended in another state, but was successful with extradition proceedings and was admitted to bail. Miss King had furnished the bail.

He admitted his relations with the young woman and that she had showered gifts of money, jewels, and clothes upon him. He had opened a brokerage office with funds given to him by Miss King. In his cuffs at the time I talked with him were a pair of diamond links which he admitted Marshall had given to Miss King. It was established, however, that this gift to Guimares was made long before the young woman's death. He had no knowledge of the murder and no suspicions. On the evening before Miss

King's death he had dined at a popular café with two young men who were members of prominent New York families. After dinner he had made a tour of night clubs. At 2:30 A. M. he reached his hotel. He called Miss King on the telephone but got no response. He went to bed. Breakfast was served at about 7:30 or 8 in his room. His whereabouts at the time of the murder were clearly established.

While examining him, however, it was observed that there were several bruises on his right hand. He said he had been scratched in a fight in one of the night clubs the night before, but had only a dim recollection of the incident, as he had been drinking. This part of his story was checked and found to be accurate.

A gun was found in his room and he was held on a charge of violating the pistol-carrying law. While he was incarcerated a thorough investigation of his movements was made, and it was found that he could not have been in the King apartment immediately before, during, or after the murder.

The ingredients for a sensational newspaper mystery had been mixed. The connection of the mysterious Mr. Marshall with the case, our difficulties in locating him, his suspected prominence, supplied the elements that haul a killing from back to front pages. Guimares supplied that other element which builds mysteries, the protagonist whost past and current difficulties gave the newspaper accounts a second figure to manipulate and around which to build absorbing conjectures. He was a night-club hanger-on; the lover of the dead woman; he had been in trouble and he owned a revolver. He was referred to as a blackmailer, yet there was no basis for this. A tag was found for Marshall. Newspapers referred to him as Miss King's "heavy sugar daddy," and this expression, now much in use, was invented to describe old gentlemen who supplied prepossessing young women with much money or "heavy sugar." Again, as in the Elwell case, an elaborate background was built up. The young woman's past was revealed in infinite detail. Public interest switched from Guimares, the less prominent figure, to Marshall, the unfound figure. The girl's life possessed possibilities for much imaginative writing. She had cut a wide swath in the night life, boasting of her rich protector and displaying her jewels, clothes, and finery before the eyes of café habitués, among whom there are always professional thieves on the lookout for women of her type—young, indiscreet women known to possess loot attractive to thieves and to be under the protection of rich men.

Backgrounds such as these are sometimes useful to the murder man. They may not offer legal evidence upon which he can act, but they often point to the incentive which thieves look for, a situation into which they can project themselves, knowing that suspicion will point instantly away from them and at the figures of others involved clandestinely with their victims.

Dorothy King had been born in poor circumstances. She was the youngest of four children and had been christened Anna Marie Keenan. At eighteen she had developed into a good-looking girl with blue eyes and golden hair. In 1912 she married a chauffeur. They were divorced ten years later, and Anna went to work as a model in a fashionable shop and became known as Dorothy King. She was not averse to being entertained by men. She became the intimate of night-club owners and patrons.

She met Marshall and presently began to appear in expensive clothes and jewels. She left the small hotel in which she had been living and established herself in the little studio apartment where she was found dead.

In the vernacular of glib Broadway she had "made the grade." Here, where success is measured by standards other than would prevail on Main Street, her poor start in life was forgotten in the more glamorous setting which Broadway furnished. A wild story was put into circulation that her protector had attempted to gain possession of his amorous letters, but the letters had been found intact in her possession.

The name of Draper Daugherty, son of a former United States Attorney General, appeared in newspaper accounts. He was spoken of as one of the dead woman's intimate friends. In the war young Daugherty had been a major. He had been in army camps in this country and abroad, and out of this service came the gossip that he had had more than one opportunity to lay his hands on a supply of chloroform! He might have taken it from army medical supplies!

An old chloroform bottle had been found on Miss King's bed. She had been killed by an anæsthetic! But when we checked up on army medical matters it was found that the government received all of its chloroform in tins, not bottles, and so young Daugherty was quickly dropped from the intriguing background.

Our search for Marshall was going on. Suddenly an assistant district attorney was advised by a prominent lawyer that his client, John Marshall, desired to lay his version of the King case before the prosecutor and police. He appeared in the prosecutor's office and I questioned him at length.

He admitted that Marshall was not his right name. I do not propose to give his right name and have these memoirs make a permanent record of an indiscretion which his children and grandchildren may have pointed out to them. He is a man of distinguished family and prominence in the social and business world. For several uncomfortable hours he sat and revealed his relations with Dorothy King. He admitted many facts about that relationship—the letters, the gifts, and other matters. He even volunteered facts that both Billy the maid and the elevator man had concealed to protect him.

I was convinced then, and am now, that he had no more to do with the slaying of Dorothy King than I had. His story was checked, his movements traced, and even an attempt was made to blackmail him as a result of his connection with the affair. Some newspapers were not very kind to us and to the assistant district attorney because we had refused to violate the condition that we had agreed upon with him—that his voluntary visit and the details of his story be not given out to the public unless we decided that he was involved in the killing. It is quite easy to understand this newspaper attitude. We had eliminated the most glamorous figure in the picture!

Guimares was turned loose upon the pistol-carrying charge, but later was tried and convicted in the federal courts for swindling and was sent to a penitentiary and later paroled.

No two murders are, or can be, alike in all their details, but a most striking similarity exists between the King case and the murder of Louise Lawson. This likeness is not strange to a man who has become accustomed to sorting his cases into patterns. Among these patterns are other forgotten Dorothy Kings and Louise Lawsons who were a little less and sometimes a little more glamorous.

Miss Lawson was an attractive music student of twenty-five. On the morning of February 8, 1924, little less than a year after the King tragedy, her body was discovered also by a colored maid in her small studio apartment at No. 22 West Seventy-seventh Street, about twenty blocks north of the King apartment.

She had been slain between 7 and 9 A. M. The body was found face down on a mahogany bed. Her feet and hands were bound with strips of gray silk stockings and toweling. Over her mouth were bands of adhesive tape, and a towel covered her face.

American Beauty roses, taken from a large basket, were scattered over the floor and had been stepped upon. A pet wire-haired fox terrier was tied to a chair. The hand loop of his leash had been slipped over her foot.

Miss Lawson, like Miss King, had known many men. Letters from them were found in the apartment together with photographs of various admirers. A record was found among her papers showing that she had about twelve thousand to her credit in a Wall Street brokerage firm. A member of this firm, who was prominent in social and club circles, admitted having taken a deep interest in the young woman, although he was married, and from time to time had supplied her with funds, jewelry, and clothing. The jewels and money were missing from the apartment.

Ostensibly Miss Lawson was a student of the piano. She had come to New York several years before from Walnut Springs, Texas, had worked a short time in motion pictures, but gave up this work and became a conspicuous figure in the night life. She made lavish display of her jewels wherever she went. Among these were a diamond platinum wrist watch and a two-and-a-half-carat diamond ring—the gifts of an admirer. These were gone from her jewel box. An ermine cape was missing. A small assortment of liquors was found in the apartment, and from the maid it was learned that she drank. Men friends sent her liquor.

Along Broadway the young woman was well known. She was described as "a perfect blaze of jewels" and she took pains to see that they could be seen and admired.

The medical examiner determined that Miss Lawson had died from suffocation, and that the position of her arms, which were tied at her back, and of the bed indicated that she had been overcome by a man, or men, of powerful build. No anæsthetic was used.

Lillian Harvey, the colored maid, said she had found

the body at 10 A. M. A Miss Peggy Tompkins, who occupied the adjoining apartment, said that at 8:30 A. M. she heard the Lawson apartment bell ring and the voice of Miss Lawson sounded, inquiring "Who's there?" A man's voice replied: "A couple of expressmen with a package for you." Miss Lawson said she was not dressed and asked the man to wait. A few minutes later the door opened, and Miss Tompkins heard no more.

The body was found clad in a blue silk nightgown over which was thrown a pink silk kimono, thus supporting the story told by Miss Tompkins. The kimono clearly indicated that Miss Lawson had thrown it over her night attire to open the door.

The apartment-house elevator operator told of taking two men to the apartment at about 8:30. One carried a package in brown paper. The elevator operator had refused to take them up without first telling him what apartment they intended to visit. He let them out on the fifth and top floor and he saw the men walk toward Apartment 56, which was occupied by Miss Lawson.

About twenty minutes later the elevator bell rang and the operator ascended in the lift to the fifth floor. One of the two men he had previously carried up entered the elevator and, on the way down, remarked that Miss Lawson wanted Scotch, not rye, and added: "You never can tell what they want." The inference to be drawn from this remark, dropped as a screen, was that the two men were bootleggers. They knew something of Miss Lawson's habits, for she often received packages of liquor from callers. The man lighted a cigarette, took only two puffs, and threw it away, indicating, if anything, that he was under a nervous strain.

The second man did not come down in the lift, nor did the elevator operator see him leave the house. It would have been possible for him to walk down the stairs while his companion was descending in the lift and in this way carry the ermine wrap without being observed, which probably is what happened.

Two weeks before a burglary was committed in an apartment on the floor above Miss Lawson's and a month before two men, representing themselves as expressmen, had called at her apartment between 8 and 9 A. M. They rang the bell. Miss Lawson answered without opening the door, and when her callers announced that they had "a case for her" she told them she was not expecting a package and the men left. The elevator men had not seen these two callers.

Newspapers played up Miss Lawson's relations with men, particularly with the well-to-do married broker. The background thus created was not unlike that in the King case. There were men friends, jewels, letters, night life, and amours. But the knowledge that two strange men, unidentified and probably thieves, had called at her apartment, and the previous attempt to enter her apartment, robbed the case of the elements that were mystifying in the King case. A few days of exploitation by the newspapers, and the case dropped into the limbo of unsolved crimes.

As in the King case, no trace was ever found of Miss Lawson's stolen property, nor identification made of her slayers, so we were up against a stone wall.

Miss Lawson was another magnetic butterfly, "a perfect blaze of jewels," an attraction for men, including professional thieves, who had ample opportunity to appraise her as a possible victim for robbery and to learn something of her habits and the fact that she was living a protected existence. It is probable that her slayers reasoned that if they robbed her after gagging her and she recovered consciousness she would scarcely report the matter to the police, knowing that to do so would reveal the source of her income and the names of her admirers.

It is not my purpose to indulge in censorious criticism

of newspaper treatment of murder cases. But this much is apparent: In cases like the King and Lawson murders they are manifestly unfair to the police, for they arouse among the public wrongly directed suspicions, and when the police fail to apprehend rich, prominent men as the slayers public opinion unjustly suspects that the police have failed.

But now and again a thief of the killing type is found and the murder man finds himself in possession of a master pattern which guides him in analyzing the mysterious elements in cases like the Elwell, King, and Lawson murders, although it does not always aid him in the apprehension of the slayer.

Such a master pattern is discussed in the next chapter, *sans* glamorous background, because there wasn't any to build up.

CHAPTER XVIII

THE MAN WITH FIVE HUNDRED NAMES

THE slayer of Elwell, in my opinion, was an invader, most likely a type of thief known as an unoccupied houseworker or possibly a letter thief.

Dorothy King probably was slain by a professional thief or thieves, possibly by a gigolo type of thief. The crude manner in which the chloroform was administered is typical of thieves.

There is little doubt that Louise Lawson was slain by one or both of the men who entered her apartment, and in this case the manner of their entrance and exit was established.

These conclusions have not been arrived at arbitrarily. They have been built up by the pattern process in almost the same manner that a physician arrives at a diagnosis of a patient's illness by the use of cases precedent; or as a lawyer prepares his case, or a judge his decision, by following precedents in case books.

With these conclusions there may be disagreement. There are those who will say that I have elected to dispose of the three mysteries in the easiest way, or at least in a way calculated to place our inability to apprehend the slayers in a most favorable light. With this critical attitude I have no quarrel. My conclusions, as I have stated, are based on patterns gathered in a lifetime of murder inquiry, which may not have been the lot of those who take issue with me.

Many pictures of crimes form these patterns. One picture in particular seemed to fit all three murders quite precisely, and this picture has the advantage of being new and therefore very clear as to every detail. It is the case of "The Man with Five Hundred Names." In a sense it is quite a perfect pattern, for he was caught; he talked and was convicted, thus affording the opportunity to subject all phases of the crime to clinical study.

On the morning of December 29, 1927, a woman living in an apartment at No. 617 West One Hundred and Ninetieth Street observed that the hall door of an apartment on the same floor was ajar. She knocked and receiving no response called out, and again receiving no response summoned the janitor and entered the apartment.

On the floor of the bathroom she came upon the body of Mrs. Emeline Harrington, the tenant of the apartment, an actress, about thirty-nine years of age. Her attire was a nightgown over which a kimono was worn. Her legs were bare. She had been dead some days. The police were notified, and through regular channels the Homicide Bureau was set in motion. With the investigating officers I visited the apartment.

Mrs. Harrington's forehead bore a number of wounds, the shape of which convinced me that she had been beaten by an instrument with a small, round head. The body lay between the bathtub and the wall. The door was open. There were no blood marks on the door, but behind it hung a pair of stockings spattered with blood, indicating that the woman had been beaten while the door was closed. A broken bottle, which had fallen to the floor from a wall rack, pointed to a struggle. The condition of the body showed that death had occurred at least five days before. The woman's attire indicated that she had been killed either in the morning or at night, since she was dishabille. The position of the bloodstained stockings, hanging about five feet six inches above the floor, led to the conclusion that her assailant was about that height and was standing when he attacked her.

An inspection of the apartment supplied motive. A table drawer was open. It had been emptied. Articles on top of a dresser were disarranged. A thief had been in the apartment.

The woman who had found the body furnished vital details. She said that on the morning of December 23rd at about 10 A. M. she had heard a scream in Mrs. Harrington's apartment and, neighbor-like, had gone to the door of the actress's apartment. She rang the bell but got no response and, hearing no further sounds, concluded that Mrs. Harrington might have made the outcry when frightened by some slight mishap. She returned to her apartment and a few minutes later heard footsteps in the Harrington apartment and decided that all was well.

Tenants of the house spoke of the actress's husband, but he had not been seen in the house for weeks. A search for him was begun.

The wife and the daughter of a former superintendent of the apartment house, having the natural curiosity that all women have about the apparel of another, described a caracul coat, several expensive rings, a wrist watch, and other jewelry they had seen on Mrs. Harrington. These articles were missing from the apartment, as well as things to be found in every household, bills for gas and electricity and keys.

The robbery, therefore, had been consummated.

Thus the pattern up to this point is almost precisely the same as was presented in the King and Lawson murders and differed from the Elwell case in two particulars, a pistol having been the weapon in that case and the robbery had not been completed.

How did the slayer enter?

The windows and doors disclosed no marks of having been tampered with. The door was ajar, indicating that the murderer had left by this means and had either neglected to pull the door shut or had pulled it to, but it had failed to latch.

From the owner of the apartment house it was learned that on December 22nd Mrs. Harrington had spoken to him of a man who had inspected her apartment with the idea of subleasing it, furnished. Mrs. Harrington was planning to leave the city over the Christmas holidays to visit friends in Detroit and relatives in Joplin, Missouri. The prospective tenant had first called in answer to a newspaper classified ad. which Mrs. Harrington had inserted. Since the owner had insisted upon knowing something of prospective subtenants Mrs. Harrington had told him that the man who had called apparently was responsible, for he had shown her what she described as a city pay check. The man was coming the next morning to sign a sublease and take the apartment.

Other tenants in the house asserted that Mrs. Harrington was careful about admitting visitors. Usually when the doorbell rang she called out "Who's there?" without opening the door unless the person calling was known to her.

The dead woman's husband had been located in a city distant from New York, where he had been for several weeks. He, too, was on the stage and was not, in fact, her husband. The couple had been divorced but the final decree had not yet been handed down.

Newspapers made front-page stories of the murder up to the time when the woman's former husband appeared. When it became apparent that he had no knowledge of the tragedy the developments from day to day were relegated to back pages and to diminishing space. There was little glamor to the dead woman's life. She had been quite well known on the stage in younger years, but more recently had been accepting engagements in out-of-town stock companies. She had a few jewels, was good looking and attracted admiration, but she was not a magnetic butterfly and there were no amours with rich protectors. In these respects, of course, the case differed from the Elwell, King, and Lawson tragedies. It lacked rich background.

The picture we had built up was quite simple. The man who had called with the city check to take Mrs. Harrington's apartment was the murderer. No one had seen him come or go except the dead woman. He had come to the apartment through the medium of the want ad. and had promised to reappear the day following to take the apartment. But the only one who could testify to these facts was dead. The pattern had to be resorted to in order to build up the picture of the thief slayer's entry and exit. What happened probably was this: Mrs. Harrington had gone to the door and, as was her custom, before opening it had inquired who was there. The man probably said he was the prospective tenant who had called the day before. She may have opened the door slightly. He pushed in. She fled to the bathroom, which is a move most women make under the same circumstances. The thief followed her and there he beat her. He then robbed the apartment and left.

He was a professional thief. Of this there was no doubt in my mind. He had watched his chance to enter and leave without being observed. And no one had seen him. A few years of stealing furnishes the professional thief with proficiency in picking the right time to work. The greatest risk he assumes is that of being seen going to or coming from the scene of the crime by human witnesses. He knows that in modern police departments there are elaborate collections of rogues' gallery photographs out of which the persons who have seen him may select his likeness. He has built up a defensive system to meet this development in crime detection.

So to a man who has acquired patterns from hundreds of robberies and murders there is little mystery in the means of entry and exit which to the lay mind appear to be the focal points around which speculation is built as in the Elwell and King cases.

The medical examiner reported that Mrs. Harrington had been beaten with an instrument which appeared to be a hammer, but her skull had not been fractured. The wounds themselves had not caused death. The loss of blood had. It is highly probable that had the woman who found the body entered the apartment on the day of the murder she would have found Mrs. Harrington alive but unconscious, and in that case her life would have been saved. Here again the circumstances parallel the King and Lawson cases. The thief had not intended to kill. He had beaten his victim into insensibility. Comparatively a stranger to her, he had little fear that if she recovered she would identify him.

Up to this point the Harrington case follows the Elwell, King, and Lawson patterns, save for the glamorous backgrounds. When the Harrington murder was being investigated and we had reached this point my conclusions, which I recorded in official reports, were that a thief had killed her.

The patterns gave me the type of a thief he was. Police robbery charts, by which the city is laid out in sections and the crimes recorded day by day, were of material assistance. For some time prior to Mrs. Harrington's murder letter-box thieves had been busy in the general vicinity of the apartment house in which she lived. Hallway mail boxes were broken into and robbed, and in some cases the thief went a step farther and entered apartments in the same houses where apparently mail boxes had not yielded loot. A Mrs. Peterson, living with her daughter in an apartment house not far from One Hundred and Ninetieth Street, had been robbed a few weeks before Mrs. Harrington was slain. The thief's means of entry was a mystery until the daughter explained that she had left the key to the apartment in an envelope in the hall mail box for her mother. The letter box had been broken into. The robbery of the apartment had taken place a little later.

I shall not detail here how the detective machine operates when it seeks to find a thief or slayer through the medium of stolen articles. It may or may not be a secret to the reader, but I'd rather not reveal the workings of the system. At any rate, it was employed in the hope of finding Mrs. Harrington's slayer. We were hopeful that something would turn up and ran down every clue that offered a possibility. Feelers were out, although we were well aware that sometimes they reach out and trip up the man we want and then again do not. The professional thief, well versed in underworld methods and habits, has a thousand hideaways into which he can disappear and a thousand assumed names he may hide behind. But there are moments when, like all human beings, he needs excitement, amusement, and stimulants—and always, of course, money.

In January, 1928, a man signed the register at the Hotel Taft in New Haven, Connecticut, and was assigned to a room. He carried a suitcase. Within a few hours he was in touch by telephone with two young women in a near-by city, and later they drove up to the hotel in a taxicab and he joined them.

A few days later he presented a check to Julian Lavin, manager of the hotel, and asked that it be cashed. The guest seemed to have been dissipating. His hand was unsteady and his eyes bloodshot. Lavin recalled that the guest had come in with only a suitcase and refused to cash the check. The guest left the hotel hurriedly, apparently disgruntled, but did not take the suitcase with him. When he failed to reappear and pay his bill Lavin visited his room. He found the suitcase and opened it. There was a packet of letters addressed to a man, but not with the name the guest had signed when registering. Lavin's suspicions were aroused. He inspected other articles in the suitcase and found a bunch of keys, fifteen in number, several receipted gas and electricity bills, and a wedding ring bearing the engraved inscription, "Guy to Emma." The bills were made out to Mrs. E. Harrington, No. 617 West One Hundred and Ninetieth Street, New York City.

Lavin looked again at the letters. They were addressed to Frederick W. Edel, No. 121 West Ninetieth Street, New York City. This was not the name signed to the register. Lavin, who had been a hotel manager in New York City, still read New York newspapers and recalled the name Harrington and the West One Hundred and Ninetieth Street address and the bare details of the tragedy.

He called in the New Haven police. Instantly they recognized the name Edel as that of a man who had been tried and acquitted of the murder of a man in Meriden, Connecticut, in 1925, and who later had been implicated in the killing of David C. Dudley, whose body was found in a woods near Meriden. Reference to current parole reports showed that Edel was out on parole from Dannemora Prison in New York and had failed to report to the parole authorities. He had been imprisoned for robbery of a taxicab driver.

New Haven police immediately notified us. Detectives Winkelman and Roge of the Homicide Bureau were sent to New Haven armed with photographs, fingerprints, and description of Edel. These were incorporated into a circular and broadcast to five thousand police departments throughout the United States. Other detectives were sent to cover the address in West Ninetieth Street which was found on the letters,

The suitcase was brought to the Homicide Bureau. Winkelman and Roge remained in New Haven and interviewed the two women who had been with Edel. He had given one of them a caracul coat to "save for him." This was identified as Mrs. Harrington's missing garment. They told of money Edel had spent.

In the suitcase we found a box opener—a nickel-plated combination tool, half claw hammer and half jimmy. It was bloodstained. The letters were of greater importance. They told something of Edel's past. For some years he had been a bartender in the Snelling Hotel, St. Paul, Minnesota, and reference was made to a number of persons in that city who seemed to be on intimate terms with him. I concluded that if Edel claimed any city as his home it was St. Paul. The police in that city were immediately communicated with, but had no information about him. However, he did answer the description of a man who had been cashing forged money orders in small cities in Minnesota. In the meantime post-office inspectors who were looking for the man were in possession of our circulars. They wanted Edel for letter stealing as well as money-order forgeries.

In March a man appeared at the money-order window in a post office at Hopkins, Minnesota, and asked to have a small money order cashed. The clerk had seen a circular describing Edel and also had been warned that it was his practice to buy a small money order, then raise it to a large denomination and cash it.

"Wait a minute," said the clerk. He stepped away from the window and sent for the town marshal. Edel dashed out of the post office, and after being pursued a mile or so fell exhausted and was arrested. He was brought back to New York City to face a charge of murder.

Thus the investigation of Mrs. Harrington's murder was advanced a step beyond the unsolved mysteries of the killing of Elwell, Dorothy King, and Louise Lawson. A suspect had been arrested to answer for a crime which had been almost as complete a mystery as the other three slayings.

A man working with patterns and applying them to situations the truth of which is not known is interested in getting a statement from a suspect for more than one reason. It is fair to the prisoner, since it gives him an opportunity to establish his innocence. It is fair to the State, for if he is guilty the statement expedites procedure in the processes which lead to trial. Finally it tells the detective whether his pattern method has justified itself.

Securing statements or confessions from accused persons is a somewhat difficult task. As evidence in a court of law they are subject to various tests and safeguards. Before they are admissible under rules of evidence the judge must determine by inquiry the conditions under which they were secured; that is, whether made voluntarily by the accused. To meet this requirement I developed a special technique in taking statements from suspects. In addition to questioning them in my office at the Homicide Bureau I have always taken them out in a police automobile to the scene of their alleged crimes, accompanied by a Bureau stenographer and investigating officers. As we went along in plain view of whoever might be passing, I have put my questions. This not only precludes the possibility of having the issue raised by the lawyers of the accused that their clients were unfairly treated, but it has other distinct advantages. One of these is that the suspect voluntarily, without coaching or leading, *may point out while he is making his statement* the various places where he lived, his movements, and the manner in which he committed the crime. This process has been referred to in newspaper accounts as reconstructing the crime.

Often I have had accused men and women while on such tours point out places they had robbed or visited that we knew nothing about, or develop facts about a murder which were vital but were not apparent except to the eye and the memory of the murderer himself. Cases have been frequent where men were taken out like this to visit the scene of only one crime we knew about, but the day has ended in the suspect's leading us to a dozen places he had robbed about which we had received no information.

Moreover, from the questions asked the accused, and his answers, which were recorded verbatim by the stenographer and later reduced to writing and signed by the accused, it is possible for judge and jury to determine, from context and circumstances, what was in my mind when the questions were asked and in the mind of the accused, thus forestalling any attempt upon the part of the defense to claim that the accused was unjustly or brutally treated.

Upon his return to New York Edel was taken on such a trip as I have just described. We drove first to the vicinity of the furnished room house where he had lived. He was uncertain as to the house. We drove around the block several times. Finally he pointed it out and we entered and he led us to the room he had occupied. In it we found an antique clock which he said he had stolen from a house uptown. He encountered the landlady and spoke to her. She recalled him.

"Let us go now to the house where you stole the clock," I suggested.

We entered the car, Edel directing its course. We halted in front of a large apartment house and Edel escorted us to the apartment of Mrs. Peterson, which he had robbed previous to the Harrington murder, effecting entrance by means of the key he found in a mail box in the hallway which he had broken open. We stepped into the Peterson apartment, and in the presence of Mrs. Peterson Edel went through the motions he had gone through while robbing the place, much to the amazement of the woman standing by. We exhibited the clock. She identified it as hers. Edel readily answered all questions.

We reëntered the automobile. The driver was instructed to take us to West One Hundred and Ninetieth Street. On the way I talked to Edel about his past. He admitted that he had been a thief for many years; that he had used in his time more than five hundred aliases. He explained how he had fled from New Haven to St. Paul, using a different name each day.

Finally we approached the apartment house in which Mrs. Harrington was murdered.

"Have you ever worked in this vicinity?" I asked Edel.

"Never," he snapped.

We halted in front of the apartment house.

"Have you ever been in this house?" I asked.

"Never in my life."

As we ascended the stairs to the floor on which the Harrington apartment was located Edel became restless, halting.

A detective took out the bunch of fifteen keys found in the suitcase and inserted one into the door lock and opened it. We stepped inside.

"What hour did you come to this apartment?" I queried.

Edel did not answer. He hung back. We stepped into the bathroom.

"Do you recognize this place?"

He did not answer.

"What did you use to gain entrance into the apartment?"

He was silent.

"Where did you take the articles from which were found in your suitcase, and which belonged to Mrs. Harrington?"

"She sent them to me," he said. "A taxi driver brought them to me one morning."

"Then you knew Mrs. Harrington?"

"I met her in a restaurant several years ago," he said, quite eagerly. "We flirted. She wrote me letters, and when I got here she sent the stuff to me."

Here I may interject the explanation that this admission is the typical strategy of the professional criminal. The only person who could testify and deny the story which Edel had just told was dead—Mrs. Harrington. And the only person who could establish the contact between Mrs. Harrington and Edel the day before she was murdered was the apartment-house owner to whom she had mentioned the man with the city check. But this evidence, being hearsay, would be inadmissible. He was compelled to admit possession of the dead woman's property. We had it, but this did not place him on the spot at the time of the murder, except circumstantially.

We returned to headquarters. It was soon established by facts which could not be introduced in evidence that prior to the day Edel called to inspect the Harrington apartment he had never seen or heard of the woman in his life. He had selected her apartment for attack through the medium of the want ad.

It is interesting to note that the aspersions thrown upon the woman's character by Edel placed her, so far as he was concerned, in the same class with the King and Lawson women. They not only served him as an explanation of how he happened to be in possession of her stolen property but suggested the possibility that she was of loose character and therefore, as he reasoned, a target for attack by others. In a motion for a new trial Edel's attorney vigorously attacked the woman's character.

The most damaging thing about Edel's statement was the big hole in it, the denial that he had ever been near, or in, the apartment house. And we were unable to establish his means of entry and he knew we were up against it in this particular. We found the keys to the apartment in his possession, yet it could not be proved that he had ever used them, nor could it be proved that he had them before or after he entered the apartment.

He was willing to admit, and did admit, other crimes, but not murder. The reason was obvious. He was eager to go back to jail on any charge save murder; eager to get out of the hands of the police and prosecutors. He was willing to pay for crimes that did not involve the death penalty. He admitted that he had gone from city to city stealing letters. I believe he would have admitted any crime except that murder.

Edel was convicted and sentenced to death. He had himself strengthened the case against him by leaving the gap in his statement which was read to the jury.

Edel was in the death house awaiting execution when he was granted a reprieve by Governor Franklin D. Roosevelt. His attorney urged that since the Court of Appeals had affirmed his conviction and sentence new evidence in his favor had been discovered. This evidence was largely an attack upon Mrs. Harrington's character. Application for a new trial was made and subsequently three additional reprieves were granted while the Court considered the motion.

CHAPTER XIX

IDEAL MURDER INQUIRY

On New Year's Day, 1926, George V. McLaughlin was appointed police commissioner. He resigned the state superintendency of banks to accept the office. He was without previous police experience, but was both an expert accountant and a lawyer, and an all-round executive. He was tall, square shouldered, with a rich understanding of men. He had risen to public life from an office boy's bench in a small bank. He came into the Police Department at a time when a so-called crime wave was at its height, and he made one of the quickest clean-ups in the history of American police departments.

The men were glad to see him come. Morale instantly improved. There were no shake-ups, just a gradual readjustment. He gave politicians a wide berth and struck at crime at its sources. He singled out for special attack the professional receivers of stolen property and thus broke up the market for stolen goods. He stopped gambling, which dammed the outlet for most of the money that thieves steal, at the same time closing up the favorite hiding places of criminals. When men of no matter what rank did a good piece of work he rewarded them—with promotions for those who could be advanced; commendation for those who could not be promoted.

In a short time he built up one of the most efficient police machines it has been my pleasure to work with.

He had been in office three months when he sent for me.

"How long have you been on the force, Captain?" he asked.

"Thirty-seven years."

"Why haven't you been promoted to a higher rank?"

"I can't explain that," I said. "I don't know." And neither did I. I had never asked for promotion and had never sought the aid of anyone else in that direction. I was too busy with murder for one thing, and for another I never believed in "working the wires" for promotion.

"Well," said McLaughlin, "I'm going to promote you."

That afternoon my appointment as deputy inspector came through. It was the first advancement in nineteen years. It made me very happy. It was recompense for the many vacationless years I had put in; for days of toil when I had gone without sleep. It justified, too, my belief in men of the McLaughlin type, of which unfortunately there are too few in public life.

As I have said, the whole Department, man for man, was on its toes ready to show that, given a fair break under a real leader, they would respond.

On February 26th Patrolman Biegel, on night duty in Queens Borough, an outlying section of New York City, saw a tall, slender man wearing a gray cap and a light overcoat hurrying along the sidewalk. He stopped him and addressed to him the usual inquiries. The man reached into his coat as if to draw out papers to establish his identity, but instead of papers he whipped out a pistol and shot Biegel in the side of the neck. The wound was not fatal.

Exactly a month later in the same borough Detectives Frank Donnelly and Arthur Kenny saw a man enter a house and presently observed a light flash. The two detectives were not together when they saw this. Kenny, however, went to the front door of the house and Donnelly to the rear door. Kenny rapped on the door and a woman upstairs put out her head. Kenny told her to open the door and admit him as he was a detective looking for a burglar.

Almost at the same time this was happening a slender man in a gray topcoat came to the back door at which Donnelly was standing.

"What's up?" the man asked the detective.

"There's a thief in this house."

"What!" the man exclaimed, blinking his eyes.

"And who are you?" the detective demanded.

"Me? I'm all right. I'm——" and he dug his hand into the inner pocket of his coat ostensibly for credentials. Donnelly stepped into the hallway, came up close to the man to look at whatever credentials he might produce. In a flash the man drew a gun from the coat pocket and shot the detective in the side of the neck.

Donnelly fell. The man fled across the back yard. Kenny, hearing the shot, sprinted around the house in the darkness and saw a form hurdling a fence. He gave chase, but the man had disappeared. At the corner of a dark alley Kenny saw a man.

"Did you see a man running this way from over that back fence?" asked the detective.

"Somebody ran up that way," said the man, pointing over Kenny's shoulder and blinking. Kenny turned his head to look and was shot in the side of the neck. He died three hours later. Donnelly recovered.

A few weeks later Detective George McCarthy spotted a man ambling along a Queens street with a box under his arm. It was late at night. There had been numerous complaints in the district about the loss of expensive radio sets. McCarthy halted the man and asked him if the box was a radio set.

"Yes," said the man. "I got a set in the box. It's my set."

"And who are you, and what you doing?" McCarthy demanded.

"Oh, I'm O. K.," said the man, thrusting his hand under the fold of his coat. "I got the sales check to show that I——" He fumbled in his pocket. McCarthy stepped closer to examine papers he expected to see, but instead a pistol flashed and he fell with a bullet in the side of the neck. The man fled. McCarthy emptied his pistol after him, but he escaped. The detective described his assailant as a man with a light overcoat, gray cap, scarlet muffler and with a queer way of blinking.

The morning following a pocketbook was found on the sidewalk near where McCarthy had fallen. It contained two bill folders, one stamped "William Cody" in gilt letters, and the other bore the imprint "Frank Merriwell." The former was the real name of Buffalo Bill; the latter the nom de plume of a hero in the blood-and-thunder dime thrillers of a bygone age. The bill folders were empty.

McCarthy recovered.

Kenny having died, the task of finding his slayer was assigned to the Homicide Bureau. It was obvious that the same man had shot the four policemen. He had one peculiarity that seemed present in all the descriptions we had of the murder. He had a way of nervously blinking his eyes. Yet almost any man accosted suddenly by a policeman is likely to blink. As for the rest of his description—the light overcoat, gray cap, and red muffler—men who would answer it might be found any place at any time by the scores. I reasoned that McCarthy, who had fired at the man several times, might have a fair picture of him in his mind.

McCarthy looked through the rogues' gallery in the Bureau of Criminal Identification and settled upon the photograph of a man known as Paul Emanuel Hilton as the one picture that bore closest resemblance to his assailant. Hilton had been an inmate of reformatories and a prison.

In the Detective Division at the time was a young man, James A. Pyke. He had joined the force in 1921. During the war he had served as chauffeur to Major General John F. O'Ryan, commanding the New York Twenty-seventh Division. He had been detailed to duty in Queens Borough in the hunt for the man who had shot the four policemen. Also, Pyke was fond of baseball. He looked to me like a man who had the makings of a homicide investigator, patient and painstaking. He was twenty-eight, slender, snappy, with plenty of nerve, soft spoken and bright. These qualities especially fit a man for homicide work. I asked Chief Inspector John D. Coughlin of the Detective Division if he would let Pyke come into the Homicide Bureau for a tryout. He was transferred.

Pyke was gratified when I assigned him to work with Detective Sergeant William Jackson on the case. The killing of Kenny and the wounding of the other officers had stirred the Department.

I offered them this caution: "Look out for that inside-pocket stall."

It would not be likely that Hilton, if he were the killer, would be going by his right name. More than likely Cody or Merriwell would be his current alias. Among a class of reckless young criminals who have no talent for inventing original names these two aliases are in common use. Pyke and Jackson started out to look for Hilton under these names. They put out gentle feelers for thieves who were using them.

A wizened little man was found who told the detectives that he knew an ex-convict who used both aliases; that he had done a stretch with him in a Rhode Island prison. His right name was Tilton, Milton, Hilton, Wilton, or something similar to these. The man picked out Hilton's prison photograph as that of the man he knew in the Rhode Island prison. He added that when Hilton left prison he had stolen a high sheriff's revolver.

Prison records showed that Hilton, as a boy, had been incarcerated in the Elmira, New York, Reformatory, the county penitentiary on Blackwell's Island, New York City, and the Rhode Island institution from which he had been released in 1924 after a term for burglary.

Where Hilton might now be the informant did not know. He scattered his patronage among speakeasies all over town, but he most often had been seen in the vicinity of Third Avenue and Fourteenth Street, where there are many cheap theaters, dancehalls, and poolrooms. He hadn't been in this locality for months.

In the Murder Clinic men were instructed that one of the most valuable indexes to a crook's whereabouts are incidents that may be picked up from his life's history. These frequently reveal a man's habits, idiosyncrasies, hobbies, and his friends. Hobbies usually show themselves in youth and follow a man to the end of his days.

Hilton had spent a good many years in penal institutions. Most certainly the characteristics that mark one man from another would be observed in prisons where the inmates have little else to look at but one another and listen to a man's boastful accounts of the things he is proficient at or very fond of.

Pyke and Jackson gathered information about Hilton's prison life from guards and men who had been doing time with him. One thing stood out above all others. He had a heavy hobby. It was baseball. He wouldn't play on prison teams unless he could hold down third base. When he didn't get this position he sat, or stood, as near third base as he could get, watching the game intently, blinking. He had boasted in prison that when he was on the outside he went to every baseball game played by the New York or Brooklyn teams in the National League. He was a rabid follower of the New York Giants.

Their search for Hilton had now brought them into April. One afternoon the two detectives wandered into a poolroom near Third Avenue and Fourteenth Street and sat down at a round-topped table. They began a heated argument about baseball. In a chair against the wall sat a young man who had known Hilton but from whom the detectives had been unable to get a word.

Suddenly Jackson's fist hit the table and he shouted at Pyke: "Am I right about that or not?"

"Aw, if that bird Hilton was only around, he'd settle this argument in a minute," said Pyke in a loud voice. "He knows baseball. I wonder where he is, anyway?" He cast his glance around the room.

The man in the chair against the wall leaned forward.

"That guy Hilton?" he asked. "He hasn't been around here for weeks. And he don't know nothing about baseball except third base. All he can think and talk about is Heinie Groh, the Giant's third baseman. He thinks Heinie oughta be president of the United States. When he hears his name mentioned he blinks and chatters like a monkey."

That afternoon the Giants were to open the baseball season at the Polo Grounds uptown. Pyke and Jackson left the poolroom, picked up a newspaper, and found that Groh was booked to play third base in the opening game.

The two detectives reasoned that if Hilton were such a rabid Groh fan he would attend this game and see his hero play; and, judging from recent descriptions of the man they wanted, he would likely be found in a cheap bleachers seat as near third base as he could get.

Pyke and Jackson went to the Polo Grounds. An hour and a half before the game was to start they stood at the gate nearest third base scanning the faces of thousands who came up, bought tickets, and entered. Their minds were focussed on a slender man with a light overcoat and gray cap possibly with a red muffler around his neck. While they were waiting Sergeant George Ciquette came along and asked them why, if they wanted to see the game, they didn't go down to the pass gate and walk in. Pyke told him to wait around. They were looking for something. Ciquette waited with them.

Suddenly Pyke exclaimed: "There he is. Third man from the end of the line." There stood the man with light overcoat and gray cap, the visor of which was pulled down over his eyes, which were blinking. Jackson walked along one side of the line, Pyke along the other. Ciquette followed behind a few paces.

Pyke caught the man and pulled him out of the line.

"Say," the suspect protested, "what's this?"

"Never mind that but come out here," said Pyke.

"What right you got to stop me?" the suspect demanded. "I'm all right. I'll show you——" He reached for the inside pocket of his coat.

Pyke's hand snapped out and caught the man's wrist. "No, none of that old stall this time," said the detective. He thrust his hand into the coat pocket and drew out the revolver later identified as the one he had stolen from the Rhode Island high sheriff. Ciquette grabbed the man's free arm. He fought back ferociously. Finally he wilted and gave up.

He was Paul Emanuel Hilton.

I questioned him in my private office. He was boastful of his coat-pocket trick. "If I carried my gun in my hip pocket," he explained, "the minute I reached for it a cop would know what I was after, but when I shoved my left hand into my inside coat pocket they thought I was after a wallet or papers. I flashed the gat on them before they knew it."

This accounted for the fact that each policeman shot had been hit in the side of the neck. I took Hilton out in a police automobile, and with utter bravado he pointed out the spots where he had hit each policeman and, in addition, designated a dozen houses from which he had stolen radio sets. Radio was not his hobby. He merely had a fence who gave him a good price for homemade radio outfits. He went about Queens Borough, where almost everyone lives in two-family houses. When he heard a good radio set he marked the house, and when he thought the time right stepped in and stole it. He was widely exploited as the Radio Burglar.

Hilton was convicted of the murder of Detective Kenny and sentenced to the electric chair. There had been a number of policemen shot in the neck before the four fell before Hilton's gun in Queens. One of these men died. I was certain Hilton had killed him. An effort was made to get Hilton to admit this killing while he was in the deathhouse. He said he was through talking. He was through, too, with life. He was executed February 17, 1927.

Hilton's course in life followed the average way that nearly all modern professionals go. He was burglar as a boy. He went on and on at this game until he thought himself sufficiently schooled to try murder. He was one of those who would have been saved from himself, and victims saved from his murderous impulse, if he had been classed earlier as an habitual criminal and isolated from society. A thing that struck me forcefully was his name—Paul Emanuel Hilton. A good name, apparently the name of a respectable family. But when I got to digging into his history I encountered the same old story. The boy had never had a chance to climb out of squalor and unhappy surroundings.

Pyke and Jackson were advanced in grade by Commissioner McLaughlin. To my way of thinking the capture of Hilton was a perfect piece of crime detection, good headwork all the way through, sound reasoning, and keen, safe judgment at the end of the chase. It was what I would call an ideal murder inquiry. It comes about as near being a story-book achievement as any case I have encountered.

Cases which at first possess all appearances of an absolute mystery and then unfold themselves smoothly when the murder man gets the faintest suggestion for his picture have lingered for years in my memory as ideal from the standpoint of detection.

A case I handled many years back comes to mind as an example of the ideal.

The body of a priest was found in the West Drive of Central Park one morning. He had been shot through the head and was breathing when found by a couple strolling through the park. He died later in a hospital. Papers in his pocket revealed that he was Father Arturo Ascencio, a Santo Domingo clergyman. No money, jewelry, or watch were found on his body.

The killing had been done with a bulldog revolver, which lay near the wounded man. The wound in his head was jagged, and this was explained by the bullets in the gun. Their noses had been flattened apparently to make them fit into the chamber of the revolver.

It looked to others like suicide. Yet the last man in the world to take his own life would be a priest. I was certain that it was murder.

Father Ascencio recently had arrived from Santo Domingo and was staying at the Ingleterra Hotel, whose guests were mostly South Americans. The night before he was shot he had mentioned to the hotel clerk that he was going out to keep an engagement with a friend, whom he was to meet at One Hundred and Tenth Street and Eighth Avenue, which is near the upper end of Central Park. The clerk had seen the clergyman standing on the hotel stoop looking at a chronometer which he took from his vest pocket. Then he moved on.

The chronometer was not found on the body, which

supplied the first element the murder man looks for, the motive.

A postcard found in the priest's room had the name H. Henriquez signed to it and the address, No. 257 West One Hundred and Tenth Street, which was in the vicinity of the place where the priest had told the hotel clerk he would meet his companion. The hotel management reported that a few days before his death the priest had reported that two watches and money were missing from his trunk. It was his habit when visiting America to bring along watches which his parishioners gave him to have repaired in this country.

Among the priest's visitors was a young man known as De Lara, who had come up from Santo Domingo with the priest on the same steamer. They were apparently good friends.

I started out in search of the person whose name was signed to the postcard. I found no such address in West One Hundred and Tenth Street, but reasoned that a mistake might have been made in the address; that probably it was meant for a street above One Hundred and Tenth. In this section were a number of South American boarding houses. At No. 257 West One Hundred and Twelfth Street I found the name Henriquez on a door bell and rang. A woman admitted me, and I was ushered into the parlor.

She was well acquainted with Father Ascencio, and the youth known as De Lara was a boarder in her house. The night before the priest was killed he had visited her and upon leaving said he was going to One Hundred and Forty-seventh Street.

"Was the father in the habit of going into Central Park?" I asked.

"Oh, yes. He and De Lara often walked through the park." The woman described De Lara as a youth of seventeen and a student. He was not in at present. I left. At the head of the stairs I encountered a man who said he was the brother of the woman I had just talked to. A minute later a young man came running up the stairs. He was about to brush past me.

"Hello, De Lara," I cried. He swung around quickly and stopped.

"Where's the gun you own?" I shot at him.

"I own no gun."

The brother looked at him. "De Lara," he said, "you do own a pistol. I saw you with bullets last Sunday night." The man looked at me. "He was pounding the noses of the bullets to make them fit the gun, and I saw him doing it," said the man.

With these few sentences the bulldog gun found at the priest's side was placed in the hands of the youth through the medium of the stub-nosed bullets.

I started to question De Lara about visits to Central Park with the priest. He was evasive. I then searched his room and found pawn tickets for watches, a chain, and a locket. De Lara said these had been given to him by a strange man he met on a steamship pier. I started with him to headquarters. We entered the subway. We sat in silence for some time. The youth's face was beaded with sweat.

The psychological moment had arrived.

"That story about getting the watches from the man on the pier is not the truth," I said to him.

"It's the truth," he said.

"You killed Father Ascencio."

"I did," he replied, "but I never stole his watches."

Later he confessed the murder to me in detail, but stoutly maintained that the watches, chain, and locket, which we found in the pawnshop and which were identified as the property of the slain priest, all had been given to him by the man on the pier.

On a visit to his cell a day later I found him in a half-comatose condition and had him sent to the prison hospital ward. After confessing he had wanted to die and had taken morphine. In oiled paper tucked in the toe of his shoes I found packets of the drug. Because of his youth he was permitted to plead guilty to murder in the second degree and sentenced to twenty years to life in state's prison. He was out in twelve years. I heard of him later. He had been arrested by the Buffalo, New York, police. There had been a murder and De Lara was found in the vicinity with a revolver in his possession. The murder had been committed in a public park. Twelve years in prison had not cured him of the gun-carrying habit. I am not aware what happened to him as the result of the Buffalo arrest, but I know that if he was carrying a gun he was going along like most of them do who deliberately kill for the purpose of robbery and instead of getting the law's prescribed penalty only serve a few years. I believe they call that "getting away with murder."

The De Lara case at the start offered confusing possibilities—the wrong address and the suicide theory. After these were straightened out developments came with speed and precision. The murderer was in our hands within a few hours after his victim's body was found; indeed before the victim was in his grave. This case from the murder man's technical standpoint worked out ideally, and from a bad start.

A famous jiujitsu murder was another inquiry that fits the pattern of ideal mystery solution.

A 'phone call one afternoon took me to the Empire Hotel. Upon arrival I found that a young Japanese had been found dead in a room upstairs, but that there was nothing to indicate foul play.

The body lay on a floor rug under a bed, and around the Japanese's neck was a linen table cover, loosely tied. There were no visible marks upon the body, no signs of poisoning or other violent means of death. The dead man was fully dressed. His pockets contained no money. Nothing had been taken from the room and there were no signs of a struggle.

Suicide was suggested to me, but I declined to entertain it. It was urged that the table cover about the man's neck was merely put there by the dead man in an effort to make suicide seem implausible. But my picture offered other possibilities which pointed to murder. The body and the rug had together been *pushed* under the bed. A suicide could not possibly have pushed himself and the rug into the position in which the body was found. I reasoned that the man had been robbed, but that before this act could be accomplished his assailant had struck him a blow which rendered him unconscious and had then fastened the linen cover around his neck, held it tight until strangulation had been effected, loosened it, and then robbed the victim. No man would have permitted his assailant to tie a table cover around his neck without making a violent struggle, of which the room offered no evidence.

Moreover, the victim was an Oriental. There is a blow in jiujitsu that may be fatal. It is delivered under the heart, and while it is not always fatal it renders its recipient unconscious.

The coroner's physician set all conjecture at rest. Death, it was determined, had been caused by strangulation, but the victim had been unconscious when death occurred, made so by a blow under his heart!

The next step was to find the murderer. From the hotel management we learned that the dead man was known as Yoshihara and that at different times he had displayed sums of money. But the hotel room had been rented not by him but by another Japanese whose name upon the register could not be deciphered. The day before his death Yoshihara had been seen in the hall talking with the Japanese who had rented the room. The latter, a maid said, wore a brown suit with a thin red stripe in it.

For weeks our men circulated among the Japanese boarding houses and steamship offices on a search for the murderer. It was a more or less blind hunt, for we did not have the name of the suspect, and his description might have fitted any Japanese. We found that Yoshihara had worked aboard steamships and at sanitariums. Now and again as the search went on we encountered the figure of the same little brown man in the brown suit with the thin red stripes. But even with a description of the cloth in our possession it was difficult for our men to make themselves understood in Japanese quarters. Finally we learned that Yoshihara and the man with the brown suit had frequently eaten together in a Japanese restaurant in Cranford, New Jersey.

At this eating place we found that the suspect had had a suit made by a near-by tailor. From this tailor we got a piece of the brown red-striped cloth from which the suit had been made. Armed with samples of this material, our men redoubled on their tracks, and where they had been unable to make clear the purpose of their quest on previous visits the pieces of goods were displayed, and instantly they were recognized as stuff worn by a Japanese who had come to America on a steamship with Yoshihara.

We found the slayer within three days after our men had come into possession of the sample of goods. He confessed to me, declaring that he had rented the room for the purpose of luring Yoshihara to it and killing and robbing him. He had fastened the linen table cover about his neck, drew it tight, and strangled him.

"But he put up a fight, didn't he?" I asked the slayer.

"Nuh, nuh," said the little man. "I do this——" And he described by gestures the jiujitsu blow which he delivered under his victim's heart. He would never admit the exact amount of money he had stolen from Yoshihara.

He admitted a smaller amount than we knew the dead man had. Why murderers always claim that the money they steal from their victims is less than the actual amount I have never fully understood. It may be that robbery to them is a worse crime than murder, or they may think that admitting a lesser amount reduces the degree of murder. Of course it doesn't. The theft of a half inch of old thread is sufficient to establish robbery as a motive for murder.

The jiujitsu case had more than one ideal aspect. In the first place, the inquiry was conducted against great odds among a people with whom we were little familiar. In the second place, it might easily have gone down in the records as a suicide, for few would have missed the little brown man. In fact, his friends hadn't missed him. They thought he had gone to sea. And the final aspect—in spite of the handicap of language and only a very limited knowledge of Oriental minds and customs—a little piece of woolen cloth not larger than the palm of a man's hand brought the slayer to book.

He was executed for the crime.

CHAPTER XX

FAULTY PICTURES BY FEMININE HANDS

MURDERESSES, especially those who slay their husbands, invariably make the same slip-up. Seeking to throw suspicion upon another they build elaborate pictures or "set ups," as the police saying goes. They do this to throw the police off the right track. But they overdo the picture. It is never real. It smacks of an effort to be overmelodramatic which, I suppose, is due to woman's highly emotional make-up. It is perhaps for the same reason that women seldom are successful detectives. They are tempted to overdo the pictures they set out to build; to make too much out of circumstances that really are of little or no consequence.

The murderess runs to a heavy plot. Frequently it is years in the making and yet, with all the care and time given to it, glaring defects appear. Their chief concern as plot builders seems to be to throw blame for their crime upon one man or several, seldom upon another woman. Male slayers most often offer alibis or farfetched defenses when accused. If they do try to throw the crime upon another the target is usually one of their own sex. The woman slayer relies upon the presumption that the male and not her own sex has the natural or inherited propensity to kill. When she slays her plot is so arranged that an issue is raised between the sexes. She expects popular opinion to favor her against the man. She looks to man for protection in crime as in other affairs of life.

There are murder patterns to support this conclusion. Two of my more recent cases were so much alike as to suggest that murderesses, too, work by pattern.

Daniel F. Kaber was a well-known publisher of Cleveland, Ohio. On the morning of July 18, 1919, he was found in a dying condition on his bed in his home in Lakewood, Ohio, where he lived with his wife Eva, and her daughter by former marriage, Marion McArdle. He had been stabbed twenty-three times with a sharp file. He died in a hospital after making a deathbed declaration that he believed that someone close to him had instigated the stabbing. He had been confined to his bed for six weeks under care of a male nurse. On the night of the attack, while the nurse was in another part of the house, two roughly dressed men stole in and stabbed Kaber.

The house had apparently been robbed. A drawer in the dining-room buffet had been broken open and family plate was missing. Shortly after Kaber's death his relatives instituted litigation to prevent his widow from coming into control of his estate, which was quite large and included the home in which he was attacked.

No one was arrested for the crime. Two years elapsed.

On Friday, June 2, 1921, the district attorney of Cuyahoga County, Ohio, wired the New York Police Department to find and arrest Mrs. Eva Kaber, who was believed to be in New York with her daughter. Marion, we learned, had arrived in New York the day before, followed by two Lakewood detectives and several reporters. She became aware that she was being followed, and to prevent her from disappearing she was brought to the Harlem police station. She refused to talk and was released. Private detectives, hired by the Lakewood authorities, shadowed her as she left the station house, hoping to be led to the mother, but she threw them off. Mrs. Kaber, in the meantime, had moved. Through sources unnecessary to disclose I learned where she was living. I took up watch on the house, and when she appeared I caused her arrest. Marion, upon visiting her mother in prison, was arrested. The two were kept apart.

In my mind, as I considered questioning the two women, were patterns of earlier husband slayings where wives had resorted to the conventional means of making it appear that the motive for murder was robbery. I sought information from the Lakewood detectives as to the condition of the Kaber house when the stabbing was reported. They informed me that the buffet drawer had been broken open with an ice pick, which is not the tool used by thieves. Moreover, rugs had been dragged from the house to the porch and pieces of silver were scattered about the lawn in the front of the house, which, again, is not the practice of professional thieves. With these facts I put the patterns to work.

I first talked with Marion. She told me she had been educated in one of the leading women's colleges in the East. She was shrewdly evasive, that is, talkative, but gave little information that was incriminating or valuable. She was blasé, modern. After many hours of questioning she told a story. It was that her mother had asked her to break open the buffet drawer and she had done so with an ice pick; had taken out the silver and scattered some of it on the front lawn; had upset the rooms to make it appear that robbery had been done.

A few days before the murder, Marion told me, she was in her mother's motor car when they met two rough-looking men. Mrs. Kaber left the car and talked with them. When she returned she told her daughter that she "was going to get rid of him," meaning her husband.

"What are you thinking of?" the daughter demanded.

"I'm going to have my own way, once," said the mother.

The following morning Kaber was found dying.

With these admissions in my possession I talked with Mrs. Kaber. For hours she sat, stolidly refusing to answer my questions. She was unlike her daughter. Marion had the confidence and naïveté of one better educated; her mother had not been to college and could not carry on a shrewdly evasive conversation as the daughter did. She had no skill at fencing. Finally, after I had repeated to her all that Marion had told me, Mrs. Kaber began to weaken. She admitted that many months before her husband was murdered she had consulted a midwife about "doing something to her husband that would cure him of his meanness." In nearly every answer she attempted to show that Kaber had mistreated her, although the information from Lakewood indicated that he was a jovial, generous husband.

The midwife, she said, had given her a bottle of fluid whose contents she poured into Kaber's morning coffee. He became ill and took to his bed, but recovered. She denied that the bottle contained arsenic, saying that she did not know what the midwife had put into it.

"But why did you ask your daughter to break open the dining-room buffet and try to make it appear that the house had been robbed?" I put to her repeatedly. "And you knew the two men who stabbed your husband?"

There were at first long lapses of silence when I put these inquiries to her.

Suddenly her head shot up.

"The midwife told me to hire ghosts to frighten my husband out of his meanness," she said. She went on to say that she found two men who would play the rôle of "ghosts," and she instructed them to give her husband "a rough shaking to scare him." She would not admit that she had hired them to kill Kaber.

The ghost story smacked of movie-plot influence. Obviously men hired to give a man a shaking would not come armed with sharp files. After seventeen hours of steady questioning her stolidity broke. She made other admissions, but always qualified them with a statement that Kaber had been mean to her; that his meanness had goaded her on.

Mrs. Kaber was not an unattractive woman. Her features were heavy; her face large and square. She had a determined jaw, large, popping blue eyes, and her hair was light. Her jaw moved with determined shifts. Her age was thirty-nine. When we discussed the details of her past life, and other matters not connected with her husband's murder, she was affable and soft spoken, but when we returned to the murder her features became animated and she moved restlessly in her chair. She resembled so closely in features and mannerisms another noted murderess, whom I shall presently discuss, that the resemblance was strikingly uncanny. Almost anyone might have taken the two women for twins. Their crimes also were alike in many particulars.

Marion was young, vivacious, the college type. When pressed hard she would say in a soft, pleasant voice: "Now, Inspector, you don't really expect me to answer that." She was constantly asking after her mother and seemed to me to be talking, accepting some of the guilt, to lift the burden from her mother's shoulders. They were not permitted to meet until after they had been questioned separately. They ran into each other's arms and wept profusely. They were returned to separate cells.

On the night of June 8th Mrs. Kaber slashed her wrists and was saved from death by a prison matron. In her extremity this was the only means of flight available. This act was precipitated by the news from Lakewood that the supposedly stolen silverware had been found in the home of Mrs. Kaber's friends, to whom she had given it three days before her husband was slain;

and by the more menacing news that several unnamed men were dickering with the Lakewood police to reveal the slayers for the reward of twenty-five hundred dollars offered by the city. Mrs. Kaber, it was disclosed, had not paid in full the money she had promised to the two thugs who had attacked her husband, and they were seeking the balance by negotiating for the reward.

Mrs. Kaber and Marion were returned to Lakewood on extradition papers. Before the trial was called three generations of women in the same family were involved. Mrs. Mary Brickel, the sixty-nine-year-old mother of Mrs. Kaber, was indicted for complicity and became a witness for the State against her daughter. She admitted setting fire to the Kaber home a year before her son-in-law's murder because her daughter was "tired of home life and wanted to go to a hotel." This attempt having failed, Mrs. Kaber told her that she was "going to have Dan killed," and on the night of the stabbing she was in the house with Marion at Mrs. Kaber's request to lend plausibility to the picture of robbery by two thugs. She accused her granddaughter of throwing the silverware on the front lawn and dragging the rugs onto the porch.

It was obvious from the assistance called in by Mrs. Kaber to arrange the defensive features of her plot that she had not the plotting ability to take care of these details, and leaving them to her mother and daughter found herself the victim of her own sex's, indeed her own kin's, faulty picture building.

Mrs. Ernimine Colavito, the midwife, upon whose shoulders Mrs. Kaber placed responsibility for the "ghost attack," was indicted and admitted that on Wednesday before the attack upon Kaber she went to his home, at Mrs. Kaber's direction, with two men, Sam and Tony, and rehearsed the stabbing of Kaber. While they were tramping about the hall and rooms upstairs, going through the motions of the attack, Kaber lay ill from the effects of arsenic, which had not worked quickly enough to suit the wife. Marion, by prearrangement, sat at a piano downstairs drumming loudly to drown the noise of the plotters upstairs.

The actual killing was left to hirelings, Salvatori Cola and Vittario Pisselli, the two men with whom Mrs. Kaber had made arrangements. The weapons they used, files made into stilletto-like knives, were not unlike the home-made weapons used in the killing of Madonia in the famous Lupo the Wolf-Morello-Petto the Ox conspiracy, which I have covered in an earlier chapter. These two men, having failed to gain the reward offered by Lakewood authorities, fled Ohio. One was later arrested in Buffalo, convicted, and sent away for life; the other escaped to Italy and was imprisoned there.

Mrs. Kaber was found guilty of murder in the first degree and a jury recommendation of mercy resulted in her imprisonment for life. Marion was tried and acquitted. Mrs. Brickel, having aided the State, was released. The midwife was tried, but the case was nol-prossed.

The motive for the crime was Mrs. Kaber's desire to get rid of housekeeping. She was ill-suited to her husband. She craved a gayer life than he wanted.

There is no way of telling whether Ruth Brown Snyder ever had read about the Kaber case. She may have. Newspapers were full of it about the time Mrs. Snyder began concocting an elaborate plot to get rid of her husband, with the same motive in mind that impelled Mrs. Kaber to resort to desperate means to free herself from the cares of a home.

Between the two women there was a striking resemblance in age, features, habits, mannerisms, and plot manipulation. There was one great difference: Mrs. Snyder had the shrewder mind. She tried to improve upon the Kaber plot by eliminating hired assassins. In their stead she brought into her famous conspiracy a lover who was completely under her domination. She tried, however, to throw the crime upon the shoulders of a phantom robber and, failing in this, shifted the blame to the lover.

And what a faulty picture she fabricated!

Newspapers on the morning of March 21, 1927, had upon their front pages a story which may be briefed as follows:

Little Lorraine Snyder, the nine-year-old daughter of Albert and Ruth Brown Snyder, had been awakened the morning before at 7:30 by the sound of tapping on the floor of the hallway just outside her bedroom door. Frightened, the child called to her mother, whose bedroom adjoined, and receiving no response, called to her father. Husband and wife occupied a front room on the same floor. No reply came from her father, so the child arose and went into the hall.

Here she found her mother lying on the floor, her wrists and ankles bound by wire.

"Mother!" the child cried. "What's the matter?"

"Run to the telephone," Mrs. Snyder gasped. "Call Mr. Mulhausen. They hit me over the head and I'm afraid for your father."

The child called Mulhausen, a neighbor. He carried Mrs. Snyder into a bedroom, laid her upon the bed, and loosed the wire about her wrists and ankles. He then went into the couple's bedroom in the front and found the body of Albert Snyder on a bed. There were two wounds upon his head. His body was rigid. He had been dead some hours. Mrs. Snyder, hair disheveled, came in and screamed at sight of her husband's body. She could not speak, but pointed to various objects on the floor. The room was in disorder. Incoherently she told Mulhausen of two men who had attacked her, then her husband, and who had carried her out into the hallway where she had fainted. They then bound her. She looked for her jewels. They were gone.

Newspapers printed the story of the attack and robbery. They told of the little home, the happy couple and their child, and of the sudden intrusion of robbers who had beat Snyder to death. The couple were quite well known and highly respected. Before her marriage Mrs. Snyder had been her husband's secretary. He was art editor of a well-known motor-boating magazine. He was forty-five, a muscular, athletic man of quiet disposition and devoted to his family and home. There had been no disagreements between the couple. Mrs. Snyder was liked by her neighbors. She was a vivacious woman who had a broad smile for everybody. Friends called her "Tommy."

In company with other men from headquarters and local police precincts I arrived at the Snyder home soon after the tragedy was reported.

The house was a single family dwelling. Its grounds were in apple-pie order. A lawn surrounded the white Colonial house. There were bird baths and sanctuaries among maple trees on the grounds. There were crumbs of bread about the bird refuges, showing someone's kindly interest in the feathered family.

A door in the side of the house was unlocked. Its key lay upon the floor inside. I examined the key and its lock. The story that had reached me was that the robbers had entered and left through this doorway. If they had it didn't seem right that they would have taken the key from its lock and thrown it on the floor. It was the kind of lock from which the key would not fall and, moreover, professional thieves after a robbery and killing would not bother to take a key from a lock and throw it down. If they left through that door they were on hurried flight.

The Kaber case with its faulty picture came to mind.

Entering the house I found the rooms as they had been described in newspapers, in great disorder. Sofa pillows were thrown about the floor. They had been taken from settees and chairs. A thief, looking for valuables, hardly would have hunted for them on settees and chairs, nor would he have gone to the pains to toss pillows on the floor in the center of the room.

In the bedroom I found Snyder's body. There were two wounds on his head, one on the back and one on the side. They had been made by a round, blunt, heavy object. About his throat were wound several strands of new picture wire. Each strand was made of sixteen thin threads of wire woven together. Why would a thief go to this trouble when, with the instrument he had used, he could have made certain of death by one or two more blows? Why had the wire been added?

On Snyder's upper lip, under his nostrils, was a small piece of soiled cotton waste caught upon the stubble of his mustache. To me it looked as if someone had brushed a handful of cotton waste across his mouth and a piece had caught upon a hair. I could find no other waste about the room.

The tiny thread of waste challenged my attention. Instinctively I searched my memory for patterns to fit this little circumstance. I recalled a number of cases where similar threads and wisps of cotton had been left behind on the victim's upper lip by the administration of chloroform. There was no odor of chloroform in the room, yet I was quite certain it had been used.

That two professionals would have struck, strangled, and then chloroformed their victim seemed implausible to me. I turned to the medical examiner and suggested that when the autopsy was performed special care be taken to look for traces of chloroform.

A revolver lay upon the bed, its chamber open, and

shells scattered about the bedclothes. I was told that it was Snyder's gun. Would thieves have left the gun and cartridges where they could have been picked up and used upon them by someone in the house as they, the thieves, were fleeing? Thieves show more caution than this.

Also on the bed was a blue bandanna handkerchief and a piece of newspaper, a corner torn from an Italian newspaper. I got the complete picture it was intended that the police should get but not necessarily believe—robbery by dark-skinned thugs, motion-picture villains. But in this day and age robbers seldom go masked; if they do they seldom leave behind their masks and a piece of newspaper tending to establish their nationality. And the three objects, handkerchief, piece of newspaper, and revolver, seemed in unnatural positions, like an arrangement devised by the property man in a motion-picture scene.

Before I had arrived Mrs. Snyder had told of the disappearance of her jewels, but they were found under a mattress in the room. In her confusion, she explained, she had hidden the jewels there and had forgotten about it!

And from Lorraine it was learned that the bindings about her mother's ankles and wrists were loosely applied. Two professional thieves, knowing that the revolver and cartridges lay upon the bed, would have made certain that the woman was bound securely so that she might not have used the weapon against them.

I was ready to talk to Mrs. Snyder.

I entered the room where she lay upon a bed. For a moment I studied her in silence. She was lying on her side, groaning, but her sharp blue eyes, squinting out of their corners, observed my movements. I caught the face of a woman which, it seemed to me, I had seen at close range before. The same square jaw and face, high cheek bones, cold blue eyes, light hair, about thirty-five years of age, and of buxom stature.

I hadn't seen this woman before, but the image of Mrs.

Kaber lay before me on the bed. In my time I have never seen two women who resembled each other so closely.

"How are you feeling, madam?" I asked her.

Mrs. Snyder moaned. I asked her to tell me her story. She related what she had told others previously; the story of the stockily built dark-skinned thugs with heavy mustaches and about thirty-five years old who had seized her in the bedroom and dragged her into the hall where they bound her. She had heard suspicious noises in her daughter's bedroom and arising to investigate had been seized by the intruder. She fainted and fell to the floor. She could not remember what happened after that.

"You fainted, madam?" I queried.

She nodded.

"About what time did you faint?"

"When they first came in. About 2:30 in the morning."

"And you were found by your daughter about 7:30 A. M.? Is that right?"

"Yes."

"Then you lay upon the floor insensible from 2:30 until about 7:30 A. M. in a dead faint?"

"Yes."

"That couldn't possibly have happened," I insisted. "You couldn't have lain five hours in a faint." She insisted she had. It is an established fact that in fainting the blood leaves the head for only a short period. If the body lies flat consciousness returns within a few minutes. But she was stolid in her insistence, another quality which Mrs. Kaber possessed.

I passed on to the woman's history. She brightened as she went back to her girlhood and her marriage. I got down to the amount of money her husband allowed her out of his weekly salary. She was quite chipper in supplying answers to these questions.

"And you carry insurance on your husband's life?" I asked casually.

"Oh, yes," she replied, lifting herself to a sitting position. "A thousand dollars." She paused. "It was a thousand dollars," she added in a low voice.

"Not what it was, madam, but what is it now?"

"Now," she said. "Oh, it's twenty-five thousand dollars now."

"What kind of a policy is it?" I asked.

"Accident and death," she said.

"How long has the policy to run?"

"Three years."

"And it's paid up for——?"

"A year."

For the time being I was through with Mrs. Snyder. My mind was quite satisfied as to a probable motive for the murder of her husband. The dark-skinned thugs passed completely out of my mind. The faulty picture vanished when I learned that the insurance which Mrs. Snyder carried on her husband's life was for forty-five thousand dollars, with double indemnity if death were caused by violence!

A more intensive search of the house was undertaken. In the hope of finding picture wire of sixteen strands, like that found around Snyder's neck, every picture and nook in the house were examined, but no such wire was found. A window sash weight was found in the basement. Among canceled bank checks signed by Mrs. Snyder I found one made out to H. Judd Gray for $200 and indorsed with that name in a masculine handwriting. I got a new figure coming dimly into the real picture—a man. In the dining room a bottle of whisky sat upon a table and near by a whisky glass filled with liquor from the bottle. The bottle had recently been opened. At least five drinks had been poured out of it. Mulhausen, who had seen Mrs. Snyder first on the morning of the murder, had said her breath did not smell of whisky and that she was not intoxicated in the slightest degree. Someone else, then, had drunk from the bottle, and the glass filled to the brim indicated a drink of a man's and not a woman's size.

I turned my attention next to the autopsy. Dr. Archibald McNeaill, an assistant medical examiner, performed it. The two wounds, he had found, had not fractured the skull. The blows with the instrument had not been heavy enough to break the skull.

The doctor turned to me. "Say, Inspector," he said, "this man was insensible, almost completely out, when the wire was fastened around his neck. It looks like death was caused by strangulation while he was unconscious. The two blows did not fracture the skull."

"Have you examined for chloroform?" I asked. The doctor hadn't yet gone that far. In my presence he exposed the skull. Snyder's brain was sent to the pathologist. The day following it was established that Snyder had been chloroformed and that this and strangulation had caused his death.

The sash weight found in the basement of the Snyder home was found under chemical examination to be stained with human blood. It was a heavy affair such as a woman would have had difficulty in lifting and striking an effective blow with. The wounds upon Snyder's head indicated that the blows had been lightly or weakly inflicted.

Up to this point, however, nothing tangible had developed to indicate either a disagreement between Mrs. Snyder and her husband or to detract from her respectability. There had been occasional tiffs between them, but they were light affairs such as usually happen between husband and wife.

It was Chief Inspector Coughlin of the Detective Division who started breaking down the picture of domestic tranquillity when he asked Mrs. Snyder what sort of a husband he was; how he treated her.

"He was just the opposite to me," she smiled. "I am

younger and like to have a good time. He likes to stay around the house and fix it up and dig in the grounds and feed the birds. I like to go out on parties and dances. I like hotel life, dinners, gay affairs. He has never liked them."

And so again this side of the woman's nature fell into the mold of the Kaber woman. And so also had developed a motive for killing Snyder—his insurance, which would have amounted to ninety thousand dollars in the event of violent death, and the lack of affection upon Mrs. Snyder's part, out of which would come the impulse to kill him in cold blood.

She was taken to the precinct station house, questioned by the district attorney and later by Police Commissioner McLaughlin. For hours she sat stolid, refusing to answer questions. She was incensed that anyone should suspect a woman of her respectability.

Then one of those unanticipated forces crept into the situation.

Mrs. Snyder was sitting in a small office, silent and sullen. Suddenly the door opened. A young man looked in.

"Why, hello, Ruth," he smiled.

"Oh, are you——?" she started to reply, greatly surprised to see him. He whispered to her, something that was never disclosed. The veil of respectability fell. The man knew a great deal of the woman's past, hidden chapters. She weakened. Her stolidity vanished. For the best part of a night she sat in the little room revealing the details of how she had murdered her husband. At first she denied that she had been aided by an accomplice. Then finally she admitted that a man had helped her kill her husband.

"And is this the man?" I asked her, showing her the canceled check which had been cashed by H. Judd Gray.

"Yes, he helped me," she said.

And so her companion in murder came into the picture.

Mrs. Snyder revealed that she had met Gray, a corset salesman, through a flirtation and they had become intimate. After a few meetings she bluntly asked him to help her get rid of her husband. He refused to be a party to it. Finally on the night of the murder, while the Snyders—husband, wife, and daughter—were at a whist party in a neighbor's home, Gray by prearrangement entered the Snyder home and concealed himself.

Early next morning Mrs. Snyder arose, called Gray from his hiding place, and told him she was ready to kill her husband. Gray was unwilling to participate in the crime. Mrs. Snyder brought out the bottle of whisky. Gray drank it from glasses which she filled to the brim. She flattered him; embraced him; told him what a vastly more manly man he was than her husband and how much more attractive. Gray, a weakling, was pleased. His vanity was struck and his mind befuddled with drink. He was completely in the woman's power.

They went into the bedroom where Snyder was asleep. Gray, whose hand was unsteady from drink, hit him a light blow with the sash weight and Snyder fought back. Mrs. Snyder then took the weight and administered a second light blow, but sufficient to stun Snyder. Then chloroform was applied and the wire bound around his neck.

The murder itself was encompassed within a few minutes. But it was hours before Gray left the house. He was delayed by the work of building up the faulty picture, the fake robbery. The time taken to accomplish this indicates to what pains murderesses go to build up pictures and in building overdo them. Between the time Snyder was killed and the time Gray left the house five hours had elapsed. This time was spent throwing pillows about the floors, arranging revolver and shells, blue bandanna handkerchief, the torn piece of Italian newspaper, and taking the key out of the lock of the side door.

The final act was the fastening of wire about Mrs. Snyder's ankles and wrists. The drink with which she had plied Gray so unsteadied his hands that he was unable to twist the wire about her wrist. Her hands kept slipping from him. Finally in anger, Mrs. Snyder bound herself and with a furious gesture dismissed Gray from the house. He had made a miserable botch of the last act in the drama.

Mrs. Snyder was far from being a woman of low mentality. My last session with her led to an incident that had never occurred before, nor has it since, in my career. From a newspaper account, printed while the inquiry was under way, I quote this excerpt:

> When Inspector Carey told Mrs. Snyder when they first met that it did not look to him like a real burglary she became highly indignant.
>
> "What do you mean?" she cried at him.
>
> "It doesn't look just right," said Carey.
>
> "How can you tell?"
>
> "We see lots of burglaries," said the inspector. "They are not done this way."

She was the first person, man or woman, brought before me for murder who could forget their plight long enough to ask a murder man about the secrets of his technique. And so the faultiness of her elaborate picture was brought home to her, but too late to be of any value.

Only a few minutes elapsed between the electrocution of Ruth Brown Snyder and H. Judd Gray.

CHAPTER XXI

BUNGLERS' BUNDLES

LAY minds imagine that the most atrocious murders are those in which the slayer kills, cuts his victim to pieces, totes them away in bundles, and scatters them. This type of slayer is popularly conceived to be a diabolical plotter as well as a particularly savage killer. On the contrary, the plots of such murderers are the least effective. The mere fact that they resort to hacking the body indicates that they were incapable of conceiving enough plot to fit their crime and, caught with a corpse on their hands, resorted to the quickest and crudest means of getting rid of it.

The actual killing usually is accomplished in the simplest and quite often in the most primitive way. One of the strange sidelights on this type of murder is that the victim's head is seldom found. Doubtless the murderer reasons that the most important part of the body to get rid of is the head, believing that the disappearance of this will prevent identification and thus forestall a murder charge. As a matter of fact, the first thing a murder man looks for in a dismemberment case is evidence that the death had been caused feloniously, which is the law's vital prerequisite. Invariably the slayer who has hacked a body into sections goes to great pains to destroy or hide the head and usually succeeds, but drops in most obvious places those parts which reveal the cause of death.

A few years ago a young colored woman had an altercation with her man and in the heat of the fight stabbed and killed him. She had warned him that if he mistreated her she would make him suffer, so she had conceived the stabbing with some premeditation.

The slaying was unearthed through the finding of the man's torso under a sink in the woman's apartment. The head and other parts wrapped in paper were thrown into a pail and ultimately dumped into the ocean by the street-cleaning department. She had disappeared, but we found and arrested her. She would not admit the stabbing, although the torso revealed the fatal knife wound.

She was a woman of average intelligence. I put the ghastliest question first.

"How did you take off his head?"

"Oh, I doan know, mister," she said in a singsong voice. "Jes' kep' a-cuttin'."

"How did you take off his arm?"

"Jes' kep' a-cuttin', cuttin', cuttin'."

"Where did you put his head?"

"Jes' let it fall into a pail. I didn't know what I could do with that corpse, mister. I had to git it out befo' the ghosts began walkin'."

She was nonchalant about the cutting up of the body, but never did admit the stabbing. She finally pleaded guilty to manslaughter.

In spite of their gruesome aspects, dismemberment cases interest a large audience, for they receive much attention in the newspapers. The finding of a human hand, arm, or leg in a city of millions of inhabitants offers intriguing possibilities to the lay mind. Interest is heightened by the fact that it would seem, offhand, almost impossible to trace the find and solve the mystery. Human limbs have been brought to me on more than one occasion, and as a rule a cursory examination tells the murder man the story. Familiarity with medical college practices discloses at once whether the limb has come from a dissection room and, as a rule, that is their origin. But, under certain circumstances, even a medical college specimen has dramatic and mysterious possibilities.

Late one afternoon an excited voice, speaking from a district attorney's office in the county in which Sing Sing Prison is located, informed me that the head keeper of the prison had reported finding a human ear in a basket of lunch brought to an inmate. The prisoner was a notorious bad man of the gangs. His wife had brought him the lunch. In searching the basket a turnkey had found the human ear. It looked like a real, life-sized murder mystery.

"The prison officials are inclined to believe that someone on the outside had murdered an enemy of the inmate who received the lunch and was sending the ear along to show the job had been done," said my informant.

Well, murder on the C. O. D. basis had been done before, but about this instance I refused to get excited.

I examined the ear and started a hunt for the wife of the convict. After three days she was found and was surprised to learn about the ear.

"Oh, my," she exclaimed, "that must've spoiled Jim's lunch! And I went to such trouble to get him up a nice basket! Chicken and everything!"

She had bought the chicken, she explained, and had taken it to a restaurant where it was cooked for her. She ate half of the fowl and the remainder was packed into a basket with other food to be taken to her incarcerated husband. The son of the restaurant keeper had packed the lunch. He was a chubby-faced youth.

"Say, youngster," I said to him, "what in the world did you put that ear in the lunch for?"

He snickered. "Aw haw, jes' to give them a laugh up at the prison."

"Where did you get it?" I demanded sternly.

"A tailor's boy around the corner gave it to me."

The tailor's son explained to me, as I anticipated he would, that he had finished his first term at medical college and, as a departing souvenir, had taken the ear from the dissecting room. Then the fat-faced boy in the restaurant asked him for something suitable with which to decorate a convict's lunch. The most appropriate thing he could think of, which was handy, was the ear which he drew from his pocket and gave to the boy.

A summer passed. One day the tailor's son appeared in my office with a long face. The notoriety which had come to him through the ear episode had caused the medical college faculty to think seriously of not admitting him to finish his education. I called the dean of the college and cleared up the situation. I advised the young man to be more careful in the future about picking out suitable decorations for convicts' basket lunches.

Not all dismemberment mysteries turn out so ludicrously.

The Doll's House Murder had more serious consequences. The body of a man was found in the water along the Rockaway peninsula. The legs and arms were tied; the body had been hacked but not severed. There was a knife wound in the throat. Through the medium of a laundry mark on the man's shirt collar I established his identity and learned that he had been on friendly terms with a young woman who worked in the same office with him but who had married an older man.

I called at the young woman's home and found her in. It was a small house, kept spotlessly. It was in perfect order. It reminded me of a doll's house and seemed not to have been lived in. In the kitchen was evidence of the young woman's neatness and order. On hooks were envelopes labeled "For Gas," "For Electricity," "For Laundry," and "Pin Money." Into these envelopes the meticulous housewife put her funds. I wandered through the rooms, rather enjoying this example of housekeeping. The young woman was pleased to see that I observed the evidence of her tidiness. But as my eyes roved the living room I saw that one of two portières was missing from a double doorway; that there was a light square on the dark oak floor, where apparently a rug had lain and recently had been taken up. These circumstances did not harmonize with the rest of the picture of orderliness.

Sudden confrontation frequently accomplishes quick results, especially with women.

"There were two portières hanging between these rooms?" I asked.

"Yes, sir," said the young woman. "I took one down because it was soiled. It's in another room."

"And there was a small rug on the floor right there?" I asked, indicating the light square on the floor.

"Yes, I took that up," she replied. "It's in the room with the portière." Her face flushed red.

An officer who accompanied me went into the other room and brought out the portière and the rug. The former was bloodstained and the latter cut into strips and also bloodstained. I went into the kitchen and searched for a weapon with which the victim's throat might have been cut. I found a grapefruit knife with curved blade. I showed it to the woman and asked if it had been used to murder the man. She made an emphatic denial.

There were tiny holes where the blade of the knife fitted into the wooden handle. I turned it over to Dr. Alexander Gettler, the medical examiner's pathologist, who found human blood in the little holes. Confronted with this evidence, the young woman broke down and confessed. After marrying the older man she had been unable to repulse the man who was dead. He kept annoying her, trying to get her to leave her husband. But she was very fond of the home she had made, the doll's house. The only menace to her happiness was the younger man who insisted upon calling when her husband was out.

The night before the body was found she met her annoyer, and he walked with her to the apartment. Her husband entered, flew into a rage, and attacked the man. The latter seemed to be getting the best of the combat, and the young woman ran into the kitchen, got the grapefruit knife, and handed it to her husband. A blow felled his wife's annoyer, and it was then that his throat was cut, the blood spurting onto the portière and rug. The body was put in a bedroom. An effort was made to cut it up, but the job was only partially done. The corpse was put into an automobile, carted to the beach, and hurled into the sea.

Husband and wife were convicted of manslaughter. The young woman had no deep affection for her husband. The dead man had been a threat to her happiness in the doll's house, and so she arranged to have him removed from the scene. The disposition of the body furnished evidence of consciousness of guilt, otherwise the husband might successfully have urged in his defense the so-called unwritten law.

Bundle bunglers are not as a rule mentally deficient. They are stolid types, capable of working out a plot to a certain point, but no farther.

Ludwig Lee, a stocky Norwegian, had a natively alert, shrewd mind. He was perhaps the worst bundle bungler that I encountered in my experience, and I have seen a goodly number.

Around two o'clock on the morning of July 9, 1927, a patrolman was going through Battery Park, the southernmost tip of Manhattan Island. He had his nightstick out, and now and then as he came upon a man asleep upon a park bench he tapped him on the soles of his feet and roused him. In the course of his travels he saw a fat bundle at the corner of an air vent of the subway. He poked at it with his nightstick. Brown cord around the bundle came apart. He investigated a little further and found within a wrapper of cheap brown paper two laundry bags, a towel made from a white cotton bedspread, a pair of oil-stained, brown denim trousers, and the right and left leg of a human being, each in a laundry bag.

From an examination of the limbs I determined that they were the legs of an aged woman, and that they had been severed from the body by an axe. The denim trousers were made to fit a thin man about five feet six inches. There were no identifying marks on the laundry bags or towel.

But upon the brown wrapping paper I found a column of penciled figures, written hurriedly:

10
49
15
39
10
10
13
25
33
———
204

They were large Spencerian figures such as a clerk in a grocery store might write in figuring up sales to a customer. And the paper was of cheap quality, such as chain grocery stores would use. Moreover, I reasoned that the nine articles for which the figures stood were commodities likely to have been purchased in a chain store. The sale they represented must have been made a day or so before the murder, since wrapping paper does not ordinarily lay long about a house.

I tapped those sources of expert advice which I have already referred to as the unofficial consulting faculty of the Murder Clinic. Paper manufacturers were called in. They informed me that brown paper of the color, quality, and size found around the legs was purchased in large quantities by two groups of chain stores—Bohack's and the Atlantic & Pacific stores. There are several hundreds of these stores in New York City. A search among all of them for the clerk who had made the column of figures would be long drawn out, and while it was under way the slayer might flee or cover up his tracks.

The paper and figures were photographed and at my request published in several newspapers with a note asking the man who had written them to get in touch with me. I did not believe that the slayer had made the figures. Had he done so he would not have used the paper. In the meantime records in the Missing Persons Bureau of the Police Department were searched for reports of aged women who had disappeared within the fortnight.

The next day was Sunday, July 10th. At 6:35 A. M. a sixteen-year-old boy playing on the lawn of a Catholic church in Brooklyn called the attention of a woman to a bundle on the edge of the lawn, which, it seemed to him, had been placed there while his back was turned as he played. It was wrapped in a rose and white checkered blanket. The woman, thinking it might be an abandoned infant, placed there to catch the eye of churchgoers, called a patrolman.

He unwrapped the blanket. In a thickness of cheap brown wrapping paper were found the hips and back section of a woman's torso. A medical examiner reported that the torso had been severed with an axe.

At 10:30 A. M. a motion-picture theater manager found the arm and left shoulder of a woman's body at the base of a fire escape on his theater a dozen blocks from the church where the torso had been found. The ring finger had been cut off and in the clenched hand were gripped several strands of black hair about the length that a man wears his hair. This parcel was wrapped in a red and white blanket and cheap brown paper. The medical examiner said that death had taken place about three days before and that the instrument used in severance was a sharp axe.

A few hours after this ghastly find Alfred Bennett, of No. 16 Lincoln Place, Brooklyn, reported to the police that his wife, the mother of four children, had been missing since seven o'clock Saturday night, July 9th. His son, John, aged nineteen, had last seen his mother cross the backyard and go into a house at No. 28 Prospect Place, which she formerly had conducted as a rooming house but had sold to Sarah Elizabeth Brownell, a seventy-six-year-old spinster, who now occupied the house and rented furnished rooms. Mrs. Bennett's oldest son, Carl, still lived in the house as one of the spinster's roomers.

In the meantime I was eagerly awaiting word from the grocery clerk who might recognize his figures in the facsimile published in the newspapers. He did not show up for reasons which presently will appear obvious. I anticipated also that other parts of the body would be found, for invariably the bundle bungler scatters his parcels in many places. And they were found—not only the remnants of the body of an aged woman but parts of a second woman's body! All were picked up in Brooklyn, thus narrowing the hunt for the slayer to that borough of the greater city.

From John Bennett, the nineteen-year-old son of the missing woman, detectives learned that his mother had gone into Miss Brownell's to see her about an installment due on the purchase price of the house. The detectives called at the Brownell house. The doorbell was answered by a short, thickset man with a bull neck, about thirty-eight years old. His hair was black.

He gave his name as Ludwig Lee and said he was a Norwegian. He had been rooming with Miss Brownell for several years. He also knew Mrs. Bennett. She had complained to Miss Brownell on Saturday that the water pipes in the house were leaking and that her yard had been flooded. He went with Mrs. Bennett into the basement and had left her standing near the furnace looking at the pipes. As to Miss Brownell, Lee said that on July 4th she had left for Gloversville, New York, to visit relatives over the holiday and had not returned.

The detectives noted a strange, damp odor in the house as they stood at the door talking with Lee. Finally the investigators separated, one going into the basement, the other calling on a Mrs. Emma Lohman, whose house adjoined the Brownell place. Mrs. Lohman told the detective that Mrs. Bennett had been with her about seven o'clock Saturday night waiting for Lee to enter the Brownell yard and admit her to the basement. A little while later the Norwegian came into the yard, and Mrs. Bennett jumped up and went to him. And Mrs. Lohman was certain that she had seen Miss Brownell in the house since July 4th!

Flashing about in the basement with a hand lamp, the detective who had remained in the Brownell house came upon a woman's torso half buried in an ash can, and other parts of a human body. Standing against the side of the furnace was a sharp axe recently washed and polished.

Lee was taken to Brooklyn police headquarters for further questioning. As he stood in the detectives' room the peculiar damp odor detected in the basement permeated the place. It was that strange, repulsive odor one encounters often at the scene of murder where human bodies have been dismembered.

Detectives left on guard at the Brownell house heard

the doorbell ring and opened the door. A man walked in. He gave his name as Christian Jensen and said he was calling to see his friend Lee, with whom he had formerly roomed in a house previously owned by Miss Brownell. Jensen said he had been out to get a morning paper. He had a copy of one in his hand, but had not yet seen it. He told the detectives that he was a clerk in a Brooklyn Atlantic & Pacific grocery store.

On the front page of the newspaper in his pocket was the facsimile of the brown wrapping paper with the column of figures on it that I had caused to be printed. He explained to the detectives that he was going up to Lee's room to look over the paper. He was sent to Brooklyn police headquarters for further questioning.

A search was made of Lee's room. In his trunk was found a passbook on Miss Brownell's savings bank account which contained four thousand dollars. Penciled on the wall above the trunk was the name Otto Nielson and an address in Brooklyn.

Two assistant medical examiners arrived at the house and on the floor of the kitchen they pieced together the sections of the bodies found in the basement and elsewhere. Several parts were still missing. They were found in an alcove in the basement. One head was missing—that of Miss Brownell. A police emergency squad drained the basement and found human fingers, one of which wore a ring identified as Miss Brownell's.

Neighbors reported that on Sunday morning they had seen Lee leave the house early with a bundle, return half an hour later, and carry out two more bundles. Nielson, upon being interviewed, stated that about 9 P. M. Saturday night, two hours after Mrs. Bennett had last been seen alive, he had called at the Brownell house with Jensen, but had some trouble in getting an answer to the doorbell. After a while Lee appeared, nude, and said he was taking a bath. Nielsen and Jensen went upstairs to

Lee's room, and after waiting for him an hour Nielson went to the basement door, found it locked, and rattled it. Lee cried out from within the basement, "Don't do that." His voice was angry.

Faced with this incriminating evidence, Lee stoutly denied that he had killed the two women and insisted that Miss Brownell had gone to Gloversville and had not returned; that he had left Mrs. Bennett standing in the basement. He admitted, however, that on several occasions, at Miss Brownell's request, he had cashed checks against her savings account and had spent the money.

He was taken back to the Brownell house and led into the kitchen where the pieced-together bodies of the two women lay.

"Who killed them?" he was asked.

He became sullen and ferocious. "I don't know!" he cried. "How should I know?" He added spitefully that "the old woman had begged me to marry her and I first refused, then consented."

Jensen came into the room. He heard Lee's last remark. He spoke up and said that on Thursday night, July 7th, he brought home a package from the store where he worked. It contained a lamp. It was wrapped in brown paper which he had taken from the counter in the store. Lee had seen him with the package and asked him if he was going to throw away the wrapping paper. He said he was. Lee asked him to let him have it. He did.

This was the piece of paper which had the figures on it. They were Jensen's figures, a column he had written down hurriedly when a customer who had bought a bill of groceries had asked him, "What are the damages?" This disclosure fell into a damning niche, for it established that the legs found at the air vent in Battery Park were those of Miss Brownell; that she was dead at the time Lee asked for the paper or he would not have asked for it. Moreover, it definitely put the bundle in Lee's hands.

What had happened to Miss Brownell and Mrs. Bennett was clear. Lee had first killed the older woman, striking her on the head with the axe. This happened on Thursday night, the night Jensen had handed Lee the wrapping paper. He had her body on his hands, but his plot had not taken into consideration the disposition of the remains. Then on Saturday night, the night Neilson and Jensen had called, Mrs. Bennett went into the basement to find the leaking pipes. It was about that time that Lee was cutting up the body of Miss Brownell. And to prevent Mrs. Bennett from telling of the ghastly sight she must have seen as she entered the basement he killed her.

Thus he had two bodies on his hands. His plot had not encompassed the disposition of a second body. Confused, he hacked them both to pieces, bundled them, and dropped them about Brooklyn with disastrous consequences.

He was electrocuted in 1928.

I am inclined to believe that even had the other sections of the body not been found, even had the detectives not entered the basement or had been taken elsewhere in their search, we would have been led to Lee. The piece of paper with Jensen's figures on it had already put us on the right trail, for Jensen later said that when he did look at the Sunday newspaper he instantly recognized the figures as his and had the case not come to such a sudden climax would have gotten into touch with us.

And so it runs with bundle bunglers. The Lee case was a striking example of what can be done in modern murder detection, with medical experts working, on one hand; and, on the other hand, trained detectives selecting the most direct clue, like the paper and the figures, which lead to the murderer in the shortest possible time. And the work of the Murder Clinic in calling in consulting experts like the paper manufacturers whose advice narrowed the hunt for the maker of the figures to two groups of chain stores.

I call the dismembering murderer a bundle bungler because the bundle usually traps him. It is a strange play of fate that a good many slayers of this type will get as far as the bundle, but lack the nerve to take it out, or, when they do take it out, they drop it in places where it is most likely to be seen.

In 1910 Ruth Wheeler, an attractive girl in her teens, was a student at the Bankers' and Merchants' Business College in New York City. A postcard reached the school one day asking that an advanced student in stenography, preferably a woman, be sent to an address in East Seventy-fifth Street. The writer, Albert Wolter, had work for such a girl.

Ruth was sent. She did not return that night to her home. Her sister learned that she had been sent to the East Seventy-fifth Street house. Accompanied by two patrolmen she went to the house and interviewed Wolter. He insisted that Ruth had been there, but had gone home. Wolter said that he was a German stenographer and lived in the small apartment with his wife.

Wolter displayed signs of undue nervousness. The sister did not like his appearance or his actions. At her request Wolter was taken to the station house and held upon a charge of abduction.

The day following tenants of the apartment next to that of Wolter noticed a bundle on the fire escape near their window. Peeved because it had been pushed near their outlet to the sunlight the tenants shoved the bundle over the edge of the fire escape. It fell into the yard below, where the janitor picked it up. He found it to contain the charred torso of a human being.

McCafferty, my old partner, who had been elevated to the rank of inspector, accompanied me to the Wolter apartment. I examined the torso and from the charred throat extricated a small gold chain which Ruth Wheeler's sister identified as one owned by the missing girl. Thus identification was clearly established. The girl had been assaulted, then choked, and her body put into the fireplace. But burning it was a slow process, and while Wolter was doing this he momentarily expected his wife, who was that only in name, to come in. Thinking the policemen's knock was hers, he hauled the body out of the fire, hurriedly wrapped it, and put it on the fire escape, pushing it over to one side so that his consort would not see it.

Wolter was electrocuted—another bundle bungler who had fallen short of plot.

Once in a great while this type of slayer is nipped red handed in the act of disposing of his bundle. Many years back an acrobat living in a cheap boarding house heard a shot in the room next to him. He waited half an hour, heard sawing and chopping, and heard a man leave the room where the shot had been fired. He peeked out and saw the man carrying a suitcase. The acrobat notified a policeman of what he had heard and seen. The policeman learned that the man with the suitcase was a pork butcher.

When he came out of the boarding house again with a suitcase and a wicker carrier the policeman accosted him. Upon opening the two pieces of luggage the officer found sections of a human body in them. The body was nearly complete, but as usual the head was missing. The murderer had done what all slayers of this type do—gotten rid of the head first. It was found in a lumber yard near by and the slayer was convicted and sent to prison for manslaughter in the second degree.

They all seem to forget that it is one thing to kill a person, but another thing to get rid of the bodies of their victims. For some reason bundle bunglers never think of fleeing themselves. They are almost always caught at the scene of their crime. Fate seems to pin them to the spot.

CHAPTER XXII

MURDER BY INVITATION

A RARE experience befell me on the morning of February 6, 1928. I stood again at the desk of the Grand Hotel in Thirty-first Street, where I had stood thirty years before getting the first dim picture of the murder of Dolly Reynolds. Murder had called me to the hotel this time—a tragedy so much like the Reynolds case up to a certain point that one might have believed that the same type of mind, if not the same slayer, had conceived both.

Strange developments arose in this case. People have often asked me what would happen as a matter of law if one person invited another to kill him; whether in that case it would be murder as the courts see it. It's a rather grotesque situation, but this case supplies the answer.

The body of a young woman, clad in a kimono, had been found in a room in the Grand Hotel annex. She had been beaten to death. Before me on the hotel desk were the registry cards. Upon one, in masculine handwriting, were the names of Mr. and Mrs. T. J. James, Troy, New York. The room to which they had been assigned was the room in which the woman's body was found. Apparently she was Mrs. James.

It has always been my practice to run back through the pages of a hotel register. In this case guests registered on cards. I ran through the cards, and under date of January 10th, a little more than a month before, I found the same names. The "J's" in the two entries were similar, both having been made with a peculiar flourish which made them look like a character on a printed music staff. The previous entry, however, gave Gouverneur, New York, as the couple's address, and not Troy.

Closer study of the two handwritings revealed other peculiarities. The January 10th entry was bold and steady, whereas the recent entry was ragged and wavering. From this difference I reasoned that the man who had written both entries was under a strain when he wrote the last one; that possibly something was upsetting him when he wrote it. The woman had not been in the room long when she was beaten to death.

I entered the room where the body lay. The woman's features were refined. She was in her middle thirties. Wounds on her forehead indicated that she had been struck by a hammer, and this was supported by the finding of a cheap hammer in the room. The body lay upon a bed.

Search of the room disclosed these articles:

A time-table of the New York, New Haven & Hartford Railroad, which runs between New York City and New England points. This was found in the bottom of a waste basket, where it might have been thrown by the occupants of the room, a maid, or someone who had previously used the room.

A woman's new hat which bore the label of a Fifth Avenue store located close to the Grand Central Terminal, where New York Central and New York, New Haven & Hartford railroad trains arrive and depart.

A black silk underskirt, or slip, which bore the tag of another Fifth Avenue store not far from the same railroad terminal.

A small patent leather handbag, quite worn, and filled with toilet requisites, which offered no clue to the woman's identification.

A pair of 4AA snakeskin pumps of ornate design bearing the name of a well-known shoe manufacturer.

And several undergarments.

From these articles and the woman's body the picture had to be built. The task which confronted me was to make a quick, decisive move which in the shortest possible time would lead to the identification of the woman and her slayer and lead to the apprehension of the latter. The reader is in possession of the same clues we had to work upon.

One bit of additional information was gathered from a hotel maid. About 9:30 A. M. she was passing down the hall when she saw a man locking the door of the room in which the body was later found. He was a tall man with a florid face and an erect, military bearing. The maid had been impressed by his stature and observed that he "looked very much like a member of the King's Guard in London." He stopped the maid and explained in a soft voice that his wife was asleep in the room and did not want to be disturbed, so he was leaving quietly. She was sleeping late because they were checking out at noon and had a long railroad journey ahead of them. He left, taking the room key with him. He did not leave the key at the desk downstairs.

The clerk at the desk described the man as tall, military in his bearing. He was the same man who had inscribed the names on the registry card.

When the man did not appear at noon the maid entered the room with her pass-key and found the body.

A few more details are added to the picture. Undoubtedly the murder was committed by the tall, military man known as Mr. James, who was the same man that on January 10th had written the entry on the registry card.

I reasoned that the woman had been shopping immediately before she was slain, and that this shopping had been done in Fifth Avenue at stores near the Grand Central railroad terminal. Thus the articles found in the room established the relevancy of the New York, New Haven & Hartford time-table found in the waste basket. The time-table lay open at pages giving the time of arrival and departure of trains operating between New York City and Stamford, Connecticut, which is a suburban city about an hour's ride from New York on the New York, New Haven & Hartford Railroad. Many of the intermediate towns and cities are in Westchester County, which adjoins New York City on the north. Hundreds of thousands of commuters travel daily between New York City and Stamford and the intermediate points.

My conclusion was that Mrs. James had traveled from one of these cities or towns to do her shopping. The absence of luggage convinced me that the trip was a shopping trip.

The body was photographed from various angles, as is done in every homicide case. A good likeness of her face was obtained. The Bureau of Missing Persons was notified.

Detectives were then detailed to locate the store in which the hammer was purchased, with instructions to concentrate their search among five-and-ten-cent stores in the vicinity of the hotel. The hammer was a cheap tool. Its head had been cast in a mold. There were defects in the metal casting—notches and furrows which usually are found on tools sold to low-price stores in large job lots. A detective reported that in a five-and-ten-cent store two blocks from the hotel he had found hammers of the same make and with the same defects. He had bought one for ten cents and upon comparison with the hammer found in the room its head proved to have come from the same mold. The salesgirl who had charge of the booth could not recall anyone to whom she had sold hammers on the day before.

The hammer, as a lead, petered out.

In the meantime I had sent detectives to scour the cities and towns along the route of the New York, New Haven & Hartford Railroad. They were armed with photographs of the woman—a complete description of her attire and the articles found in the room. The only facts about the man which they had in their possession was the meager information that he had a florid face, was tall, and deported himself like a man who had seen, or was in, military service. And as far as we knew he was T. J. James and the woman his wife. The aid of police detectives in the towns and cities was enlisted.

Some days passed before our inquiries developed. Then a New Rochelle police detective, who had made it a point to interrogate commuters that boarded trains at that point, found a man who recalled having been impressed by the uncommonly erect carriage of a tall man with red face whom he had seen several times on the train, and who apparently had boarded it at one of the cities farther north.

This transferred the search to cities above New Rochelle. At Mamaroneck, several stops above New Rochelle, a commuter was found who recalled having seen a woman step aboard a morning train with a man of florid countenance and military bearing. He was especially attracted by ornate snakeskin pumps worn by the woman. They seemed to be out of keeping with the rest of her costume, which was plain and severe. He had seen the tall man help her aboard the train, then got aboard himself. The train was New York bound. This had happened several days before the body was found.

In Mamaroneck shopkeepers, ticket agents, newsboys, taxi drivers, and real estate agents were interviewed. A man was found who had seen the couple described come out of an apartment house. The detectives made inquiries at this house and learned that no one lived there named James, but when the description of the tall, military man with red face was announced the owners of the apartment house instantly recognized it as that of "the Major," but not Major James. The name he had given here was Cecil Campbell and the woman was his wife. They had occupied a two-room studio apartment with bath. They had given up this apartment some time back at the request of the owners, upon whom the major had passed several worthless checks. The couple had then moved to a cottage on the edge of the town.

The major had been a non-communicative person, the apartment house owners said. He had only once gotten into a lengthy conversation and upon this occasion spoke of his military service. He had been all over the world and had encountered much adventure, soldiering in Mexico and India and leading troops in China. Luck had downed him in recent years, he told his hearers. He did what he could get to do, anything. He grinned when a woman in the apartment called him a soldier of fortune. His wife was a retiring woman. She had spoken only to tradespeople while she lived in the house.

The cottage on the edge of town was located. It was unoccupied but furnished. Neighbors knew nothing of the couple, for they neither visited nor were visited and had seemed anxious not to know anyone around them. The cottage was watched for three days. The Campbells not having appeared, detectives entered and searched the house. They found letters indicating that Campbell had lived in South Wyndham and Portland, Maine, and had worked in New Jersey as a military disciplinarian in a boys' school. More recently the couple had lived in Rye, a town adjoining Mamaroneck, and thither the detectives carried their investigation. Here it was learned that the couple had lived in Lynn, Massachusetts. Detective Martin was sent to New Jersey to find additional traces of Campbell; Detective Jackson went to various towns in Westchester County, and Pyke hurried to Lynn to talk with a Mr. and Mrs. Haskell, to whom Mrs. Campbell had sent a child's coat a few days before Christmas while she was living in Rye.

The Haskells had not heard from the Campbells since Christmas, but, they told Pyke, there were other friends who might know where they were. One of these was Mrs. John Murphy, who before her marriage had worked in an office with Campbell. Also in the office at the time was Mary Lyle McLean. Campbell had married Miss McLean after he had given up the office and had gone to work as an instructor in military tactics at a boys' institution at Shirley, Massachusetts. This marriage had taken place in May, 1922. Shortly afterward Campbell left the institution and went to Boston and later to New Jersey. It was impossible for him to stick at one job.

Four years later he was appointed superintendent of a disciplinary institution at South Wyndham. The appointment was announced in South Wyndham and in Boston newspapers with complete and somewhat thrilling accounts of Major Campbell's adventurous life. A young woman, known only as Cornelia, and who was employed as a telephone operator in South Wyndham, read the account. She was amazed. Back in 1917 she had married Campbell and had a child by him, now aged eight. Campbell had disappeared shortly after the marriage. Tired of waiting for him to return, Cornelia had filed suit for divorce in September, 1925.

Miss McLean, whom he had married in 1922, was the dead woman. He had contracted a bigamous marriage with her. The first wife knew nothing of Campbell's present whereabouts. He was a rover, she said. It would take years to find him. She had hunted for him eight years without success.

However, Pyke brought back a photograph of Campbell and his dead wife. Officials of New Jersey correctional institutions recognized the photograph of Campbell as an instructor who had been employed by them a month past and who had told them when he left that he was going to Philadelphia. The major acted strangely, they said, as though he had come to an impasse with life. Detectives Martin and Jackson were sent to Philadelphia and located an institution where Campbell was believed to be a visitor. It was a refuge for derelict men. Martin entered the place and saw a tall, military-looking man sitting erect at a desk staring blankly out a window. He went over to the man.

"Campbell, we want you in New York," said the detective. The man looked up, nodded, then arose.

"What happened to your wife?" Martin asked him outside.

In a low voice he said, "She's dead."

The major told me one of the strangest stories I had ever listened to. He admitted killing his wife with the hammer. The two had come to New York to carry out a suicide pact. He was at the end of his rope. The couple were deeply in love. They went to the Grand Hotel to talk over plans of their pact. They both agreed that they were through with life, but the means to encompass their destruction could not be agreed upon.

Finally they boarded a Hudson River ferry, intending to throw themselves into the water when the boat reached midstream. She would be first to go and he would follow. There was some disagreement about this, Campbell said. He thought he should go first. But when the time to jump arrived he looked about. Too many persons were standing by, so the attempt was abandoned and they came back to the hotel and entered the room on the fourth floor.

They had twenty-five cents between them. The woman suggested that she take ten cents and buy a hammer. Campbell gave her the money. She left the hotel. He went out, intending to take a ferry boat and leap into the river. At the ferry house he changed his mind and returned to the hotel. His wife was on the bed in her kimono. The ten-cent hammer lay upon the dresser. She suggested that he kill her with it.

And so while she lay upon the bed he struck her on the forehead and killed her. Alone with her body on his hands, he turned to complete his part of the pact. He opened a window and was about to jump but his nerve sagged.

"Why didn't you jump?" I asked him.

In a lifeless voice he replied: "There was a ledge below the window and so many people down on the street that I couldn't bring myself to do it. I was afraid I might hit the ledge and fall on the sidewalk and injure someone."

On the witness stand Campbell admitted the crime and described the act in detail. He went into his life at great length. He was an abject figure, a man completely beaten by life. He was convicted of murder in the second degree; and sentenced to from twenty years to life. The jury was moved to pity for him in spite of the fact that he had wanted to die and expressed a willingness in court to do so.

The jury's verdict settles the grotesque issue as to what would happen if one person asked another to kill him. It is murder just the same.

A strange thing occurred during this case. I took Campbell in a motor car to show me the store where his wife bought the hammer and to have him point out his movements on the day of the murder. I asked him what he had done with the key to the hotel room. He said that on February 6th, while wandering about Brooklyn trying to make up his mind to die, he had thrown the key into a rubbish can in Brooklyn miles from the hotel.

At 3:30 that same afternoon Patrolman Charles Reicher on duty in Brooklyn saw a key on top of a rubbish can, read the address on its fiber tag, and mailed it back to the hotel. It was then turned over to the property clerk's office at police headquarters and a few minutes later came into my possession. It was identified as the key to the room in which Campbell had slain his wife. It was an important link in the chain of evidence against Campbell, for it proved action on his part to conceal the crime, albeit the woman had invited him to kill her.

A great French detective once was asked to name the greatest detective.

"Monsieur Bon Chance," he replied—Mr. Good Luck. In so far as the finding of the key was concerned Mr. Good Luck was on the job working through the alert eyes of Patrolman Reicher, who, however, had a little picture come to his mind when he saw boys playing around the rubbish can. It was not the thing for boys to be doing. It was an offense against the sanitary code. He did his duty. Then he saw the key on top of the rubbish. He, no doubt, decided that the key did not belong there. People seldom throw away keys, even though they are useless. Usually they put them in a box or drawer or on a ring and keep them. He picked up the key and sent it to the hotel.

Patrolman Reicher in his way was working with pictures, too, and the key finally was fitted into its right place in the right picture.

The Campbell case stands alone in my mind as a pattern. No case ever paralleled that picture of a soldier of fortune standing over the form of his wife and at her invitation beating her to death with a ten-cent hammer which she herself had purchased. In a way I can conceive what brought him to that terrible extremity. He had lived a life of real adventure; had been near death or in its presence many times. Perhaps he had lived too full a life too soon, and when adversity overtook him there was nothing more to live for.

The soldier of fortune had become a soldier of misfortune—the strange human paradox which I call a murderer by invitation.

It was one of the last important cases I concluded before my retirement in 1928. And one of the weirdest—perhaps the sort of finish that might be expected to the career of a man who had been probing into murder for nearly forty years. And as I look back—time-tables, whisky glasses, keys, bits of writing, wisps of cotton waste, bottles and bottle'holders, men's false moves, and women's faulty pictures—they are like tiny peaks of paint on an artist's palette. The mind and memory furnish the sensitive brush with which you touch the colors to the canvas, and at last you get the finished picture, but always in heavy tones, the blackness of murder.

You get highlights, too—lurid, tempting, distracting, like brilliant sunsets. These are the glamorous backgrounds. You have to look out that they don't dazzle the eye and destroy the fine detail of the picture. In a way the murder man is like an artist, but a very practical one. And his pictures are not for sale. They may cost a man or woman a life.

And out of it all, out of the many pictures, as they pass in review, a man will come to some general conclusions about murder and the reasons for it, and why we have so much of it to-day.

CHAPTER XXIII

A PHILOSOPHY OF MURDER

PURELY by coincidence the writing of this chapter was begun on April 3, 1929. Just forty years ago to the day and month began the career which is the basis of these memoirs. After that length of time on one job a man, if he has been at all observant, if he can piece together his experiences and has a retentive memory, should have a philosophy about the thing he has been doing; if not a philosophy at least a pattern for one.

I have never kept track of my cases by numbers; have never counted them. Somewhere in the thousands lies the total number of homicide investigations I have worked upon or have directed. Nor is the number important. The patterns are, for they are what I've worked by. They are stored away to come into use when a face, an act, a scene, or a circumstance in a current murder suggests a parallel to something encountered before in my experience.

The murder scene in America has undergone vast alterations since I first set about getting the picture of a thief. In those days murder was a rarity. But in twenty years, the statisticians tell us, the homicide rate in this prosperous and progressive nation has doubled. Forty years ago if sixty persons met violent death in a year in New

York City at the hands of another the homicide rate was abnormal. The normal rate to-day is between six and eight killings a week, not including an average of one hundred who meet death each week in accidents. A week without murder or accidental killing sometimes happens and is viewed as a phenomenon. Yet New York City, the statisticians also advise, has next to the lowest homicide rate in the large American cities.

If the homicide rate has doubled the increase has not occurred among the class which furnished the slayers of Mrs. Adams, Mrs. Buchanan, and William Rice. If murderers of this type can be classified they would fall into the category of murderers who kill for escape. They were, as near as I can see, misplaced human units. Had Buchanan not been a doctor, Molineux not a chemist, and Patrick not a lawyer, it is probable that their lives would have taken vastly different courses. I dare say that in their cases the motive to kill grew out of their professional activities. They were at that age where people begin to think about settling down or readjusting themselves. None was an outstanding member of his profession, and each may have realized that he was misplaced. In an attempt to capitalize upon what mediocre skill they possessed they turned to murder—Buchanan and Patrick to get money enough to escape from professions which had failed to yield the returns they expected; Molineux to escape from a sense of inferiority which stood in his way as clubman and wooer of women.

Their plots were elaborate, indicating minds that were capable of concentration—trained minds. Of this type of murderer there has been a decrease in the last forty years. I hardly think this is attributable to the skeptic's reasoning that minds of to-day are less capable of concentration or elaborate plotting. Rather prosperity, the processes of civilization, and the wider accessibility of amusements have greatly reduced the number of trained minds that turn to murder. Human relationships are freer, education is more accessible, luxuries are not hard to get, and the great industrialization of the country has made it easier for people to get what they want—to lift and readjust themselves, find places for themselves, and become more satisfied with life.

In short, escape from unhappy conditions is more easily achieved, and those whose minds grasp this situation can find no reason to slay. They also are the ones most likely to comprehend the futility of attempting to win by murder.

Ruth Snyder and Mrs. Eva Kaber were of yet another type, products of the new desire to gain luxury quickly, which unfortunately is one of the penalties which prosperity exacts. The Buchanan and Patrick types were patient plotters, produced by an age not in such a hurry to acquire wealth. Mrs. Snyder and Mrs. Kaber were impetuous, impulsive. Their plots were the fruits of impatience, the hurry to get what others had. They, too, were seeking escape, not from impoverished conditions which Buchanan and Patrick faced by reason of their professional mediocrity, but to make a quick jump from middle-class comforts to the luxury that greater wealth would bring. Nor is it among this class of slayers that the increase in homicides has occurred. We probably shall have slayers of both classes as long as there are divisions in human society.

The increase has been chiefly among another and more modern class, to describe which I can think of no more appropriate classification than murderers by privilege. How great the increase has been in this class is reflected in a current newspaper. It records that in 1929 A. D. in the second largest city in the United States seven men were lined up along a garage wall and their lives snuffed out in the flash of a minute by professional killers. Seven a minute doubtless is a record, and if not massacre as we know it is at least a first cousin.

Killers of this type have come to be known in this age of speed and slang as the "murder mob." The act itself, like all others of the same type, is described in the light language of the era as giving somebody "the ride," "bumping them off," or "croaking them." When these expressions appear upon the motion-picture screen there are titters in the audience, and from this reaction one comes to the conclusion that a large part of the public, represented by the seats occupied in our massive motion-picture theaters, publicly and tacitly share in the light-hearted view of murder as the professional killer sees it.

If there is any philosophy to be made out of this spectacle, it is that the authors of this type of murder look upon murder as a privilege conceded to them by their own lawless world and not over-aggressively disputed by the populace. It is termed a phenomenon, but then we are fond of calling anything we do not understand, haven't got the time to understand, or do not care to face frankly, a phenomenon. It doesn't strike me that way.

I've watched the thing grow. The old type of professional criminal was not a killer. His world granted him the privilege to steal, but he avoided killing. A thief was unwise to kill and by so doing bring on violent eruptions in crookdom. Cunning, rather than an ability to kill, was the test of eligibility among criminals in that sparsely populated underworld of thirty and forty years ago.

If caught, and they made a pretense of injured innocence, it was just a flash in the pan. There was a certain sportiveness among the old-time crooks. When the cards were set against them they knew enough to drop their hands. They availed themselves of the services of lawyers, but these men were practitioners of the old school who relied upon forensic skill and open battle rather than shrewd, underhanded manipulation of legal technicalities and baseless defenses to win their causes. There was a time when the orations of criminal practitioners in the defense of noted professional crooks were considered masterpieces of oratorical skill and logic, and great speeches to juries were often reduced to brochures and widely distributed and read. It has been a long time since a great speech at a criminal trial has been reduced to type even in a newspaper.

Lawyers rose to great eminence as criminal practitioners. To-day one of the quickest ways to draw resentful fire from a successful lawyer is to call him a specialist in criminal law. The bar in America seems to have withdrawn itself from its once important place in the administration of criminal justice, leaving the field to a small coterie of practitioners over whom bar associations seem to exercise little control.

This precisely is what the modern, organized criminal wants. He is not looking for high-class lawyers who will fight cases on merit. He much prefers the man who is short on all the professional qualities that once made lawyers great, but who possesses an intimate knowledge of legal trickery and will put it to adroit use in getting the criminal off, so that he may resume the privilege of working again to make up for lost time and pay off the debts that legal difficulties have brought on.

The professional criminal calls this type of practitioner his "mouthpiece." I have commented already upon the appropriateness of this title. Anyone who has observed the process of trial in a criminal court where the defendant is known to be a seasoned veteran at crime will note how infrequently the accused and his lawyer will confer and also how infrequently such a defendant will take the witness stand. Planning and talking seems to be left entirely to the lawyer whose capacity is not a defender but a spokesman or mouthpiece.

And it is the criminal's law-given privilege thus to be defended. Perhaps a better way to picture the part the mouthpiece plays is to tell a true story. It has been told by a young lawyer who served for some years as an unpaid defender of penniless criminals. The accused, a young but active thief, was in jail for robbery. He did not get the loot he set out for, hence the scarcity of attorneys to offer their services. He mistook the unpaid defender for a regular mouthpiece. They were conferring for the first time in jail, in anticipation of the prisoner's approaching arraignment in court.

"Well, my friend, what is your story?" the lawyer asked.

"I was pulled into this job by accident," the defendant began. He went on with a long rigmarole, claiming not only an accidental intrusion upon the job but eventually offering all other defenses, including an alibi, police frame-up, mistaken identity, and first time in trouble. It was obvious that he was guilty.

The lawyer listened in patience, then smiled. "And is *that* your story?" he asked in surprise.

"That's it," grinned the thief. "You asked me for it and I'm telling it to you." He bent toward the lawyer. "But, counsellor," he added, "if you know a better one, well, spring it. Ain't that what you're here for?"

From the defenses I have seen projected in court where the accused were known to be professionals and were charged with murder I am inclined to think that many of them were born of just such a conference as this.

I recall an incident which will give the reader a picture of the professional's defense advanced another stage. Five notorious young bandits of the new crop, who had tried murder as a part of the robbery job but had failed, were called for trial. We had them almost red handed. One of them had been shot in the get-away, but he had been thrown out of the gang's car on the sidewalk in front of what the mob leader mistook for a hospital but was an apartment house. Here he was left to die, his companions fleeing. Our men found him. The cold-blooded manner in which his gang had left him to die had embittered him, and when he recovered he told us the story and became a state's witness against the gang.

The leader of the mob as he came into court on the first day encountered some of the officers inside the railing.

"When you guys get us," he sneered, "aëroplanes'll be selling for a nickel apiece."

They had no legitimate defense we knew of and indeed had made overtures to plead guilty if the degree of the crime were reduced. This overture was rejected. But the defense interposed in their behalf was interesting if often used. They cried police third degree, for which there was not the slightest foundation, as was proved when two of the gangsters took the witness stand. They were convicted. Their defense had been manufactured, but it proved futile.

There are lawyers, of course, who are above reproach. They come into the practice of criminal law with lofty ideals and ethical standards, but if they stick to them their business dwindles to nothing. They are generally found defending criminals by appointment from the court, where the State pays for their defense, since they were without funds sufficiently large to be attractive to paid counsel. The cream of the business falls to the established mouthpieces. The others do not prosper because they are unwilling to absorb the viewpoint of the criminal element—that deeply instilled and arrogant belief that pillage and murder is the privilege of their class.

In their own world, as I have pointed out in earlier chapters, this privilege to kill is undisputed and protected. The rule of self-extermination indicates how this privilege is availed of in the endless chain of underworld killings.

The American murder scene seems to have entered upon its greatest change at the begininng of the present century. I have made no intensive study of the history of murder in this country, but I am aware that in my own time the class of self-privileged murderers has grown. Many elements contributed to the growth.

It was about 1900 that the greatest influx of foreign elements began and uncontrolled immigration permitted the bad to come with the good. Concurrently criminals began to drop their masks and become more brazen and less fearful of the law. The murder rate began to rise. Laws to safeguard the privileges of criminals began to pile up on statute books. New defenses to murder were invented, including *dementia Americana,* which now has been lost sight of in a maze of other defenses invented and invoked by shrewd lawyers. It was about 1900, too, that American prosperity began to increase and to become more accessible to classes which previously had not had their share of it.

Of the criminally inclined aliens admitted under unrestrictive immigration not a few brought with them a traditional viewpoint that murder was a privilege. This tradition in many cases was inherited from medieval times when kings were privileged to murder and brigands setting themselves up as kings intrenched themselves behind the privilege. If the relation of race to murder is emphasized here it is because my clinical observations give dominance to this phase. I have given much thought to weapons in all murder cases, for they are not only the first thing a murder man looks for to establish the felonious intent of the slayer but they indicate the part that racial instincts play in homicide.

The knife, for instance, betrays a slayer of lower order, and almost invariably where the wielder of the knife is apprehended he is a member, or a descendant, of a racial group from southern Europe, Asia, or is colored. The knife as a weapon of murder is of primitive origin. It came before gunpowder. It is the weapon of slayers who have been pretty close to poverty.

The club, hammer, axe, and other tools commonly used by mechanics usually disclose a murder committed by other groups of foreign origin. In many parts of Europe and Asia pistols and knives remain in the luxury class, while the club or tool is a common household possession. Murderers who use these weapons select them instinctively because of a native familiarity with them. Moreover, the races from which this type of slayer is most often recruited have been oppressed for centuries, and the club was the common weapon of their marauding oppressors and also a weapon of defense against them. They were born, or their ancestors were, to the sight of the club or tool as an instrument of attack and defense.

Bombs and other explosives are the weapons most used in industrial and political sabotage and by nihilistic radicals. They are group weapons where the motive is not only to kill but to spread terror. In recent years the blackmailing racketeer has resorted to the bomb or an abbreviated form of it called the "pineapple," his purpose being not only to kill enemies but to increase his power by terrorism. The reader may trace the origin of this weapon by a study of the names of those who have been convicted for manufacturing and planting them. With few exceptions the stock from which the bombers were recruited did not come over on the *Mayflower*. The "pineapple" is nothing more than a military hand grenade first used in the late war, and for its introduction into the American murder scene the war, rather than any one racial group, may be blamed.

Arson as a means of murder is no longer common. When it is resorted to the act is that of a pyromaniac, whose motive is to destroy property and not murder, an insurance cheat, or a murderer employing fire to destroy evidence of his crime. Insurance company records disclose that the arsonist invariably is of foreign birth or extraction. As this was being written New York City newspapers were recording the third of a series of so-called "torch" murders where the victims' bodies were burned. The very fact that they occurred in series and that the murder was first accomplished by other means explains both the cycle and the use of fire. The first suggested the second and the second the third to minds that had been unable to decide upon other ways to dispose of the bodies. The murderers were not foreigners but of the lower type of mind found in bundle bunglers.

The strangler belongs to no one racial group. He is invariably a man, never a woman, and usually of large stature and strength. The killing is done on a sudden impulse, where the motive is anger, passion, or drunken frenzy. Now and again an Oriental strangler is encountered who has become adept in the use of his strength and can apply it with fatal consequences.

Murder by poison is, of course, of ancient origin. It is the choice of no particular racial group, but rather the weapon employed by a class, a superior or educated class whose members possess minds which can concoct elaborate plots, but who shrink from the sight of death and resort to poison because it does not involve their presence at the time death takes place. They are superegotists, but too smart, too confident, or too eager; they overdo the job. I am firmly of the belief that the will to poison has been pretty well educated out of would-be poisoners by the fatal consequences which have overtaken murderers of this type.

Murders committed by the means just referred to have greatly decreased in recent years. The common weapons in America to-day are firearms. No one race or group of races holds a monopoly upon their use, nor does any class of murderers, professional or otherwise, resort to them because of any racial or traditional instinct. Firearms are just handy and their use involves no degree of skill.

Except in recent years little restraint has been imposed upon the purchase of firearms. They are for sale everywhere, and those who haven't the price steal them. There are laws against carrying them or possessing them, but the task of enforcing these laws is beset with great difficulties. Policemen are not privileged to go about tapping hip pockets indiscriminately to find gun carriers. How effective the gun-carrying permit system is may be judged by the fact that in the great majority of murders committed with firearms the perpetrators had no permits. Obviously a professional gunman would be the last person to ask for a permit. Shotguns, machine guns, and automatic rifles are the accouterments of the professional murder mob of to-day making war upon society to intrench themselves in privilege.

It is no source of wonderment to me that the older and more primitive weapons have been discarded for the firearm. Not only does the criminally inclined immigrant find the privilege to possess these weapons, cheaper, freer, and easier than abroad, but the native-born also is influenced toward them by their accessibility.

And laws extend other privileges to criminals. If a defendant accused of murder (until recently in New York State) declined the opportunity to take the witness stand in his own behalf to explain away damaging evidence this was his law-given privilege, but the public prosecutor was restrained by law from exercising in behalf of society the privilege of commenting upon the fact that the accused did not take the stand. If a receiver of stolen goods, the creator of the market in which thieves sell their loot, were arrested the thief who sold him the goods—and who by reason of that fact was the only one who could testify to the secret illicit transaction—went on the witness stand his testimony had to be corroborated or was worthless. This was a handy privilege for both receiver and thief. If a habitual criminal with a long prison record were arrested the law extended to him the privilege of putting up bail *in spite of his known record.* Thus he enjoyed equal privileges with a person never before accused of crime or persons who might later be found innocent. And when known criminals furnished bail the law gave them the privilege of using stolen property as indemnity!

These are a few of the laws which force the criminal to the not illogical conclusion that though he may be a habitual offender the law specifically singles him out for privileges. And from this class of criminals the murderers responsible for to-day's increased homicides are recruited. My philosophy of murder is concerned chiefly with them, for they make the murder scene what it is to-day.

Who sponsored such laws? How did they get on the statute books? For answers one must turn to legislators. Our legislative bodies are made up largely of lawyers. A certificate admitting a man to the practice of law has become almost a prerequisite to entering politics. Bankers, merchants, and farmers are seen less and less in American legislative assemblies. Nor are the lawyers who enter law-making bodies always the most brilliant successes in their profession. Politics, and not the law, attracts them. And the legally trained mind is an adaptable one. Though the guilt of a client may be clear, it is required of the lawyer that he see beyond, around, or through his client's guilt, or not see it at all. This gives the lawyer an elasticity of viewpoint. By this process he becomes the fervent defender of his client, and it frequently works out that the greater the guilt the more intense the fervor. For this the lawyer is hardly to blame. The ancient ethics of his profession fix his conduct toward his client.

When he becomes a legislator he carries this elasticity of viewpoint and fervency with him and exercises it, not in behalf of one, two, or three clients, but in behalf of all accused persons. Any law that tightens the hold of courts, jails, and police upon criminals becomes at once a menace to man's liberty and an infringement of constitutional rights. It is always made to appear that some great principle of justice is at stake and that innocent persons will suffer if the laws are passed. And that law is talked to its doom. On the other hand, a law that weakens society's effort to protect itself against the criminal element is lauded as a modern, humane development. More than likely when it becomes operative it is found to bestow one more privilege upon the criminal class.

Of course there are good and bad lawyers, just as there are good and bad policemen, soldiers, and business men. But their position in our law-making and enforcing machinery is odd, to say the least. It is paradoxical. Lawyers both make and unmake the laws; they enforce them as prosecutors and tear them apart as defenders of accused persons. They interpret them as judicial officers. I do not mean to imply that they are actuated by venal motives. They are merely taking care of things closest to them; the sources of their livelihood. A physician-legislator would oppose laws inimical to his profession; a farmer-legislator would do likewise. The difficulty, in my opinion, lies in giving the lawyer-legislator the balance of power in framing and enacting penal laws. It is this one-sided complexion of legislatures that causes the criminal to believe that the one agency he must employ when he runs up against the law—the lawyer—will, in the matter of legislation, instinctively favor that class of clients, like himself, who in the aggregate mean most to a lawyer. Criminals do not have to lobby to protect their interests or gain privileges.

A development that has struck me with great force in recent years is the readiness with which the modern type of killer admits his guilt or confesses his crime. It has led me to believe that they have little dread of our elaborate machinery for justice. I have watched men sweat and twitch through a confession; observed the quieting effect that it had upon their demeanor when once their guilt is acknowledged, but I have also seen the same men assume an attitude of bravado in court when their skilled lawyers tore the confessions to pieces, or attacked the police, not, however, by putting their clients upon the witness stand, but by attacking the States' case by innuendo or false defense. In this way they achieve a more subtle effect with a jury, and they avoid the risk that lies in putting a guilty murderer upon the witness stand.

What has happened, as near as I can measure it, is this: Criminals have learned to look with hope beyond police, confessions, and that sort of thing. In court, in the hands of a lawyer, they expect to find, and do find, their privileges. Why worry about a confession, being caught red handed, previous criminal records, and evidence the police uncover when the giant machine which society has set up to mete out justice yields privileges to the criminal class?

Add to the situation I have just pictured the specter of prohibition and the unprecedented, widely distributed prosperity, and the final, lurid touch is added to the picture of murder in the United States in 1929. When one talks about prohibition nowadays it is customary to classify him as a wet or dry. I am neutral. I do not use and never have used liquor, having neither desire nor need for it. The country could be stone dry, dewy, or wringing wet; it would not affect me personally. And I am looking at it now in its relation to murder.

Perhaps the statement about prohibition should be qualified and the trouble that it has caused be diagnosed as an unwillingness to obey prohibition laws. At any rate, it plays a dual part in the murder scene. On the one hand it has created a disrespect for law and on the other has built up a new school for crime.

Both the youth and the mature man with law-breaking

tendencies observes that while the law stands plain upon the statute books, and has been upheld by courts, there are two classes who feel privileged to violate it: the man who wants a drink, and the man who supplies the want. Both have arrogated to themselves the privilege of disobeying the law, which as I have attempted to point out is what the habitual criminal has been doing for years. It so happens that a large mass of otherwise law-abiding citizens now refuse to accept the law, and so with even more logic than hitherto has supported the criminal's viewpoint he comes to understand that at last the rest of the world sees laws as he does. The criminal now becomes one of the larger mass, or, to put it conversely, a large part of the so-called honest world has accepted his philosophy. And this, he reasons, must make his philosophy right, where before there was doubt about it.

And if men are slain in their attempt to keep flowing the supply of liquor—well, the criminal reasons, they were primarily serving the interest of wet citizens whom an undesirable law robbed of certain privileges. Precisely this is what the criminal has been battling for since time began. He would prefer no laws at all. He has done his best to make murder and robbery profitable if not lawful, which is neither more nor less than prohibition has accomplished with liquor. This all has a bearing upon the murder rate.

There is still another important angle to prohibition, or this widespread unwillingness to obey the law, which the murder man encounters in his daily work. It breeds criminals of the killing type faster than they ever were bred before. A gregarious youth seeking adventure, as all do, finds it awaiting him in the bootlegging industry. It could hardly be unlawful, he reasons, when so many citizens are getting their supply from sources which are provided in almost every community. He tries his hand at rum running. He finds that the hazards of the occupation require him to go armed to fight off hijackers. Or he may have gone into the hijacking end of the game. At any rate, he becomes a gun carrier. He discovers the power that a loaded weapon has to compel men and women to hand over their property. He acquires the knack of handling a gun and finds he has little to fear after the first experience at holdup is encountered. He never knew that before.

"Where did you get your experience with a gun?" I have asked many of the young murderers brought in.

"Handling booze," is the usual reply.

"How did you get into robbery?"

"Just went after the bigger stuff."

This exchange of question and answer sums up the situation. Why bother about all the roundabout tricks involved in handling liquor when it has become apparent to the youth that men and women at the flash of a gun will yield up their valuables as quickly as rum runners yielded up their contraband supplies? Bootlegging is abandoned, now that the gun-carrying experience has been obtained, for the type of robberies so common and in which most of the lives lost are now lost through murder. When the thief robs and kills he has refuges without number where no one will ask him questions—speakeasies, into which he can throw himself and enjoy protection. He knows that the protection will be quite secure, otherwise the speakeasy would not be operating. If his means of livelihood is not apparent, and people ask questions of him, he is in "the booze racket," and this explains a lot and disarms suspicion. On every hand, at every step, he finds privileges awaiting him.

Prosperity, too, at least a misconceived notion of what prosperity is, has affected this new class of slayers. They are no longer satisfied with purses, the family plate, and odds and ends of jewelry. The old-time type of thief has almost disappeared from the scene. It is interesting to note how pickpockets have disappeared since women began to strap their handbags around their wrists and to carry checks and not currency. Million-dollar robberies have been common in recent years. Robberies that yield loot in five or six figures are daily occurrences throughout the United States. The underworld octopus, which slang usage dubs the "racketeer," is not content with one gang. He seeks to build an empire of murder mobs and to have his hand in every easy-money activity. The big idea seems to be to grasp the greatest amount of wealth in the quickest way, with murder merely an incidental to robbery.

The great wave of installment buying in America may have been an influence in creating this desire to gain possession of the thing desired at the quickest possible moment and pay later, or perhaps not at all. Then, too, in this age people cling with greater tenacity to their property, which of course is the right organized government guarantees. By far the greatest number of murders to-day are committed in the course of robberies and attempted robberies. Men and women not only show greater courage in facing armed bandits, but they display a more determined resistance to attempts to take their property. Thus in the conflict that occurs between victim and thief two irresistible forces meet—the bandit who will kill to steal because he must have his easy money at once and the owner of the property who puts his material possessions above life itself.

On top of this is the age-old belief of the criminal that he and his world are right and that other people and systems are all wrong. He is not unlike the old lady who with uncontrollable pride saw her awkward son marching away with his regiment. He was the only one out of step, but to her not he but all the others were wrong. To the misfits of the human family whom we call criminals crime is not a descent in the social and moral scale. Almost every act associated with their criminal careers to them marks an ascent. When they are sent to prison they never speak of going down. It's always "going up." When youthful slayers and old ones, too, are asked where they started in crime, and who schooled them, it's always "up there," referring to some penal institution in which they served time. Every move as they get down deeper into crime is an upward trend. They see themselves as holders of privileges. Every down is an up. They attain full stature as big men of crime when they have done a job or two of murder.

There is quite a mass of murderers by privilege. Just what society will do to rid itself of the menace is hardly for me to say. My business for almost forty years has been to catch them after they turned criminal and let the law finish the picture.

CHAPTER XXIV

MURDER AS A SPECTACLE

THE criticism most frequently directed at the police in murder cases is that they catch only criminals whose mentality and ability are inferior to their own. Because of this, it is urged, a great percentage of murder mysteries go unsolved, and to satisfy an inherent desire to see detectives of superior mentality go after and catch criminals of superlative ability and mentality the public turns to fiction mystery.

In these memoirs I have tried to give the reader a variety of cases so that he might judge for himself whether this criticism is true. Perhaps the average murder in real life falls short of supplying a need which becomes more pressing as life's complexities increase. Or is it need or impulse, an impulse which lies deep in human nature and which finds satisfaction only in seeing a fellow being of superior mental attainments and social position dragged down to the lowest levels? This is a harsh criticism to make of human society; yet I am quite certain that if every murderer I had arrested had been eminently successful, prominent, and above the average in intelligence I would have succeeded to international fame as the world's greatest detective.

I am also quite certain that if I had arrested, without

legal evidence that would satisfy a jury, every person of success, prominence, and intelligence at whom the finger of popular suspicion pointed, I also would have been known, not as a fairly successful detective, but as one of the world's worst blunderers. Most assuredly I never would have been permitted to serve for nearly forty years as a guardian of public safety.

What a glamorous spectacle these hundred of successful, prominent, and bright though sometimes indiscreet persons would have made, haled into court to answer to murder charges merely because they might have known the deceased; might have been seen with him or her; or, having been indiscreet in their relations with the murdered person, as a consequence invited suspicion. On occasion, the popular demand has been met by arrests in cases such as the Patrick and Molineux cases, but the peculiar dénouement that invariably arises in cases like these and many others is that mass emotions reverse themselves. Almost without exception the popular cry goes up that such persons when finally brought up for trial are being pilloried because of their wealth, success, or position in life. Great public sympathy is aroused. The populace splits into factions. The contest which justice brings on becomes a spectacle like football played between a home and a visiting team, with the home team attracting the heaviest rooting because the stands are filled with alumni, students, and local residents—all ardent supporters of the home team.

On the other hand, when the police capture a peculiarly diabolical killer from a low station in life the killing and the capture attract a flash of interest, for almost as soon as it is known that he comes from an inferior station, or is an habitual criminal, popular interest subsides. Yet, if there has been a scarcity of what might be called a "better class" of murders, the newer order of journalism reflected in newspapers which specialize in murder and scandal single out the low-type murder for special treatment, discovering some morbid phase about the crime or a mental quirk in the murderer and playing these up.

The difficulty with the average murder from the spectacle standpoint, or what is known in the theatrical profession as "box office value," is that the accused was not bright, was unsuccessful, not prominent, and had no social standing. The inference always seems to be that if he were bright he would not have been caught, and since he was stupid enough to be caught he merits little attention.

Against this situation the practical detective must work, attracting condemnation if he catches only poor criminals and condemnation also, in the end, if he gets a so-called bright one in his net. Well, the detective must perforce ask himself, what kind of murderers do they want us to catch? Only bright ones? After my experience I can only say that there are few, if any, bright murderers. If they were bright they wouldn't be murderers. The popular theory seems to be that the bright ones get away and leave their crimes on the hands of the police unsolved.

A good deal depends upon the meaning you give the word "bright," and your interpretation of the term "unsolved crime." If a murderer is bright because he has committed an unsolved crime the implication is that he is bright because he escaped punishment. If watching men and women confess their crimes entitles me to speak with authority upon the subject, I would say that no murderer ever escapes punishment—those caught and uncaught. I do not pose as a metaphysician analyzing the operation of human conscience. I only know from practical observation, watching the things that touch murderers' consciences and torture them, that no sane murderer can live, even though the world does not know him as a murderer, and escape the contacts that make the conscience sting. Anyone who puts his conscience in that trying situation is, to my way of thinking, hardly entitled to be called bright. As one looks at them, studying their lives, their plots, their crimes, the conclusion is reached that practically all murderers, those in high as well as low station, are cracked vessels of life. They could not hold what life put into them.

Nor is this popular idea that our murderers should come from a better class shared only by laymen. Juries and even prosecutors sometimes swing that way. I recall a very efficient assistant prosecutor, new to the job, who was amazed at the type of witnesses we procured to testify against a criminal who was a well-known figure in the underworld. The witnesses nearly all were criminals like himself and by reason of that fact the only ones who could furnish evidence the State required to prove its case.

"Why, these witnesses are a pretty low class themselves, Captain," the prosecutor said, surprised and disappointed. "They are all thieves and jailbirds."

"Well," I replied, "we have to get along with what we are able to find in crookdom. They are all associates of the defendant. What did you expect us to find as witnesses? Professors, teachers, clergymen, and bankers?"

Perhaps a so-called transcendent detective who had developed a psychic sense might have found other witnesses, but by what peculiar processes I am unable to say. I have never seen what might be termed a true scientific detective who had reduced to a pure science the solution of a crime, the capture of the perpetrator, and his conviction. They exist in the story books, but then these are written for amusement, and I observe that few of them end where the crime mysteries of real life end—in capital punishment or prison sentences. All that science has been able to devise to help find criminals and fasten crimes upon them is available to the practical police detective if he knows what he wants and has kept in touch with affairs so that he knows to whom he may turn for competent scientific advice and aid. This system has been employed in the Homicide Bureau and other branches of the New York Police Department. Scotland Yard uses it. Continental European detective systems have brought the scientific expert a little closer to the police department. In some cases medico-legal experts are attached to European police departments. America's scientific resources are unlimited. Why not use them as business in America uses them—in consulting capacities?

In the main, outstanding police detectives in Europe differ little from those in America. Indeed, there always has been an interchange of ideas and methods. To be sure, European detectives seem more romantic figures to Americans, but this is largely because they are so distant and a literature has been built up around them which invests them with supernatural qualities and perfectibility. Those whom I have known, or whose work I have studied, possess the same underlying faculties. They have learned to know crimes and criminals and, knowing both, a detective will instinctively acquire a pretty accurate picture of the operation of the crime-bent mind. From time to time I have had contact with European detectives. I have never found one yet who boasts that in Europe the police catch brighter criminals than we catch on this side of the water. On the other hand, murderers of the mass type, like Bluebeards, will go along in Europe from one crime to another for years without being caught until that final slip-up, which is the betrayer of almost all criminals, guides the police to them. Murder in Europe is less of a spectacle than in America. But this is a young nation.

The belief is common, too, that we have more unsolved murders in America than abroad. A favorite comparison by which our police are judged is the low murder rate in England and other European countries. Better scientific methods of detection as well as greater certainty of punishment share credit for this salutary condition, but the comparison is unfair to those American police departments which have striven to keep pace with the times.

In the first place, this country's large cities comprise a great melting pot. In England the police deal mostly with members of their own race and understand better their motives and acts, being themselves of the same race. This is true of other European countries. Moreover, the system of registration among natives as well as aliens provides European police with a check upon the population, transient as well as fixed. A similar system in this country would be thought of as espionage repulsive to American ideals of liberty. In the course of a month's work a member of the Homicide Bureau in New York City may be called upon to investigate a dozen murders committed by the members of as many different races, each case involving some different hidden racial tradition or motive and necessitating inquiry among persons who speak foreign languages.

In the administration of criminal justice in Continental Europe there is a still more important factor that works against the criminal and in favor of the police. In America the basic law requires that the burden of proving the guilt of an accused rests upon the State. Upon the State then—and chiefly upon its evidence-gathering arm, the police, without which the costly machinery of justice would not function—rests the responsibility of making out a case *without the aid* of the accused and in nearly every instance against the machinations of the accused and his defenders. In Continental Europe the burden is upon the accused to establish his innocence. Thus the law in these countries commits the accused to the necessity of aiding the police and courts or suffering the consequences of silence and trickery.

To the unsolved murder problem in America there is still another side. To each state is given the sovereign right to make its own penal laws, establish its courts, prisons, and police systems. There is no methodical, unerring exchange of criminal identification data between all states, although in recent years a national bureau serving as a clearing house for this data has been established. Thus a man wanted for murder in one state may be arrested for robbery in another and sent away for that crime while the murder charge goes unanswered. The case of Edel, the slayer of Mrs. Harrington, is one of many examples. The exchange of information about him with police and postal authorities in Minnesota resulted in bringing him to book in New York City for murder. But had this not taken place, Edel might never have been found and convicted of murder. He might easily have gotten into prison in, say, Texas or Georgia for thievery, served his time, come out, taken a new alias, and resumed his criminal career. A criminal who has committed murder, but who has not been revealed as the murderer, is not likely to confess to a crime that may cost him his life when he finds himself in prison for a lesser crime.

There is a desire on the part of most seasoned criminals when caught for lesser crimes to plead guilty to them in a hurry, which to me is a sign that they are glad to be imprisoned for the lesser crime because some greater crime which has not been fastened upon them will likely be forgotten by the time their sentences are served.

To blame all police detectives and departments for failing to solve all or a larger percentage of crimes when they are faced by a situation like this is on a par with condemning a doctor for failing to cure every patient or a lawyer for not winning every case. But the public's readiness to criticize the police and not the doctor and the lawyer lies in the fact that the former are paid public servants. An old newspaper editor once observed to his staff that when there was a dearth of sensational news at the usual sources they could "get busy and roast the police because they haven't got any come-back." Judged by the frequency of these "roasts" and the public approval that usually attends the activity known as a "police shake-up," they apparently are relished by the public regardless of how the eruption may affect their own safety and the man on the force who is trying honestly to meet increasing demands which the public makes of its paid guardians.

I'm not posing here as a defender of the police. I am merely trying to put the reader behind the scenes at the spectacle. Police forces are no different from families, armies, navies, and massed bodies of workers anywhere. There are as many efficient, bright, loyal, and honest men in police service as there are in other bodies of organized men, and of course as many who do not fit. When the police have a leader whom they respect and follow they respond, and their efficiency is favorably reflected. When they have a leader who is otherwise the morale drops as it will in an army when the leadership lies in wrong hands. It takes no expert eye to detect the effect of leadership on the men. If efficient they are on their toes; if bad they slump. The result is reflected in greater activity of the criminal element, and murder, like all other crime, increases. And murder control, after all, is effective only when the two branches of police service, the uniformed or preventive branch, and the non-uniformed, or detective branch, are functioning up to snuff.

There is such a thing as murder control. The decrease in New York City's homicide rate during the administration of Commissioner Woods and again during Commissioner McLaughlin's administration bore eloquent testimony to the fact that efficient leadership bears vitally upon murder control. Probably the greatest factor that gained whole-hearted respect and loyalty from the men under him was Woods's separation of politics from police affairs. He summed it up in 1917 in this formula:

The day I took office a general order was issued announcing that any man on the force might have a personal interview with me upon request. It was also made clear that while I was glad to see any member of the force on any subject he wished to speak to me about I wanted to see him personally and not some friend who might come to speak for him. . . . The baneful effects of political influence on a police force, leaving aside the grosser manifestations of it which take the form of crookedness and dishonesty, lies in the unavoidable conclusion that if a politician can secure favors which the policeman wants, that policeman owes favors to the politicians and the favors are always pretty sure to be paid for in a way which gives privileges to the politician and his friends which should not be given and which usually constitute a license to break the law. It was made clear by me that every member of the force was expected to stand on his own record.

A criminal or one criminally inclined reading that pronunciamento is likely to think twice before setting himself against a police department operated on such a basis. A policeman reading it senses a square deal and, satisfied he'll get it, works a little harder.

Ten years later McLaughlin, who, had he remained longer at the head of the Department, might have given the country an unparalleled example of police administration, established the policies which Woods had tried with success and made war against the denizens of easy-money street.

"I am in this job," said McLaughlin, "to curb crime and I have found that one sure way to do it is to eliminate gambling. Commercialized gambling cannot possibly exist on legitimate money. It must have easy money. No man regularly employed can afford to contribute long to a professional gambling game. And no game can thrive long on the patronage of a small group such as membership of a club. It must have outside money. No large gambling business can thrive long without some kind of protection. The police are bound to know about the place, and if there is not police protection there must be some other kind of protection. Once let the word spread that there is any kind of protection for gambling and the rush of criminals starts like the stampede of easy-money men and women to a new mining camp.

"To maintain the gambling game, its patrons must have an easy-money revenue. They cannot earn it, so they go after it in other ways. Then comes the robber, stick-up man, and the type that are committing to-day's wanton murders. It is a vicious circle. Crooks soon learn that where there is protection for gambling there is protection also for other kinds of crime. Show me where there is protection and I will show you a city where there is a high rate of crime of every kind."

Unfortunately McLaughlin remained in command of the Department only a short time, but by the end of his term in the City of New York—richest of fields for the predatory criminals—all crime had been greatly reduced and homicides had dropped sixty per cent. He stopped the flow of easy money at its source and outlet. He put an effective stop to gambling and he ran the professional receivers of stolen goods out of business, and murder dropped with the rest of crime. He had struck at the criminals, who are out for quick and easy money, the murderers by privilege as I have called them.

There is a still more vital requisite to a tighter control of murder. This is to remove the privilege as it has been built up by laws. This has been done by laws which compel courts to impose life sentences upon habitual criminals convicted more than three times of major crimes. Such a law was recently passed in New York State. By its operation a criminal who has been convicted three times of a felony receives, upon his conviction for a fourth felony, a life sentence. A law has also been passed increasing the penalty where robberies are committed or attempted with the aid of dangerous weapons.

The life-sentence law has been branded as harsh and barbaric, a throw-back to the dark ages. Yet is it? Take Edel or Hilton. Their careers at crime made them habitual criminals. They had shown no signs of redemption. Short prison sentences had not changed them. Edel was out on parole when arrested for murder; Hilton had just come from prison. Many cases follow the patterns of the Edel and Hilton matters. The law gave to them as it does to others who venture into crime the privilege of enjoying liberty when they had earned isolation from human society.

If there is anything barbaric about sending away for life men who can't get away from crime and who go from small pilfering into the realm of murder, I am unable to see it. Of course the man who is caught by the law, aided by his mouthpiece, will call it barbaric. Which savors most of barbarism—the act of the State or society in permitting a man to go along at crime for a lifetime until he is finally put to death by the State, or letting him have his life but denying him the privilege of liberty to effect eventually his own destruction and the death of innocent victims? In one case the State holds the rope and lets him dangle at the end of it till he kills and then it hauls him in. In the other case he has proved himself unsuited to society by his self-chosen career and is pulled in before he kills. In the former case society plays with him like a cat with a mouse.

The life term law saves him from himself, which, I have observed, in forty years of dealing with criminals, is the most humane thing you can do for him.

Perhaps all this advice I have given might dim the spectacle of murder as it runs along to-day, in which case the populace might find that a murderless world is quite a dull one, for a "big" murder, as it is exploited to-day, sells more newspapers than a presidential election and almost as many as a championship prize fight will sell.

Perhaps, too, there no longer would be the cry so often hurled at murder men—"Go catch us some bright murderers," when, as I have already set forth, there is no such thing.

To those who must have life seasoned with a little murder, I commend the detective fiction tale, for here the murderers are invariably bright, and the detectives, too, and the slayers are always caught.

In the world of imagination there's perfection even in murder. I've had to take murders as I've found them. If there is such a thing as a perfect crime in the domain of the murderer I've never found it, nor an approach to it.

Nor a perfect detective.

THE END

www.ingramcontent.com/pod-product-compliance
Lightning Source LLC
LaVergne TN
LVHW020610110826
845149LV00002B/430

* 9 7 8 1 4 1 8 1 8 8 0 4 7 *